SPANISH-ENGLISH ENGLISH-SPANISH DICTIONARY OF COMPUTER TERMS

Alfredo U. Chiri

HIPPOCRENE BOOKS
New York

For information, address:
HIPPOCRENE BOOKS, INC.
171 Madison Avenue
New York, NY 10016

Library of Congress Cataloging-in-Publication Data

(available)

ISBN 0-7818-0148-6

Printed in the United States of America

ACKNOWLEDGMENTS

While I was in Perú I became a listener to the complaints of my late uncle, Diogenes Uceda, who had compiled letters written in Spanish from correspondence between the U.S.A. and Latin American importers of high-tech equipment. His only reason for doing this was to prove to me the lack of a common technical traslation between English-speaking and Spanish speaking countries. One of his favorite comments was "How is it possible to understand what they mean in this letter?" and all I could say was "It is impossible. This is due to plain sheer ignorance."

I am especially pleased to thank my uncle, Diogenes Uceda, for his heroic work in helping me to obtain the proper engineering contacts throughout Latin America and Spain. Also I want to thank all those Spanish-speaking engineers who helped me in the standardization of the computer term-phrases.

I want to acknowledge my debt to my wife, Phyllis, my first proofreader and editor, who endured countless hours in adding the English phonics to the Spanish phrases. My deepest thanks for her constant dedication and patience.

I would like to thank George Blagowidow, publisher, and Amy Gillet, assistant editor, who saw the book's potential and guided it during the editorial stages on through completion.

ABBREVIATIONS USED IN THIS TRANSLATOR

ENGLISH

[adj]	adjective
[adv]	adverb
[n]	noun
[np]	noun phrase
[pre]	prefix
[v]	verb

ESPAÑOL

[adj]	adjetivo
[adv]	adverbio
[f]	femenino
[m]	masculino
[pre]	prefijo
[v]	verbo

INTRODUCTION

Today the use of computers is one of the fastest-growing and most important developments of our time. These machines are being used by more people to solve complex engineering problems and for business analysis. A major problem with any revolutionary development is the nomenclature. In a fast-moving field such as computer technology many new terms are developed with the growth of the technology. It is important that these terms be accurate and represent the definition of the originating language rather than a transliterated form.

Spanish-English / English-Spanish Dictionary of Computer Terms is a collection of more than 5700 English and Spanish computer terms that focus on the areas of programming languages, graphics, video, telecommun ications, artificial intelligence, and hardware equipment for mainframe and personal computers. These terms have been selected as the most likely to create translative differences between the English and Spanish languages. The book is written in a form which allows a computer literate to obtain the true translation of the technical terms. The meaning remains and is not changed by a poorly done translation.

All terms described in Spanish correspond to the precise usage which may override the word-for-word translation. Terms have been carefully scrutinized so that the Spanish translation represents the actual English computereze jargon.

All terms are entered in alphabetical listing. If a term has more than one translation, due to specific meanings when used in specialized fields, the same word will be presented more than once. The user will have the option of selecting the proper term.

Because many of the terms have been recently introduced, a standard of translation has been provided so that the English-speaking and Spanish-speaking countries develop a standard of common understanding among professional users. The translation must be in pure Spanish, free of colloquialism and any aberrations of the language. This translator is designed as a tool to help bring that understanding about.

SPANISH-ENGLISH

A

abortar [v] abor [a-bort']

acceso casual [m] random access [rran'-dom ak'-ses]

acceso directo [m] direct access [di-rect' ak'-ses]

acceso en serie [m] serial access [se-ryal' ak'-ses]

acceso inmediato [m] immediate access [im-me-dyat' ak'-ses]

acceso múltiple [m] multiaccess [multi-ak'-ses]

acceso paralelo [m] parallel access [para-lel' ak'-ses]

acceso secuencial [m] sequential access [se-kuen'-syal ak'-ses]

acceso semicasual [m] semirandom access [semi-rran'-dom ak'-ses]

acceso simultáneo [m] simultaneous access [simul-tane'-us ak'-ses]

accesorio [m] accessory [ak-ses'-sory]

acoplador acústico [m] acoustic coupler [a-co-us'-tic ka-pler]

acoplamiento mutuo [m] interface [inter'-feis]

acoplamiento mutuo de bucle-corriente [m] current-loop interface [ku'-rrent lup inter'-feis]

acoplamiento mutuo hombre-máquina [m] man-machine interface [man-ma-chin' inter'-feis]

actividad [f] activity [ak-ti'-bity]

actividad baja [f] low activity [lo ak-ti'-bity]

actualización diferida [f] delayed updating [de-leyd' ap-dei'-tin]

actualizar [v] update [ap-deit']

acumulación de información parásitica [f] garbage collection [gar-ba'-ich co-lek'-cion]

acumulador [m] accumulator [ak-ku'-miu-lei-tor]

adaptador [m] adapter [adap'-ter]

adaptador de canales [m] channel adapter [cha'-nel adap'-ter]

adaptador de circuitos estampados [m] adapter boards [adap'-ter bo'-ards]

adicionador completo [m] full-adder [ful ad'-der]

adjuntar [v] append [a-pend']

adquisición automática de datos [f] ADA automatic data acquisition [ADA auto-ma'-tik da'-ta ak-kui-si'-cion]

adquisición automática de datos [f] automatic data acquisition (ADA) [auto-ma'-tik da'ta ak-kui-si'-cion (ADA)]

adquisición de conocimiento [f] knowledge acquisition [nou'-led-ye ak-kui-si'-cion']

aficionado de computador [m] computernik [com-piu-ter'-nik]

agenda [f] agenda [a-llen'-da]

agregación de datos [f] data aggregate [data agre-gue'-it]

agrupación [f] clustering [clas-ter'-in]

agrupación primordial [f] primary cluster [primari clus'-ter]

agudo [m] sharpness [shaar-pe'-nes]

agujeros [m] perfs [pe'-erfs]

aislamiento [m] isolation [i-so'-lay-sion]

ajustar [v] set [set]

ajuste fino [m] tweak [tu-ik']

al alcance [m] extent [ex-ten'-t]

al azar [adv] at random [at rran'-dom]

álbum de recortes [m] scrapbook [es-crap'-buk]

alfabeto [m] alphabet [alfa'-bet]

alfanumérico [adj] alphanumeric [alfa-nu'-merik]

alfanumérico [adj] alphameric [alfa-me'-rik]

álgebra de Boole [mf] Boolean algebra [bu-le'-an al'-ye-bra]

algoritmo [m] algorithm [algo'-ryd-im]

alimentación [f] feed [fiid]

alimentación de papel por línea [f] line feed [lain fiid]

alimentación horizontal [f] horizontal feed [o-ri'-sontal fiid]

alimentación por fricción [f] friction-feed [frik'-cion fiid]

alimentación por página [f] form feed [form fiid]

alimentador de cinta [m] tape feed [teip fiid]

alimentar [v] feed [fiid]

alineación [f] alignment [a-lai'-ment]

almacenamiento de memoria [m] storage [es-tor'-aich]

almacenamiento de memoria auxiliar [m] auxiliary storage [ausi-li'-a-ry es-tor'-aich]

almacenamiento de memoria secundaria [m] secondary storage [se-con'-da-ri es-tor'-aich]

almacenamiento de memoria temporal [m] temporary storage [tem-po'-ra-ry es-tor'-aich]

almacenamiento de memoria virtual [m] VS virtual storage [bi-es vir-chu'-al es-tor'-aich]

almacenamiento de memoria virtual [m] virtual storage (VS) [vir-chu'-al es-tor'-aich (VS)]

almacenamiento principal [m] main storage [me'-in es-tor'-aich]

almacenar [v] store [es-to'-ar]

alquiler a una tercera persona [m] third-party lease [tir'-d par'-ti lis']

alternación [f] alternation [al-ter'-nei-cion]

ambiente [m] environment [en-vai'-ro-ment]

amortiguamiento [adj] damping [dam'-ping]

análisis de contorno [mf] contour analysis [con-tu'-ar ana-ly'-sis]

análisis de dibujos [mf] analysis graphics [ana-ly'-sis gra'-fiks]

análisis de redes [mf] network analysis [net'-gu-ork ana-ly'-sis]

análisis de sistemas [mf] system analysis [sis'-tem ana-ly'-sis]

análisis numérico [m] numerical analysis [nu-me'-ri-cal ana-ly'-sis]

analista [mf] analyst [a-na-list']

analista de sistemas [mf] systems analyst [sis'-tem a-na-list']

analización [f] parsing [par'-sing]

analizador [m] analyser [a-na'-lai-ser]

analizador [m] analyzer [a-na'-lai-ser]

analizador de carácteres [m] parser [par'-ser]

análizador de sistema [m] system analyzer [sis'-tem a-na'-lai-ser]

analizador diferencial [m] differential analyser [di-fe-ren'-cial a-na'-lai-ser]

analizador diferencial [m] differential analyzer [di-fe-ren'-cial a-na'-lai-ser]

analógico [m] analog [ana'-log]

anchura de banda [f] bandwidth [ban-d'-wid]

androide [mf] android [an-dro'-id]

androide [mf] gynoid [gi-no'-id]

anillo de protección del fichero [m] file-protect ring [fa-il' pro'-tec-t rin-g']

anillo que no permite escribir [m] write-inhibit ring [bra'-it in-ji'-bit rin-g']

anillo que permite escribir [m] write-enable ring [bra'-it ena'-ble rin-g']

anillo que proteje escritura [m] write-protect ring [bra'-it pro'-tec-t rin-g']

animación [f] animation [ani-mei'-cion]

anotación [f] annotation [an-no'-tei-cion]

anular [v] override [ober-rrai'-d]

añadir memoria [m] add-on [ad-d' on]

añadir un circuito [m] add-in [ad-d' in]

apagar [v] power down [pou'-guer do-un]

aparato asíncrono [m] asynchronous device [a-sin'-cro-no-us de-va'-is]

aparato binario [m] binary device [bi-na'-ri de-va'-is]

aparato de audio [m] audio device [a-u'-dio de-va'-is]

aparato de juego de video [m] video game machine [vi-de'-o ga-im ma-chi'-n]

aparato de secuencia [m] sequential device [se-ku-en'-si-al de-va'-is]

aparato fotoeléctrico [m] photoelectric devices [fo-to-elek'-trik de-va'-is]

aparato para entrar dibujos [m] graphic-input device [gra'-fik in'-put de-va'-is]

aparato para sacar dibujos [m] graphic-output device [gra'-fik o-ut'-put de-va'-is]

aplicación [f] application [a-pli-kei'-cion]

aprendizaje amplificado con ayuda del computador [m] CAL computer-augmented learning [CAL com-piu'-ter a-gu-men'-ted ler'-nin-g]

aprendizaje amplificado con ayuda del computador [m] computer-augmented learning (CAL) [com-piu'-ter a-gu-men'-ted ler'-nin-g (CAL)]

aprendizaje automatizado [m] CBL computer-based learning [c-bi-el com-piu'-ter bei'-sed ler'-nin-g]

aprendizaje automatizado [m] computer-based learning (CBL) [com-piu'-ter bei'-sed ler'-nin-g (c-bi-el)]

aprendizaje heurístico [m] heuristic learning [yu-ris'-tik ler'-nin-g]

aptitude de servicio [f] serviceability [ser-vi-sea-bi'-li-ty]

apuntador [adj] flagged [fla'-ge-d]

apuntador nulo [m] nil pointer [nil po'-in-ter]

árbol [m] tree [tri'-i]

árbol con brotes [m] spanning tree [es-pa'-nin-g tri'-i]

árbol de decisión [m] decision tree [des-si'-cion tri'-i]

árbol desordenado [m] unordered tree [an-or'-de-red tri'-i]

árbol enhebrado [m] threaded tree [tre'-ded tri'-i]

árbol óptimo [m] minimal tree [mini'-mal tri'-i]

archivado [m] archival [ar-ca'-i-bal]

archivando [adj] archiving [ar-ca'-i-bin-g]

archivo [m] file [fa'-il]

archivo con trasera [m] piggyback file [pi-gui-bak fa'-il]

archivo de mensajes sin sentido [m] dead letter box [ded le'-ter bax]

archivo de primera generación [m] grandfather file [gran'-fa-der fa'-il]

archivo de recurso [m] resource file [rre-sour'-se fa'-il]

archivo de reporte [m] report file [re'-port fa'-il]

archivo de reserva [m] file backup [fa'-il bak-ap]

archivo de texto [m] text file [teex-t fa'il]

archivo detallado [m] detail file [di-te-il' fa'-il]

archivo envuelto [m] enveloped file [en'-ve-lop-d fa'-il]

archivo inverso [m] inverted file [in-ver'-ted fa'-il]

archivo original [m] father file [fa'-der fa'-il]

área blanda de imagen [f] soft clip area [sof clip a-rea]

área constante [f] constant area [cons'-tant a-rea]

área de salida [f] output area [aut'-put a-rea]

área fuera de limite [f] hard-clip area [jard clip a-rea]

área para montar circuitos [f] land [lan-d]

área que no permite circuitos [f] keep-out areas [kip aut a-re'-as]

argumento [m] argument [ar-gu'-ment]

aritmética de longitud múltiple [f] multiple-length arithmetic [mul'-ti-ple lent a-rit-me'-tic]

aritmética de matriz [f] matrix arithmetic [ma-trix a-rit-me'-tic]

aritmética de punto fijo [f] fixed-point arithmetic [fix'-ed po'-int a-rit-me'-tic]

aritmética de punto flotante [f] floating-point arithmetic [flo-tin-g po'-int a-rit-me'-tic]

aritmética vectorial [f] vector arithmetic [vec'-tor a-rit-me'-tic]

arquitectura [f] architecture [ark-qui-tek'-chur]

arrancar [v] boot [but]

arrancar el autocargador [m] bootstrapping [but-es-tra'-pin-g]

arranque secundario [m] warm boot [wu-arm but]

arrastrado [m] drag [dra-ag]

arrastrando [adj] creeping [kri'-pin-g]

arrastre parcial [m] partial carry [par'-sial ca'-rri]

arreglo [m] array [a'-rey]

arreglo de una dimensión [m] one-dimensional array [uan di-men'-si-o-nal a'-rey]

arreglo del archivo [m] file layout [fa'-il ley'-aut]

arreglo del registro [m] record layout [re-kor'-d ley'-aut]

arreglo escaso [m] sparse array [es-par'-c a'-rey]

arreglo improvisado [m] kludge [clud'-ye]

ascenso de archivos [m] upload [ap-lo'-ad]

asidor [m] grabber [gra'-ber]

asignación [f] allocation [alo-kei'-cion]

asignación de almacenamiento de memoria [f] storage allocation [es-tor'-aich alo-kei'-cion]

asignación de recursos [f] resource allocation [re-so-ur'-se alo-kei'-cion]

asignación dinámica [f] dynamic allocation [di-na'-mik alo-kei'-cion]

asignar [v] allocate [alo-kei'-it]

asíncrono [adj] asynchronous [a-sin-cro'-nas]

asterisco [m] asterisk [as-te'-risk]

atascamiento [m] jam [llam]

atenuación [f] attenuation [a-te-nue'-cion]

atrapar [v] trap [trap]

atributo [m] attribute [a-tri'-bi-ut]

audiovisual [mf] audio-visual [au'-dio vi-su'-al]

aumentando [adj] zooming [su'-min-g]

aumento de bit [m] fat bits [fat bits]

autoadaptado [adj] self-adapting [sel'-f a-dap'-tin-g]

autocargador [m] bootstrap [but-es'-trap]

autoelección [m] autopolling [auto-pol'-lin-g]

autoestructurado [adj] self-organizing [self or-ga'-nai-sin-g]

automación [f] automation [auto-mei-cion]

autómata [mf] robot [rro'-bat]

autómata [mf] automaton [auto-ma'-ton]

automatización de la fuente de datos [f] source data automation [so-ur'-se da-ta auto-mei-cion]

automonitor [m] automonitor [auto-moni'-tor]

auto-cargador [m] auto-load [auto lo'-ud]

auto-despacho [m] auto-answer [auto an'-ser]

auto-enlace [m] auto-dial [auto dai'-al]

auto-reanudarse [m] auto-restart [auto re'-es-tar-t]

auto-retransmisión [m] auto-repeat [auto rre'-pit]

avancé [m] feed-in [fi'-id in]

avanzar [v] feed [fi'-id]

ayuda a la depuración [m] debugging aid [de-bug'-in eid]

ayuda de programación [m] programming aids [pro-gram'-min eids]

ayuda de programación [m] design aids [di-sain eids]

B

bajo de ley [m] base [be-is]

banca de prueba [f] testbed [tes'-t-bed]

banco de datos [m] data bank [da'-ta bank]

bancos de información automatizada [m] information banks [in'-for-mei-cion banks]

banda [f] band [ban'-d]

banda ancha [f] broadband [brod-ban'-d]

banda de guardar [f] guard band [gar'-d ban'-d]

banda de jebe [f] rubber banding [rra'-ber ban'-din-g]

baraja [f] deck (paper cards) [dek (pei'-per card'-s)]

baraja de tarjetas [f] pack of cards (paper) [pak of card'-s (pei'-per)]

barra de tipos [f] type bar [ta'-ip bar]

base [f] radix [ra'-dix]

base de conocimiento [f] knowledge base [no-led'-ye be-is]

base de datos [f] data base [da'-ta be-is]

base de datos en línea [f] on-line data base [on la'-in da'-ta be-is]

basura entra, basura sale [f] garbage in-garbage out (GIGO) [gar'-be-ich in gar'-be-ich a-ut (GIGO)]

basura entra, basura sale [f] GIGO garbage in-garbage out [(GIGO) gar'-be-ich in gar'-be-ich a-ut]

baudio [m] baud [ba-ud']

biblioteca [f] library [lai-bra'-ri]

biblioteca de cintas [f] tape library [te'-ip lai-bra'-ri]

biblioteca de programas [f] program library [pro-gram lai-bra'-ri]

biblioteca de programas de aplicación [f] application programs library (APL) [apli-kei'-cion pro-gram-s lai-bra'-ri (APL)]

biblioteca de programas de aplicación [f] APL application programs library [APL apli-kei'-cion pro-gram-s lai-bra'-ri]

bidireccional [adj] bi-directional [bai di-rek'-cion-al]

bifurcación [f] branch [bran-ch']

bifurcación [f] bifurcation [bi-fur'-ka-cion]

bifurcar [v] branch [bran-ch']

binario [adj] binary [bi-na-ri']

biónica [f] bionics [bi-o'-niks]

bióplaqueta [mf] biochip [ba-io'-chip]

bipolar [adj] bipolar [bay-po'-lar]

biprocesador [m] dual processor [du'-al pro-se'-sor]

bit [m] bit [bit]

bit de comienzo [m] star bit [es'-tar bit]

bit de paridad [m] parity bit [pa-ri'-ti bit]

bit de servicio [m] service bit [ser-vi'-se bit]

bit de signo [m] sign bit [sa-in' bit]

bit de verificación [m] check bit [chek bit]

bit de zona [m] zone bit [soo-ne bit]

bit dual [m] dibit [di-bit]

bit-por-segundo [m] bit-per-second (BPS) [bit per se'-con-d (BPS)]

bit-por-segundo [m] BPS bit-per-second [BPS bit per se'-con-d]

blanco [m] blank [bla'-ank]

bloc de dibujo [m] sketch pad [es-ket'-ch pad]

bloc de notas [m] scratch pad [es-kra'-ch pad]

bloque [m] block [blok]

bloque de almacenamiento de memoria [m] storage block [es-tor'-aich blok]

bloque ennidado [m] nested block [nes-ted block]

bloquear [v] lockout [lok'-aut]

bloqueo de registro [m] record blocking [re-kor'-d blo'-kin-g]

bobina [f] hub (tape drive) [jab (te'-ip dra'-ib)]

bobina [f] spool [es-pul]

bobinado [adj] spooling [es-pu'-lin]

bobinadora [f] spooler [es-pu'-ler]

bobinar [v] spool [es-pul]

bola de tipógraficos [f] typeball [ta-ip bal]

boleador [m] track ball [trak bal]

borde [m] nerd [ner-d]

borrado [adj] erased [i-rai'-sed]

borrar [v] erase [i-ra'-is]

borrar [v] scratch [es-kra'-ch]

botón de ratón [m] mouse button [ma'-us bat'-ton]

brazo de acceso [m] access arm [ak-ses arm]

brecha de fichero [f] file gap [fa'-il gap]

brillantez [f] brightness [bra'-it-nes]

brocha de pintar [f] paintbrush [pa-in-bra-ich]

bucle [m] loop [lup]

bucle de acceso rápido [m] rapid-access loop [ra'-pid ak'-ses lup]

bucle sin control [m] uncontrolled loop [an-con'-tro-led lup]

buscando ciegamente [f] blind search [bla-in-d se'-ir-ch]

buscar [v] search [se'-ir-ch]

buscar [v] look-up [luk-ap]

búsque globalmente y reponga [f] global search and replace [glo-bal' se'-ir-ch an-d re-pla'-is]

búsque y reponga [f] search and replace [se'-ir-ch an-d re-pla'-is]

búsqueda [f] search [se'-ir-ch]

búsqueda binaria [f] binary search [bi-na'-ri se'-ir-ch]

búsqueda dicotómica [f] dichotomizing search [dai-ko'-to-mai-sin se'-ir-ch]

búsqueda en el texto [f] full-text searching [ful tex-t se-ir'-chin]

búsqueda en secuencia [f] sequential search [se-cu'-en-si-al se'-ir-ch]

búsqueda encadenada [f] chaining search [che'-i-nin-g se'-ir-ch]

búsqueda sistemática [f] systematic search [sis-te-ma'-tik se'-ir-ch]

byte [m] byte [ba'-it]

C

cabecera [f] header [je'-der]

cabeza [f] head [jed']

cabeza de borrar [f] erase head [i-re'-is jed']

cabeza de escritura [f] write head [rra'-it jed']

cabeza de lectura [f] read head [rrid jed']

cabeza de lectura previa [f] pre-read head [pre'-rrid jed']

cabeza de lectura-escritura [f] read-write head [rrid-rra'-it jed']

cabeza de registro [f] record head [re'-cor-d jed']

cabeza del bloque [f] block header [blok jed-er']

cabeza reproductora [f] playback head [pley-bak jed']

cable [m] cable [ka'-ble]

cable de conexión [m] patchcord [pach-kor'-d]

cabo [m] tail [te'-il]

cabrestante [m] capstan [cap'-es-tan]

cadena puntera [f] chain [che-in]

caerse [m] drop-in [drap-in]

caja de centello [f] twinkle box [tu-in'-kel box]

caja de circuitos estampados [f] card cage [kard que-ich]

calculador [m] computer [com'-piu-ter]

calculadora mecánica [f] calculator [cal-ku-lai'-tor]

cálculo de acceso múltiple [m] multi-access computing (MAC) [mul-ti-ak'-ses com'-piu-tin-g (MAC)]

cálculo de acceso múltiple [m] MAC multi-access computing [MAC mul-ti-ak'-ses com'-piu-tin-g]

cálculo inicial [m] home computing [jom com'-piu-tin-g]

cálculo interactivo [m] interactive computing [in'-ter-ak-tib com'-piu-tin-g]

calibración [f] calibration [ka-li-bre-i'-cion]

calidad [f] grade [gre'-id]

cámara de color [f] color camera [ko'-lor ka'-me'-ra]

cambiar [v] exchange [ex-che'-in]

cambio de factores [m] tradeoff [tre-id'-of]

cambio de paso [m] step change [es'-tep che'-in]

campaneando [m] bells-and-whistles [bels an-d bui'-sels]

campo [m] field [fil'-d]

campo de control [m] control field [kon'-trol fil'-d]

campo de la cadena puntera [m] chain field [che'-in fil'-d]

campo fijo [m] fixed field [fix fil'-d]

campo libre [m] free field [fri fil'-d]

campo variable [m] variable field [va'-ri-a-ble fil'-d]

canal [m] channel [cha'-nel]

canal de comunicación [m] communication channel [ko'-mu-ni-ka-cion cha'-nel]

canal de comunicación [m] link [lin'-k]

canal de comunicación de datos [m] links [lin'-ks]

canal de duplex [m] duplex channel [du-plex cha'-nel]

canal de lectura-escritura [m] read-write channel [rrid-rra'-it cha'-nel]

canal de rango vocal [m] voice grade channel [vo-is'gre-id cha'-nel]

canal del multiplexer [m] multiplexer channel [mul'-ti-plex-er cha'-nel]

canal selector [m] selector channel [se-lek'-tor cha'-nel]

cancela [v] cancel [kan-sel]

caos [m] chaos [ka'-os]

capacidad [f] capacity [ka-pa'-si-ti]

capacidad de almacenamiento de memoria [f] storage capacity [es-tor'-aich ka-pa'-si-ti]

capacidad de tratamiento utíl [f] throughput [tru-put]

capas asociadas de gráfica [f] layering [lei-ye'-rin]

capas gráficas [f] layer [le-yer]

capítulo [m] chapter [chap'-ter]

captura de datos [f] data capturing [da'-ta cap-chu-rin'-g]

captura de datos fuente [f] source data capture [so-ur-se da'-ta cap-chur]

carácter [m] character [ka-rac'-ter]

carácter blanco [m] space character [es-peis ka-rac'-ter]

carácter de sincronización [m] sync character [sin-k ka-rac'-ter]

carácter de supresión [m] ignore character [ig-nor ka-rac'-ter]

carácter especial [m] special character [es-pe'-sial ka-rac'-ter]

carácter global [m] global character [glo-bal ka-rac'-ter]

carácter inválido [m] illegal character [i-li'-gal ka-rac'-ter]

carácter nongráfico [m] nongraphic character [non-gra'-fik ka-rac'-ter]

carácter óptico [m] optical character [op-ti-cal' ka-rac'-ter]

carácter sin uso [m] idle characters [ai-del ka-rac'-ters]

característico [m] feature [fi-chur]

carácter-por-segundo [m] character-per-second (CPS) [ka-rac'-ter per se-con-d (CPS)]

carácter-por-segundo [m] CPS character-per-second [CPS ka-rac'-ter per se-con-d]

cargador [m] loader [lou-der]

cargador automático [m] automatic loader [auto-ma'-tik lou-der]

cargador de enlace [m] linking loader [lin-kin'-g lou-der]

cargador de sistema [m] system loader [sis-tem lou-der]

cargar [v] load [loud]

cargar y ejecutar [v] load-and-go [loud an'-d go]

carrete [m] reel [ri-il]

carro automático [m] automatic carriage [auto-ma'-tik ka-rri-aich]

cartucho [m] cartridge [kar-trich]

cartucho de datos [m] data cartridge [da'-ta kar-trich]

casa especializada en programación [f] software house [sof-gue-ar ja-us]

casete [mf] cassette [ka-se-te]

casillero receptor [m] stacker [es-ta'-ker]

casual [adj] random [rran-dom]

casualmente [adj] ramdomly [rram-dom-li]

catálogo de datos [m] data catalog [da'-ta ca-ta'-log]

categoría [f] status [es-ta'-tus]

célula [f] cell [sel]

célula activa [f] active cell [ak'-ti-be sel]

célula magnética [f] magnetic cell [mag-ne'-tik sel]

centro [m] hub [jab]

centro de conmutación [m] switching center [sui-chin'-g sen-ter]

centro de procesador de texto [m] word processing center [gu-or'-d pro-se-sin'-g sen-ter]

centro de retransmisión [m] relay center [re-lai sen-ter]

cerca de computadores [f] computer enclosure [com-piu'-ter en-clo-chu-ar]

cerco de sonido acústico [m] acoustical sound enclosure [a-kus-ti-cal sa-un'-d en-clo-chu-ar]

cerner [v] sift [sif'-t]

cerniendo [adj] sifting [sif-tin'-g]

cibernética [f] cybernetics [sai-ber'-ne-tiks]

ciclo [m] cycle [sai-cle]

ciclo de procesamiento del computador [m] computer processing cycle [com-piu'-ter pro-se-sin'-g sai-cle]

ciclo nulo [m] null cycle [nul sai-cle]

cicuito de enchufe [m] plug in [plag in]

ciencia del computador [f] computer science [com-piu'-ter sai-en'-se]

cierre [m] shutdown [chat-da-un]

cierre automático [m] automatic shutdown [auto-ma'-tik chat-da-un]

cifra [f] cipher [sai-fer]

cilindro [m] cylinder [si-lin'-der]

cilindro impresor [m] print barrel [prin'-t ba'-rrel]

cincuenta-excedente [adj] excess-fifty [ex-ses fif-ti]

cinta [f] tape [te'-ip]

cinta con perforación [f] perforated tape [per-fo'-rei-ted te'-ip]

cinta creadora [f] father tape [fa-der te'-ip]

cinta de alimentación central [f] center-feed tape [sen-ter fi'-id te'-ip]

cinta de alimentación por arrastre [f] advance-feed tape [ad-van'-sed fi'-id te'-ip]

cinta de control del carro [f] carriage control tape [ka-rri-aich con-trol te'-ip]

cinta de instrucciones maestras [f] master-instruction tape (MIT) [mas'-ter ins-truk'-cion te'-ip (MIT)]

cinta de instrucciones maestras [f] MIT master-instruction tape [MIT mas'-ter ins-truk'-cion te'-ip]

cinta de maniobra [f] work tape [gu'-ork te'-ip]

cinta de papel [f] paper tape [pei-per te'-ip]

cinta de perforación completa [f] chadded tape [cha-ded te'-ip]

cinta de serpentina [f] streamer [es-tri'-mer]

cinta entintada [f] ink ribbon [ink rri'-bon]

cinta maestra [f] master tape [mas-ter te'-ip]

cinta magnética [f] magnetic tape [mag-ne'-tik te'-ip]

cinta magnética [f] magstripe [mag-es'-tra-ip]

cinta perforada [f] punched tape [pun-ched te'-ip]

cinta que lee al revés [f] backward read [bak-guar rrid]

cinta sin perforación [f] chadless tape [chad-les te'-ip]

cinta virgen [f] virgin tape [vir-llin' te'-ip]

circuito [m] circuit [sir-cu'-it]

circuito abierto [m] open loop [o'-pen lup]

circuito agitante [m] gating circuit [gai-tin'-g sir-cu'-it]

circuito biestable [m] bistable circuit [ba-is'-tei-bol sir-cu'-it]

circuito cerrado [m] closed loop [clo-sed lup]

circuito común [m] trunk circuit [trun-k sir-cu'-it]

circuito de cuatro alambres [m] four-wire circuit [fo-ar gua-yer sir-cu'-it]

circuito de disparo [m] trigger circuit [tri'-ger sir-cu'-it]

circuito estampado [m] card [kard]

circuito estampado de extensión [m] expansion card [ex-pan'-sion kard]

circuito integrado [m] IC integrated circuit [IC in-te-grei'-ted sir-cu'-it]

circuito integrado [m] integrated circuit (IC) [in-te-grei'-ted sir-cu'-it (IC)]

circuito lógico [m] logic circuit [lo-llic sir-cu'-it]

circuito regenerado [m] refresh circuitry [rre-frech sir-cu'-i-tri]

clases de tipógrafos [f] type font [ta'-ip fon'-t]

clasificación [f] sort [sor'-t]

clasificación del árbol [f] heap sort [jip sor'-t]

clasificación del árbol [f] tree sort [tri'-i sor'-t]

clasificación en onda [f] bubble sort [ba-bel' sor'-t]

clasificación en onda [f] ripple sort [rip'-pel sor'-t]

clasificación oscilante [f] oscillating sort [os-si-lai'-tin sor'-t]

clasificación-fusión [adj] sort-merge [sor'-t me-ir-ch]

clasificador alfanumérico [m] alphanumeric sort [alfa-nu-me'-rik sor'-t]

clasificador de documentos [m] document sorter [do-kiu-men'-t sor'-ter]

clasificadora [f] sorter [sor'-ter]

clasificando [adj] sorting [sor'-tin'-g]

clasificar [v] sort [sor'-t]

clasificar el intercalo [m] collating sort [co-lei-tin'-g sor'-t]

clave concatenada [f] concatenated key [con-ka'-te-nei-ted ki]

clon [mf] clone [klon]

codificación [f] coding [co-din'-g]

codificación automática [f] automatic coding [auto-ma'-tik co-din'-g]

codificar [v] code [coud]

código [m] code [coud]

código absoluto [m] absolute code [ab-so-lut coud]

código binario [m] binary code [bai-na'-ri coud]

código binario denso [m] dense binary code [den'-s bai-na'-ri coud]

código biquinario [m] biquinary code [bai-kui-na'-ri coud]

código cíclico [m] cyclic code [zai-clik coud]

código de acceso mínimo [m] minimum-access code [mi-ni-mum ak'-ses coud]

código de barras [m] bar-code [bar coud]

código de cierre [m] lock code [lok coud]

código de corrección de errores [m] error-correcting code [error co-rrec-tin'-g coud]

código de detección de errores [m] error-detecting code [error de-tek-tin'-g coud]

código de entrada [m] access code [ak'-ses coud]

código de instrucción [m] instruction code [ins-truc-cion' coud]

código de la cadena puntera [m] chain code [che-in coud]

código de máquina [m] machine code [ma-chin coud]

código de operación [m] op-code [ap coud]

código de operación mnemotécnico [m] mnemonic operation code [ne-mo-nik o-pe-ra-cion' coud]

código de orden [m] order code [or-der coud]

código de reentrada [m] reentrant code [re-en-tran'-t coud]

código de respuesta [m] answer code [ans-guer coud]

código de trazos [m] bar code [bar coud]

código del carácter [m] character code [ka-rac'-ter coud]

código del producto universal [m] universal product code [yuni-ver'-sal pro-duc'-t coud]

código esquemático [m] skeletal code [es-ke-le-tal coud]

código fuente [m] source code [so-ur'-se coud]

código Hollerith [m] Hollerith code [jo'-le-rit coud]

código líneal [m] in-line coding [in la'-in co-u-din'-g]

codigo modular [m] modular coding [mo'-du-lar co-u-din'-g]

código objeto [m] object code [ob-yet coud]

código redundante [m] redundant code [re-dun-dan'-t coud]

código relativo [m] relative code [re-la'-tib coud]

código reservado [m] private code [prai-ve-it coud]

código reubicable [m] relocatable code [re-lo'-kei-ta-bel coud]

código simbólico [m] symbolic coding [sin-bo-lik co-u-din'-g]

coeficiente de errores [m] error rate [error re-it]

coerción [f] coercion [co-er'-cion]

coherencia [f] coherence [co-ji-ren-se]

cohesión [f] cohesion [co-je-sion]

colección de programas [f] program package [pro-gram pa'-que-ich]

colgar [v] hang-up [jan ap]

colocar [v] put [put]

color [m] hue [jiu]

colores primordiales [m] primary colors [prai-ma-ri co-lor'-s]

columna [f] column [co'-lum]

columna de circuitos estampados [f] card column [kard co'-lum]

comensar el modo de diágolo [v] logging-in [lo-guin in]

comensar la sesión [v] log on [log on]

comentario [m] comment [ko-men'-t]

como cocinando [adj] cookbook [cuk-buk]

comparador [m] comparator [com-pa'-ra-tor]

comparar [v] compare [com-pe'-ar]

compatibilidad [f] compatibility [com-pa-ti'-bi-li-ti]

compatibilidad de programas [f] program compatibility [pro-gram com-pa-ti'-bi-li-ti]

compatibilidad entre equipos [f] equipment compatibility [e-ku-ip'-men-t com-pa-ti'-bi-li-ti]

compila y marcha [m] compile-and-go [com-pa-il an'-d go]

compilador cruzado [m] cross-compiler [cros com-pai-ler]

compiladora [f] compiler [com-pai-ler]

compiladora natal [f] native compiler [nei-tib com-pai-ler]

compilar [v] compile [com-pa-il]

complementar [v] complement [com-ple-men'-t]

complemento [m] complement [com-ple-men'-t]

complemento a diez [m] ten's complement [ten'-s com-ple-men'-t]

complemento a dos [m] two's complement [tu'-s com-ple-men'-t]

complemento a nueves [m] nine's complement [na-in'-s com-ple-men't]

complemento a uno [m] one's complement [u-an'-s com-ple-men'-t]

complemento de la base [m] radix complement [rra-dix com-ple-men'-t]

componente discreto [m] discrete component [dis-crit com-po-nen'-t]

componer [v] patch [pach]

composición tipográfica de computador [f] computer typesetting [com-piu'-ter ta-ip-se-tin'-g]

compresión de datos [f] data compression [da'-ta com-pre'-sion]

comprobación de suma [f] summation check [su-mei'-cion chek]

comprobación total [f] proof total [pruf to-tal]

compuesto de color [m] composite [com-po-sit]

computador [m] computer [com-piu'-ter]

computador analógico [m] analog computer [a-na'-log com-piu'-ter]

computador anfitríon [m] guest computer [ges'-t com-piu'-ter]

computador anfitrión [m] host computer [jos'-t com-piu'-ter]

computador de mesa [m] desk top computer [des'-k tap com-piu'-ter]

computador digital [m] digital computer [di-lli-tal com-piu'-ter]

computador en una plaqueta [m] computer-on-a-chip [com-piu'-ter on a chip]

computador especializado [m] special-purpose computer [es-pe-si-al pur-pos com-piu'-ter]

computador hecho en casa [m] homebrew [jom briu]

computador híbrido [m] hybrid computer [jai-bri'-d com-piu'-ter]

computador neumático [m] pneumatic computer [ne-u-ma-tik com-piu'-ter]

computador personal [m] personal computer [per-so'-nal com-piu'-ter]

computador portátil [m] portable computer [por-ta-ble com-piu'-ter]

computador principal [m] mainframe [me-in fre-im]

computador satélite [m] satellite computer [za-te-la-it com-piu'-ter]

computador síncrono [m] synchronous computer [sin-cro-no-us com-piu'-ter]

computador sólo [m] stand-alone [es-tan'-d a-lon]

computador universal [m] general-purpose computer [ye-ne-ral pur-pos com-piu'-ter]

computadores en tándem [m] tandem computers [tan-dem com-piu'-ter-es]

computar [v] compute [com-piu'-t]

computomaníaco [m] hacker [ja-ker]

comunicación [f] communication [com-mu-ni-ka'-cion]

comunicación amiga [f] handshaking [jan che-i-kin'-g]

comunicación asíncrona [f] asynchronous communication [a-sin-cro-no-us com-mu-ni-ka'-cion]

comunicación de voz [f] voice communications [vo-is com-mu-ni-ka'-cion-s]

comunicación síncronizada [f] synchronous communications [sin-cro-no-us com-mu-ni-ka'-cion-s]

comunicación telefónica [f] telephonic communication [te-le-fo-nic com-mu-ni-ka'-cion]

comunicaciones entre sistemas [f] intersystem communications [inter-sis-tem com-mu-ni-ka'-cion]

comunicaciones ópticas [f] optical communications [op-ti-kal com-mu-ni-ka'-cion-s]

concatenar [v] concatenate [con-ka-te-ne-it]

concentración de datos [f] data concentration [da'-ta con-sen-tre-i-cion]

concetrador [m] concentrator [con-sen-tre-i-tor]

condición del medio ambiente [f] ambient conditions [am-bi-en'-t con-di-cion'-s]

conductor común [m] bus [bas]

conductor común del direccional [m] address bus ad-dre'-s bas]

conductor de prueba [m] test driver [tes'-t dra-i-ver]

conectar [v] turn on [ter-n on]

conector [m] connector [con-nec-tor]

confiabilidad [f] reliability [re-la-ya-bi-li-ty]

confiable [adj] reliable [re-la-ya-ble]

configuración [f] configuration [con-fi-gu-rei'-cion]

configuración de bit [f] bit pattern [bit pa-ter'-n]

configuración de la central de redes [f] centralized network configuration [cen-tra-la-i-sed net-guor'-k con-fi-gu-rei'-cion]

configuración en telaraña [f] spider configuration [es-pa-i-der con-fi-gu-rei'-cion

confirmación negativa [f] negative acknowledgement [ne-ga-tib ak-no-bled-ment]

conjunción [f] conjunction [con-yun'-cion]

conjunto [m] set [set]

conjunto de datos secuenciales [m] sequential data set [se-ku-en-sial da'-ta set]

conmutable [adj] switch [su-ich]

conmutación automática de mensajes [f] automatic message switching [auto-ma'-tik me-ze-ich sui-chin'-g]

conmutación de líneas [f] line switching [la'-in su-i-chin]

conmutación de mensajes [f] message switching [me-sa-ich su-i-chin]

conmutación de paquetes [f] packet switching [pa-ket su-i-chin]

conmutación del bloque [f] block switching [blok su-i-chin]

conmutación digital [f] digital switching [di-lli-tal su-i-chin]

conmutación telefónica [f] telephone switching [te-le-fon su-i-chin]

conmutador [m] switch [su-ich]

conmutador [m] toggle [to-gle]

conmutador electrónico [m] electronic switch [e-lek-tro-nik su-ich]

conmutar [v] switch [su-ich]

consola [f] console [con-sol]

consola de visualización [f] display console [dis-ple-i con-sol]

consola remota [f] remote console [re-mot con-sol]

constante [adj] invariant [in-va-ri-an'-t]

constantes [f] constants [kon-es-tan'-t]

construcción de modelos [f] model building [mo-del bil-din'-g]

consulta de tablas [f] TLU table look-up [TLU tei-bol luk-ap]

consulta de tablas [f] table look-up (TLU) [tei-bol luk-ap (TLU)]

consultar [v] look-up [luk-ap]

contador [m] counter [co-un-ter]

contador de posiciones [m] location counter [lo-kei-cion co-un-ter]

contador en círculo [m] ring counter [rrin co-un-ter]

contador reversible [m] reversible counter [rre-ver-si-ble co-un-ter]

contenido [m] content [con-ten'-t]

contenido direcionable [adj] content-addressable [con-ten'-t a-dre-sa'-ble]

contenido pre-selecionado de palabras [m] KWIC key-word-in-context [KWIC ki-gu-or'-d-con-tex-t]

contenido pre-selecionado de palabras [m] key-word-in-context (KWIC) [ki-gu-or'-d-con-tex-t (KWIC)]

contorneando [m] contouring [con-to-u-rin'-g]

contra la escalera visual [adj] anti-aliasing [an-tai-a-lia-sin'-g]

contraseña [f] password [pas-gu-ord]

contraste [m] contrast [con-tras'-t]

control [m] control [con-trol]

control automático de calidad [m] automatic quality control [auto-ma-tik qu-a-li-ti con-trol]

control de paridad [m] parity check [pa-ri-ti chek]

control de paridad par-impar [m] odd-even check [od-iven chek]

control de procesos [m] process control [pro-ses con-trol]

control de realimentación [m] feedback control [fi-id bak con-trol]

control de supervisión [m] supervisory control [super-vai-so-ri con-trol]

control del cursor [m] cursor control [cur-sor con-trol]

control manual [m] manual control [ma-nu-al con-trol]

control numérico [m] numerical control [nu-me-ri-kal con-trol]

control por excepción [m] exception principle system (EPS) [e-sep-cion prin-si-pel sis-tem (EPS)]

control por excepción [m] EPS exception principle system [EPS e-sep-cion prin-si-pel sis-tem]

control proporcional [m] proportional control [pro-por-cio-nal con-trol]

controlador de agrupación [m] cluster controller [clus-ter con-tro-ler]

controlador periférico [m] peripheral controller [peri-fe'-ral con-tro-ler]

controlar [v] control [con-trol]

conversación cruzada [f] cross-talk [cros tok]

conversión [f] conversion [con-ver'-sion]

conversión automática de datos [f] automatic data conversion [auto-ma'-tik da'-ta con-ver'-sion]

conversión de binario a decimal [f] binary-to-decimal conversion [bai-na-ri tu de-si-mal con-ver'-sion]

conversión de binario a hexádecimal [f] binary-to-hexadecimal conversion [bai-na-ri to jex-sa-de-si-mal con-ver'-sion]

conversión de binario a octal [f] binary-to-octal conversion [bai-na-ri tu ok-tal con-ver'-sion]

conversión de ficheros [f] file conversion [fa-il' con-ver'-sion]

conversión de procesos [f] process conversion [pro-ses con-ver'-sion]

conversión paralela [f] parallel conversion [pa-ra-lel con-ver'-sion]

convertidor [m] converter [con-ver'-ter]

convertidor analógico-digital [m] analog-digital converter [ana-log di-lli-tal con-ver'-ter]

convertidor de teclado [m] pooler [pu-ler]

convertidor digital-analógico [m] digital-to-analog converter [di-lli-tal tu ana-log con-ver'-ter]

convertidor serie-paralelo [m] serial-parallel converter [se-rial para-lel con-ver'-ter]

convertir [v] convert [con-ver'-t]

copia blanda [f] soft copy [sof'-t co-pi]

copia de reserva [f] backup copy [bak-ap co-pi]

copia impresa [f] hard copy [jar'-d co-pi]

copiador [m] transcriber [tran-es-cra-i-ber]

copiar [v] copy [co-pi]

corrección automática de errores [f] automatic error correction [auto-ma'-tik error co-rrek-cion]

correo electrónico [m] electronic mail [elek-tro-nik me-il]

correo informático [m] computerized mail [com-piu'-ter-ai-sed me-il]

correo por voz [m] voice mail [vo-is me-il]

correspondiente [adj] match [mach]

cortar y pegar [v] cut-and-paste [cat an'-d pe-is'-t]

corutina [f] coroutine [co-ro-u-tin]

creado especialmente [adj] tailor-made [tei-lor me-id]

cromático [m] chroma [kro-ma]

crujido [m] crunch [crun'-ch]

crujido de números [m] number crunching [nan-ber crun-chin'-g]

cuadriculado [m] grid [grid]

cuadro intermedio [m] framebuffer [fre-im-ba-fer]

cualidad portátil [f] portability [por-ta-bi-li-ti]

cuántico tiempo [m] time quantum [ta-im cuan-tum]

cuantificación [f] quantization [cuan-tai-sa'-cion]

cuantificador [m] quantizer [cuan-tai-ser]

cuantificar [v] quantize [cuan-ta-is]

cuarta-generación [adj] fourth-generation [fo-urz ye-ne-ra'-cion]

cuarto de máquinas [m] machine room [ma-chin rum]

cuasi-instrucción [f] quasi-instruction [kua-sai-ins-truc-cion]

cuenta de ciclos [f] cycle count [sai-cle co-un'-t]

curiosear [m] browsing [bra-u-sin'-g]

cursar [v] path [pas]

curso [m] path [pas]

cursor [m] cursor [cur-sor]

C-electrónico [m] E-mail [I-me-il]

CH

chasis [m] chassis [cha-sis]

chasis [m] cage [ke-ich]

chasqueando [m] clicking [clik-in'-g]

choque [m] crash [kra'-ach]

choque en el disco [m] head crash [jed kra'-ach]

D

dar un tirón [v] pop [pap]

datos [m] data [da'-ta]

datos analógicos [m] analog data [ana-log da'-ta]

datos de control [m] control data [con-trol da'-ta]

datos de muestra [m] sample data [sam-ple da'-ta]

datos de transacción [m] transaction data [tran-sa-cion da'-ta]

datos del ensayo [m] test data [tes'-t da'-ta]

datos sin procesar [m] raw data [rro da'-ta]

de canto del árbol [m] outdegree [o-ut-di-gri]

de reserva [f] fall-back [fal-bak]

de tecla a direccional [f] hashing [ja'-chin-g]

debilitadamente aclopado [m] loosely coupled [lu-se-li ca-pled]

decadencia de luminosidad [f] luminance decay [lu-mi-nan'-se de'-key]

decatenar [v] decatenate [de-ka-te-ne-it]

decimal [m] decimal [de-si-mal]

decimal codificado en binario [m] binary-coded decimal (BCD) [bi-na-ri' ko-ded de-si-mal (BCD)]

decimal codificado en binario [m] BCD binary-coded decimal [BCD bi-na-ri' ko-ded de-si-mal]

declaración [f] statement [es-tei-ment]

declaración de acción [f] action statement [ak-cion es-tei-ment]

declaración de asignación [f] assignment statement [a-sai-ment es-tei-ment]

decodificador [m] decoder [de-ko-der]

decodificador del direccional [m] address decoder [a-dres de-ko-der]

decodificar [v] decode [de-cod]

decolarse [v] deque [di-kiu]

decremento [m] decrement [de-cre-men'-t]

decriptar los datos [m] decryption [de-crip-cion]

dedal [m] thimble [tim-bel]

dedicado [adj] dedicated [de-di-kei-ted]

defecto [m] bug [bag]

definición del problema [f] problem definition [pro-blem de-fi-ni'-cion]

deformación [f] distortion [dis-tor'-cion]

degausador [m] degausser [di-ga'-u-ser]

deglosador [m] decollator [di-co-lei-tor]

degradación con garbo [f] graceful degradation [gre-is-ful de-gra-dei'-cion]

deinstalar [v] deinstall [de-in-s-tal]

del fondo hacia arriba [adj] bottom-up [bo-dom ap]

delantero [m] leader [li-der]

delimitador [m] delimiter [de-li'-mi-ter]

delimitar [v] delimit [de-li'-mit]

demodulador [m] demodulator [di-mo-du-lei-tor]

densidad de almacenamiento de memoria [f] storage density [es-to'-raich den-si-ti]

densidad de bit [f] bit density [bit den-si-ti]

densidad de carácter [f] character density [ka-rac'-ter den-si-ti]

densidad de empaquetamiento [f] packing density [pak-in'-g den-si-ti]

densidad de registro [f] recording density [re-cor-din'-g den-si-ti]

dentado [m] jaggies [lla-gui-es]

dependiente de la máquina [f] machine-dependent [ma-chin di-pen-dent]

depósito [m] deposit [di-po-sit]

depósito de alimentación [m] hopper [ja-per]

depurar [v] debug [di-bag]

depurar [v] checkout [chek-aut]

derramarse [v] overflow [over-flo]

desaparece [m] drop-out [drop aut]

desbordamiento [m] overflow [over-flo]

descanso [m] interlude [inter-li-ud]

descargar [v] off load [of lo-ud]

descenso de archivos [m] download [da-un lo-ud]

desconectar [v] turn off [tur'-n of]

descriptor [m] descriptor [des-crip-tor]

descubra y sustituya [f] find and replace [fa-in'-d an'-d ri-pla-is]

descubrir [v] find [fi-in'-d]

desdesigualar [m] dejagging [di-llag-in]

desempaquetar [v] unpack [an-pak]

desenredar [v] unwind [an-gua-in'-d]

deshacer [v] undo [an-du]

deslumbrante [mf] glare [gle-ar]

despacho [m] dispatch [dis-pach]

despacho/captor [m] answer/originate [an'-ser/o-ri-lli-nei-t]

despejar [v] clear [kli-ar]

desperdicio [m] junk [yank]

desplazamiento [m] shift [chif'-t]

desplazamiento [m] panning [pa-nin'-g]

desplazamiento a la derecha [m] right shift [rra-it chif'-t]

desplazamiento a la izquierda [m] left shift [lef'-t chif'-t]

desplazamiento arimético [m] arithmetic shift [a-rit-me-tik chif'-t]

desplazamiento en círculo [m] ring shift [rrin'-g chif'-t]

desplazamiento lógico [m] logic shift [lo-llik chif'-t]

desplazamiento lógico [m] logical shift [lo-lli-cal chif'-t]

desplazar [v] shift [chif'-t]

destacando [m] highlighting [jai-lai-tin'-g]

desviación [f] loophole [lup-jol]

desviación de información [f] reroute information [ri-rou'-t in-for-ma'-cion]

detectar [v] sense [sen'-s]

diagnosis [f] diagnosis [di-ag-no-sis]

diagnosis de errores [f] error diagnostics [error di-ag-nos-tik'-s]

diagnóstico de sistema [m] system diagnostics [sis-tem di-ag-nos-tik'-s]

diagrama de cables [m] cabling diagram [kei-blin'-g dai-a-gram]

diagrama lógico [m] logic diagram [lo-llik dai-a-gram]

diagrama por bloques [m] block diagram [blok dai-a-gram]

diapositivos [m] slide [es-laid]

dibujando [adj] sketching [es-ket-chin'-g]

dibujo con líneas [m] raster graphics [rras-ter gra-fik'-s]

dibujo en computador [m] computer drawing [com-piu'-ter dro-gu'-in]

dibujos [m] graphics [gra-fik'-s]

dibujos artísticos para cortar [m] clip art [klip art]

dibujos artísticos preparados [m] click art [klik art]

dibujos de color [m] color graphics [co-lor gra-fik'-s]

diccionario [m] dictionary [dik-chio-nary]

diferenciador [m] differentiator [di-fe-ren-chie-tor]

digital [adj] digital [di-lli-tal]

digitalizador [m] digitizer [di-lli-tai-ser]

digitalizar [v] digitize [di-lli-tais]

digitilizador [m] data tablet [da'-ta ta-ble'-t]

digitilizador de gráfica [f] graphics digitizer [gra-fik'-s di-lli-tai-ser]

digitizador de video [m] video digitizer [vi-deo di-lli-tai-ser]

dígito [m] digit [di-lli'-t]

dígito de signo [m] sign digit [sa-in di-lli'-t]

dígito de verificación [m] check digit [chek di-lli'-t]

dígito de zona [m] zone digit [son di-lli'-t]

dígitos binarios equivalentes [m] equivalent binary digits [eku-i-va-len'-t bai-na-ri di-jit'-s]

dígitos significativos [m] significant digits [sig-ni-fi-can'-t di-jit'-s]

diodo [m] diode [dai'-od]

diodo luminoso [m] light-emitting diode (LED) [lait e-mi-tin'-g dai'-od (LED)]

diodo luminoso [m] LED light-emitting diode [LED lait e-mi-tin'-g dai'-od]

dirección de máquina [f] machine address [ma-chin' ad-dres]

dirección de referencia [f] reference address [re-fe-ren'-s ad-dres]

dirección de segundo nivel [f] second-level address [se-con'-d le-vel ad-dres]

dirección de uno más uno [f] one-plus-one address [uan plas uan ad-dres]

dirección indirecta [f] indirect address [in-di-rek'-t ad-dres]

dirección relativa [f] relative address [re-la-tib ad-dres]

dirección reubicable [f] relocatable address [re-lo-kei-ta-bel ad-dres]

dirección simbólica [f] symbolic address [sim-bo-lik ad-dres]

dirección virtual [f] virtual address [vir-chu-al ad-dres]

direccionado relativo [m] relative addressing [re-la-tib ad-dres-sin'-g]

direccionado repetitivo [m] repetitive addressing [re-pe-ti-tib ad-dres-sin'-g]

direccional [mf] address [ad-dres]

direccional absoluto [m] absolute address [ab-so-lut ad-dres]

direccional afectivo [m] affective address [a-fek-tib ad-dres]

direccional efectivo [m] effective address [e-fek-tib ad-dres]

direccional explícito [m] base address [be-is ad-dres]

direccional explícito [m] explicit address [ex-pli-sit ad-dres]

direccional para más tarde [m] deferred address [de-fe-rred ad-dres]

direccional verdadero [m] actual address [ak-tual ad-dres]

direccionamiento [m] addressing [ad-dres-sin'-g]

direccionamiento abreviado [m] abbreviated addressing [abre-via-ted ad-dres-sin'-g]

direccionamiento alargado [m] extended addressing [es-ten-ded ad-dres-sin'-g]

direccionamiento directo [m] direct addressing [di-rek'-t ad-dres-sin'-g]

direccionar [v] address [ad-dres]

directiva [f] directive [di-rek-tib]

directorio [m] directory [di-rek'-to-ri]

disco [m] disk [dis'-k]

disco [m] disc [dis'-k]

disco de blanco [m] target disk [tar-get dis'-k]

disco de cartucho [m] cartridge disk [car-trich dis'-k]

disco de un lado [m] single-sided disk [sin-gel sai-ded dis'-k]

disco duro [m] hard disk [jar'-d dis'-k]

disco flexible [m] diskette [dis-ket]

disco flexible [m] floppy disk [fla-pi dis'-k]

disco intermedio [m] disk buffer [dis'-k ba-fer]

disco magnético [m] magnetic disk [mag-ne-tik dis'-k]

discreto [adj] discrete [dis-kret]

diseñar [v] model [ma-del]

diseño automático de sistemas [m] automatic system design [auto-ma-tik sis-tem di-sain]

diseño central [m] centralized design [sentra-lai-sed di-sain]

diseño con ayuda del computador [m] computer-aided design (CAD) [com-piu'-ter ai-ded di-sain (CAD)]

diseño con ayuda del computador [m] CAD computer-aided design [CAD com-piu'-ter ai-ded di-sain]

diseño de computadores [m] computer design [com-piu'-ter di-sain]

diseño de elementos [m] item design [ai-tem di-sain]

diseño funcional [m] functional design [fun'-cio-nal di-sain]

diseño técnico automatizado [m] automated engineering design (AED) [auto-mei-'-ted en-lli-nee-rin'-g di-sain (AED)]

diseño técnico automatizado [m] AED automated engineering design [AED auto-mei-'-ted en-lli-nee-rin'-g di-sain]

diseño y dibujo con ayuda del computador [m] CADD computer-aided design and drafting [CADD com-piu'-ter ai-ded di-sain an'-d draf-tin'-g]

diseño y dibujo con ayuda del computador [m] computer-aided design and drafting (CADD) [com-piu'-ter ai-ded di-sain an'-d draf-tin'-g (CADD)]

disparador [m] trigger [tri'-ger]

disparar [v] trigger [tri'-ger]

dispersión [f] dispersion [dis-per'-sion]

dispositivo aclopado con carga [m] charge-coupled device (CCD) [char-aich cou-ple'-d di-vais (CCD)]

dispositivo aclopado con carga [m] CCD charge-coupled device [CCD char-aich cou-ple'-d di-vais]

dispositivo de almacenamiento de acceso directo [m] direct access storage device (DASD) [di-rec'-t ak'-ses es-tor-aich di-vais (DASD)]

dispositivo de almacenamiento de acceso directo [m] DASD direct access storage device [DASD di-rec'-t ak'-ses es-tor-aich di-vais]

dispositivo de entrada [m] input device [in-put di-vais]

dispositivo de entrada/salida [m] input/output device [in-put/aut-put di-vais]

dispositivo de salida [m] output device [aut-put di-vais]

dispositivo del almacenamiento de memoria [m] storage device [es-tor-aich di-vais]

distancia de líneas [f] leading [li-din'-g]

distancia de señal [f] signal distance [sig'-nal dis-tan'-c]

divisor [m] divider [di-vai-der]

divulgación de datos [f] data leakage [da'-ta li-ka'-ich]

doble control [m] twin control [tuin con-trol]

doble longitud [adj] double-length [do-u-ble len'-t]

doble precisión [f] double precision [do-u-ble pre-si'-sion]

dobletipo [m] typeover [taip-over]

documentación [f] documentation [do-ku-men-tei'-cion]

documento [m] document [do-ku-ment]

documento fuente [m] source document [so-ur'-c do-ku-ment]

dominio [m] domain [do-mein]

dos pasos [m] two pass [tu pas]

duendecillo [m] sprites [es-pra'-it]

duplex [mf] duplex [du-plex]

duplex todo completo [m] full-duplex [ful du-plex]

duplicación [f] duplication [du-pli-kei'-cion]

duplicar [v] duplicate [du-pli-keit]

E

econométria [f] econometrics [e-ko-no-me-trik'-s]

editación de texto [f] text editing [tex'-t edi-tin'-g]

editar [v] edit [edi'-t]

editor de pantalla llena [m] full-screen editing [ful es-crin edi-tin'g]

editor de texto [m] text editor [tex'-t edi-tor]

ejecución de programas concurrentes [f] concurrent program execution [con-ku-rren'-t pro-gram ex-se-kiu'-cion]

ejecutar [v] execute [ex-se-kiut]

ejemplo por interrogación [m] query by example [ku-eri bai ex-sam-pel]

el primero entra-el último sale [m] first in-last out (FILO)] [fir-s'-t in las'-t aut (FILO)]

el primero entra-el último sale [m] FILO first in-last out [FILO fir-s'-t in las'-t aut]

el último entra - el último sale [m] LILO last in-last out [LILO las'-t in las'-t aut]

el último entra - el último sale [m] last in-last out (LILO)[las'-t in las'-t aut (LILO)]

elección [f] polling [po-lin'-g]

eléctrico [adj] electric [e-lec'-trik]

eléctrisado [adj] electrical [e-lec'-tri-kal]

electrónico [adj] electronic [e-lec'-tro-nik]

elemento [m] element [ele-men'-t]

elemento con tres-entradas [m] three-input element [tri in-put ele-men'-t]

elemento de equivalencia [m] equivalence element [ekui-va-len-se ele-men'-t]

elemento de identidad [m] identity element [ai-den-ti-ti ele-men'-t]

elemento de matriz [m] matrix element [ma-tris ele-men'-t]

elemento de umbral [m] threshold element [tres-jold ele-men'-t]

elemento mayoritario [m] majority element [ma-llo-ri-ti ele-men't]

elemento primitivo [m] primitive element [pri-mi-tib ele-men'-t]

elementos del bloque [m] blocking factor [blo-kin fak-tor]

eliminación [f] deletion [di-li'-cion]

eliminar [v] weed [gu-id]

embaucar los datos [m] data diddling [da'-ta did-lin'-g]

empacar [v] packing [pak-in'-g]

empalmadora [f] splicer [es-plai-ser]

empaque [m] pack up [pak ap]

empaquetar [v] pack [pak]

emparejar [m] hit [jit]

empaste [m] filling [fil-in'-g]

emulación del terminal [f] terminal emulation [ter-mi-nal e-miu-lei-sion']

emulador [m] emulator [e-miu-lei-tor]

en blanco [m] blanking [blan-kin'-g]

en espera de mensajes [f] message queuing [me-saich kiu-in'-g]

en línea [adj] on-line [on lain]

en modularción [f] modularity [mo-du-la-ri-ti]

en orden de subida [f] ascending order [as-sen-din'-g or-der]

en rotación [f] round robin [raun'-d rro-bin]

encadenación del programa [f] program chaining [pro-gram chei-nin'-g]

encadenamiento de datos [m] data chaining [da'-ta chei-nin'-g]

encaminamiento de mensajes [m] message routing [me-saich rra-u-tin'-g]

encaminar [v] route [rra-ut]

encerrado [adj] lock-up [lok ap]

enchufar [v] plug in [plag in]

encodificador [m] encoder [en-kou-der]

encodificar [v] encode [en-kou'-d]

encontronazo [m] smash [es-mach]

encriptar [v] encipher [en-sai-fer]

encriptar los datos [m] data encryption [da'-ta en-crip-cion]

encuadrar [v] frame [frei'-m]

encuadre [m] frame [frei'-m]

encuadrillado [m] gridding [grid-din'-g]

enhebrar [adj] threaded [tre-a-ded]

enlace [m] linkage [link-aich]

enlace básico [m] basic linkage [bei-sik link-aich]

enlace común [m] trunk link [trun'-k lin'-k]

enlace digital [m] digital link [di-lli-tal lin'-k]

enlace para transmisión de datos [m] data link [da'-ta lin'-k]

enlazo fusible [m] fusible link [fiu-si-bel lin'-k]

enmascaramiento [m] masking [mas-kin'-g]

enmascarar [v] mask [mas'-k]

ennidar [m] nesting [nes-tin'-g]

enparejar [v] match [mach]

enpuñado [m] handler [jan-dler]

enrollamiento [m] scrolling [es-kro-lin'-g]

enrollamiento automatico [m] automatic scrolling [auto-ma-tik es-kro-lin'-g]

enrollamiento continuo [m] continous scrolling [con-ti-niu'-s es-kro-lin'-g]

enrollamiento horizontal [m] horizontal scrolling [jo-ri-son'-tal es-kro-lin'-g]

enrollamiento suave [m] smooth scrolling [es-mut es-kro-lin'-g]

enrollamiento vertical [m] vertical scrolling [ver-ti-kal es-kro-lin'-g]

enrollar [m] rollback [rrol bak]

ensamblador [m] assembler [a-sem-bler]

ensamblando [m] assembly [asem-bli]

ensamblándolo [m] assembling [asem-blin'-g]

ensamblar [v] assemble [asem-bel]

ensayo a distancia [m] remote testing [rre-mot tes-tin'-g]

ensayo del programa [m] program testing [pro-gram tes-tin'-g]

enseñanza automatizada [f] computer-based learning [com-piu'-ter bei-sed le-ar-nin'-g]

entrada [f] input [in-put]

entrada [f] access [ak-ses]

entrada [f] entry [en-tri]

entrada de datos [f] data entry [da'-ta en-tri]

entrada de microfilm al computador [f] CIM computer input microfilm [CIM com-piu'-ter in-put micro-fil'-m]

entrada de microfilm al computador [f] computer input microfilm (CIM) [com-piu'-ter in-put micro-fil'-m (CIM)]

entrada de trabajos a distancia [f] remote job entry [rre-mot llob en-tri]

entrada de voz [f] voice input [vo-is in-put]

entrada manual [f] manual input [ma-nu-al in-put]

entrada para más tarde [f] deferred entry [de-ferr en-tri]

entrada/salida [f] input/output (I/O) [in-put au-put]

entrada/salida [f] I/O input/output [I/O in-put/au-put]

entrándolo [v] inputting [in-piu-tin'-g]

entrar [v] access [ak-ses]

entrehierro [m] head gap [jead gap]

entrelazar [v] interlace [in-ter-leis]

envio solo [m] SO send only [SO sen'-d on-li]

envio solo [m] send only (SO) [sen'-d on-li (SO)]

en-el-estante [adj] off-the-shelf [of-di-chel'-f]

equipo auxiliar [m] auxiliary equipment [au-si-lia-ri e-ku-ip-men'-t]

equipo de comunicación de datos [m] data communications equipment [da'-ta co-mu-ni-kei-sion'-s e-ku-ip-men'-t]

equipo de datos telefónicos [m] telephone data set [tele-fon da'-ta set]

equipo físico [m] hardware [jar-gu'-air]

equipo para entrar dibujos [m] graphics-input hardware [gra-fik'-s in-put jar-gu'-air]

equipo para sacar dibujos [m] graphics-output hardware [gra-fik'-s ou-put jar-gu'-air]

equipo subordinado [m] ancillary equipment [an-sil-la-ri e-ku-ip-men'-t]

equivalencia [f] equivalence [eku-i-va-len'-s]

ergonomía [f] ergonomics [er-go-no-mik'-s]

error [m] error [error]

error de ambigüedad [m] ambiguity error [an-bi-gi-yu'-i-ti error]

error de paridad [m] parity error [pa-ri-ti error]

error de redondeo [m] rounding error [rra-un-din'-g error]

error de truncamiento [m] truncation error [trun-kei'-sion error]

error duro [m] hard error [jar error]

error final [m] terminal error [ter-mi-nal error]

error hereditario [m] inherited error [in-je-rit error]

error propagado [m] propagated error [pro-pa-gue-i-ted error]

error residual [m] residual error [re-si-dual error]

escala [f] scale [es-kail]

escala de gris [f] gray code [grei co-ud]

escala de tiempo [f] time scale [ta-im esc-kail]

escalada [adj] scaling [es-kai-lin'-g]

escalera visual [f] aliasing [a-lia-sin'-g]

escalónado [adj] stair-stepping [es-te-ar es-tep-pin'-g]

escondrijo de la memoria [m] cache memory [ka-che']

escotilla [f] trapdoor [trap-do-ar]

escribiendo con adelanto [m] type ahead [ta'-ip a-jed]

escribir [v] write [bra-it]

escribir con el teclado [v] type [ta'-ip]

escritor de trazos [m] stroke writer [es-trok brai-ter]

escritura agrupada [f] gather write [ga-der bra'-it]

escritura inmediata [f] demand writing [de-man'-d brai-tin'-g]

escudriñado de líneas [m] raster scan [ras-ter es-kan]

escudriñando [adj] scanning [es-ka-nin'-g]

escudriñar en cursivo [m] cursive scanning [cur'-siv es-ka-nin'-g]

espacio del direccional [m] address space [ad-dres es-peis]

espacio incremental [m] incremental spacing [in-cre-men-tal es-pei-sin'-g]

especificación [f] specification [es-pe-si-fi-ka'-sion]

especificación del programa [f] program specification [pro-gram es-pe-si-fi-ka-sion]

esperando [mf] queuing [ki-u-in]

esquema [mf] schema [es-ke-ma]

esquema del árbol [m] tree diagram [tri dai-a-gram]

esquema detallado [m] detail diagram [di-teil dai-a-gram]

esquemático [m] schematic [es-ke-ma-tik]

estación de una red [f] subscriber station [sus-crai-ber es-tei-sion]

estación de visualización [f] display station [dis-plei es-tei-sion]

estación operativa [f] operating station [ope-rei-tin'-g es-tei-sion]

estacionario continuo [m] continous stationery [con-ti-nius es-tei-sio-na-ri]

estado cero [m] zero state [si-ro es-teit]

estado de arte [m] state-of-the-art [es-teit of di art]

estado de espera [m] wait state [gu-ait es-teit]

estado de uno [m] one state [uan es-teit]

estar en espera [adv] in queue [in kiu]

estática [adj] static [es-ta-tik]

estática en la pantalla [f] hash [jach]

estera contra la estática [f] antistatic mat [an-ti-es-ta-tik mat]

estilo [m] stylus [es-tai-lus]

estroboscópico [m] strobe [es-tro-ub]

estructura [f] structure [es-trak-chur]

estructura de bucle [f] loop structure [lup es-trak-chur]

estructura de redes de sistemas [f] SNA systems network architecture [SNA sis-tem'-s net-guor'-k ar-ki-tek-chur]

estructura de redes de sistemas [f] systems network architecture (SNA) [sis-tem'-s net-guor'-k ar-ki-tek-chur (SNA)]

estructura del árbol [f] tree structure [tri es-trak-chur]

estructura jerárquica [f] hierarchical structure [ja-ie-rar-ki-cal es-trak-chur]

estructurado de datos gráficos [m] graphic-data structure [gra'-fik da'-ta es-trak-chur]

estructuras de control [f] control structures [con-trol es-trak-chur'-s]

estudio de las posibilidades [m] feasibility study [fi-sea-bi-li-ti es-ta-di]

etiqueta [f] label [lei-bel]

etiqueta [f] tag [tag]

etiqueta de cabecera [f] header label [je-der lei-bel]

etiqueta de cola [f] trailer label [trei-ler lei-bel]

etiqueta de declaración [f] statement label [es-tei-men'-t lei-bel]

etiqueta de pista [f] track label [trak lei-bel]

etiqueta del fichero [f] file label [fa'-il lei-bel]

evaluación gráfica y revisión técnica [f] graphical evaluation and review technique (GERT) [gra-fi'-kal iva-lu-ai'-sion an'-d re-viu tek-ni-ke (GERT)]

evaluación gráfica y revisión técnica [f] GERT graphical evaluation and review technique [GERT gra-fi'-kal iva-lu-ai'-sion an'-d re-viu tek-ni-k]

exactitud [f] accuracy [aku-ra-si]

examinación de la variación [f] range check [rein'-ch chek]

examinar [v] check [chek]

examinar el vuelco [m] dump check [dam'-p chek]

exedió [f] overrun [ober-ran]

expansión [f] expandability [ex-pan-da-bi-li-ti]

experiencia práctica [f] hands-on [jan'-s on]

exploración [f] scan [es-kan]

exploración de las marcas [f] mark scanning [mar'-k es-kan-nin'-g]

explorador [m] scanner [es-kan-ner]

explorador óptico [m] optical scanner [op-ti-kal es-kan-ner]

explorar [v] scan [es-kan]

explorar hacia atrás [m] backtracking [bak-trak-kin'-g]

explosión de combinaciones [f] combinatorial explosion [com-bi-na-to-ri-al ex-plo'-sion]

exportar [v] export [ex-port]

exportación de datos [f] data export [da'-ta ex-port]

expresión [f] expression [ex-pre'-sion]

expresión de relación [f] relational expression [re-lei-si-o-nal ex-pre'-sion]

extenderse sobre [v] overlap [ober-lap]

extracción caracteristica [f] feature extraction [fi-chur ex-trak'-sion]

F

fabricación con ayuda del computador [f] CAM computer-aided manufacture [CAM com-piu'-ter ai-ded ma-nu-fak-chur]

fabricación con ayuda del computador [f] computer-aided manufacture (CAM) [com-piu'-ter ai-ded ma-nu-fak-chur (CAM)]

fabricante de tapónes compatibles [m] PCM plug compatible manufacturer [PCM pla'-g com-pa-ti-bel ma-nu-fak-chur]

fabricante de tapónes compatibles [m] plug compatible manufacturer (PCM) [pla'-g com-pa-ti-bel ma-nu-fak-chur (PCM)]

fácil para el usuario [adj] user-friendly [yu-ser fri-en-d-li]

facilidades [f] facilities [fa-si-li-tis]

facsímile [m] facsimile [fak-si-mi'-le]

factor de la escala [m] scale factor [es-keil fak-tor]

fallo [m] fault [fa-ul'-t]

fallo del equipo [m] equipment failure [e-kuip-men'-t fei-lur']

fallo duro [m] hard failure [jar'-d fei-lur']

falta de arranque [f] cold fault [kol'-d fa-ul'-t]

fase de ejecución [f] execute phase [es-se-kiut fe-is]

fichero [m] file [fa-il']

fichero activo [m] active file [ak-tib fa-il']

fichero archivado [m] archived file [ar-kaib'-d fa-il']

fichero central de información [m] central information file [sen-tra in-for-mai'-sion fa-il']

fichero cerrado [m] closed file [clo-se'-d fa-il']

fichero de almacenamiento de memoria [m] file storage [fa-il' es-tor-ich]

fichero de discos [m] disk file [dis'-k fa-il']

fichero de trabajo [m] scratch file [es-cra-ich fa-il']

fichero físico [m] physical file [fi-si-cal fa-il']

fichero hijo [m] son file [son fa-il']

fichero maestro [m] master file [mas-ter fa-il']

fichero padre [m] parent [pe-ren'-t]

fichero secuencial [m] sequential file [se-ku-en-sial fa-il']

ficheros casuales [m] random files [rran-dom fa-il'-s]

ficheros compartidos [m] shared files [cha-red fa-il'-s]

ficheros de discos fijos [m] fixed-disk file [fix'-d dis'-k fa-il']

ficticio [adj] dummy [da'-mi]

fila [f] row [rrou]

filtro [m] filter [fil-ter]

fin de bloque [m] end-of-block (EOB) [en'-d of blok (EOB)]

fin de bloque [m] EOB end-of-block [EOB en'-d of blok]

fin de cinta [m] EOT end-of-tape [EOT en'-d of tei'-p]

fin de cinta [m] end-of-tape (EOT) [en'-d of tei'-p (EOT)]

fin de fichero [m] end-of-file (EOF) [en'-d of fa-il' (EOF)]

fin de fichero [m] EOF end-of-file [EOF en'-d of fa-il']

fin de pasada [m] end-of-run (EOR) [en'-d of rran (EOR)]

fin de pasada [m] EOR end-of-run [EOR en'-d of rran]

fin de trabajo [m] end-of-job (EOJ) [en'-d of yob (EOJ)]

fin de trabajo [m] EOJ end-of-job [EOJ en'-d of yob]

flujo de bit [m] bit stream [bit es-trim]

flujo de datos [m] data stream [da'-ta es-trim]

flujo de estructura [m] structure chart [es-truk-chur char'-t]

flujodatos [m] dataflow [da'-ta-flo]

flujograma [m] flowchart [flo-char'-t]

flujograma automatizado [m] automated flowchart [auto-ma-ted flo-char'-t]

flujograma de programa [m] program flowchart [pro-gram flo-char'-t]

flujograma detallado [m] detail flowchart [di-te-il flo-char'-t]

flujorama estructurado [m] structured flowchart [es-truk-chur flo-char'-t]

fondo [m] background [bak-gra-un'-d]

formador de texto [m] formatter [for-ma'-ter]

formato [m] format [for-mat]

formato de impresión [m] print format [prin'-t for-mat]

formato de la instrucción [m] instruction format [ins-truk-sion for-mat]

formato normalizado [m] standard form [es-tan-dar'-d form]

formato reducido [m] reduce format [re-dus for-mat]

forzar [v] force [for'-c]

fotoresistivo [m] photoresist [foto-rre-sis'-t]

frase de control [f] control statement [con-trol es-tei-men'-t]

frase de declaración [f] declarative statement [de-kla-ra-tib es-tei-men'-t]

frequencia de fallos [f] failure rate [fe-i-liu-re re-it]

frequencia de pulsación [f] beat frequency [bi'-it fre-kuen'-si]

frequencia de repetición de impulsos [f] PRF pulse repetition frequency [PRF pul'-s re-pe-ti-sion fre-kuen'-si]

frequencia de repetición de impulsos [f] pulse repetition frequency (PRF) [pul'-s re-pe-ti-sion fre-kuen'-si (PRF)]

frequencia del muestreo [f] sampling rate [sam-plin'-g re-it]

frequencia del portador [f] carrier frequency [ka-rri-er fre-kuen'-si]

fuente [f] source [so-ur-se]

fuente de almacenamiento [f] storage pool [es-tor-aich pul]

fuera de linea [adj] off-line [of la-in]

fuertamente acoplado [m] tightly coupled [ta-it-li ka-ple'-d]

función [f] function [fun'-cion]

función de transferencia [f] transfer function [tran-s-fer fun'-cion]

función definida por el usuario [f] user-defined function [llu-ser di-fai-ned fun'-cion]

funcionamiento en paralelo [m] parallel running [para-lel rru-nin'-g]

furtivo [adj] poaching [pou-chin-g]

fusión [f] merge [mer'-ich]

fusión óptima del árbol [f] optimal merge tree [op-ti-kal mer'-ich tri]

fusión postal [f] mail-merging [me-il mer-chin'-g]

fusionar [v] merge [mer'-ich]

G

galimatías [f] gibberish [gui-be-rich]

gama de colores [m] gamut [ga-mut]

generación de sistemas [f] systems generation (SYSGEN) [sis-tem'-s lle-ne-rei'-sion (SYSGEN)]

generación de sistemas [f] SYSGEN systems generation [SYSGEN sis-tem'-s lle-ne-rei'-sion]

generación del sistema [f] system generation [sis-tem lle-ne-rei'-sion]

generador [m] generator [lle-ne-rei'-tor]

generador de carácteres [m] character generator [ca-rak'-ter lle-ne-rei'-tor]

generador de función [m] function generator [fun-sion lle-ne-rei'-tor]

generador de informes [m] report generator [re-por'-t le-ne-rei'-tor]

generador de números casuales [m] random number generator [rran-dom nan-ber lle-ne-rei'-tor]

generador de programas [m] program generator [pro-gram lle-ne-rei'-tor]

generador de soportes lógicos [m] software generator [sof-gue-ra lle-ne-rei'-tor]

generador de video [m] video generator [vi-deo lle-ne-rei'-tor]

generar [v] generate [lle-ne-rei'-t]

genérico [adj] generic [lle-ne-rik]

geocodificación [f] geocoding [geo-ko-din'-g]

giratablas [m] thumbwheel [tum-buil]

giro total [m] turnaround [tur-na-rra-un'-d]

global [adj] global [glo'-bal]

golpe seco [m] press [pres]

golpe seco con mayúscula [m] shift-click [chif-clik]

golpecito seco [m] click [clik]

grabadora de casete [f] cassette recorder [ca-se-te re-cor-der]

grado de inclinación [m] pitch [pit'-ch]

grado de inclinación del carácter [m] character pitch [ca-rak'-ter pit'-ch]

gráfica [f] graphics [gra-fik'-s]

gráfica acentuada [f] area chart [ere'-a char'-t]

gráfica administradora [f] management graphics [ma-na-lle-men'-t gra-fik'-s]

gráfica de baja resolución [f] low-res graphics [lo res gra-fik'-s]

gráfica de computadores [f] computer graphics [com-piu'-ter gra-fik'-s]

gráfica de gran resolución [f] hi-res graphics [jai res gra-fik'-s]

gráfica de tortuga [f] turtle graphics [tur-tle gra-fik'-s]

gráfica del caligrafíco [f] calligraphic graphics [ca-li-gra'-fik gra-fik'-s]

gráfica interactiva [f] interactive graphics [inter-ak-tib gra-fik'-s]

gráfico [m] graph [graf]

gráfico en barras [m] picture graph [pik-chur graf]

gráfista de computadores [mf] computer graphicist [com-piu'-ter gra-fi-sis'-t]

grupo [m] group [grup]

grupo de árboles [m] forest [fo-res'-t]

grupo de cables [m] harness [jar-nes]

grupo de carácteres [m] character set [ca-rak'-ter set]

grupo de datos [m] data set [da'-ta set]

grupo de usuarios [m] user group [iu-ser grup]

grupos de datos concatenados [m] concatenated data set [con-ka-te-nei-ted da'-ta set]

grupos de entrada [m] input stream [in-put es-tri'-m]

grupos de salida [m] output stream [aut-put es-tri'-m]

guarde y envie [adj] store-and-forward [es-tor an'-d for-gu-ar'-d]

guía [mf] prompt [prom'-t]

guión blando [m] soft hyphen [sof'-t jai-fen]

guión duro [m] hard hyphen [jar'-d jai-fen]

H

hacer más claro [m] lightness [lait-nes]

herramienta conceptual [f] conceptual tool [con-sep-chu-al tul]

herramientas programadas automaticamente [f] APT automatically programmed tools [APT auto-ma-ti-ka-li pro-gra-med tul'-s]

herramientas programadas automaticamente [f] automatically programmed tools (APT) [auto-ma-ti-ka-li pro-gra-med tul'-s (APT)]

heurística [adj] heuristic [iu-ris-tik]

hijos nodales [m] sibling [si-blin'-g]

hilera de semiconductores [f] semiconductor array [semi-con-duk-tor a-rey]

hoja cuadriculada electrónica [f] gridsheet [grid-chi'-t]

hoja de vidrio [f] pane [pei'-n]

hoja electrónica [f] worksheet [gu-or-chi'-t]

hoja electrónica [f] spreadsheet [es-pred-chi'-t]

holografía [f] holography [jo-lo-gra'-fi]

holograma [m] hologram [jo-lo-gram]

homeostasis [f] homeostasis [jo-mos-ta-sis]

hueco de índice [m] index hole [in'-des jol]

husmeo de la memoria [m] memory sniffing [me-mo-ri es-ni-fin]

I

icono [m] icon [ai'-con]

identificación de archivos [f] file identification [fa'-il ai-den-ti-fi-kei-sion]

identificador [m] identifier [ai-den-ti-fai-ller]

identificador universal [m] universal identifier [llu-ni-ver-sal ai-den-ti-fai-ller]

iluminador [v] illuminate [ilu-mi-nei'-t]

imagen [f] image [ima'-ch]

imagen de matiz continuo [f] continuous tone image [con-ti-no-us to-un ima'-ch]

imparidad [f] odd parity [od pa-ri-ti]

implicación condicional [f] conditional implication [con-di-sio-nal im-pli-kei'-sion]

importación de datos [f] data import [da'-ta im-port]

impresadora de tambor [f] drum printer [drum prin-ter]

impresión [f] printout [prin'-t-aut]

impresión de obscuridad [f] shadow printing [cha-do prin-tin'-g]

impresión detallada [f] detail printing [de-te-il prin-tin'-g]

impresor de cadena [f] train printer [tre-in prin-ter]

impresora [f] printer [prin-ter]

impresora a percusión [f] impact printer [in-pak'-t prin-ter]

impresora bidireccional [f] bi-directional printer [bai di-rek-sio-nal prin-ter]

impresora de banda [f] band printer [ban'-d prin-ter]

impresora de barras [f] bar printer [bar prin-ter]

impresora de cadena [f] chain printer [che-in prin-ter]

impresora de color [f] color printer [co-lor prin-ter]

impresora de dedal [f] thimble printer [tim-bel prin-ter]

impresora de esfera [f] ball printer [bol prin-ter]

impresora de laser [f] laser printer [lei-ser prin-ter]

impresora de líneas [f] line printer [lain prin-ter]

impresora de martillo [f] impact printer [in-pak'-t prin-ter]

impresora de matriz [f] matrix printer [mei-trix prin-ter]

impresora de páginas [f] page printer [pe-ich prin-ter]

impresora de qualidad de letra [f] letter-quality printer [le-ter kua-li-ti prin-ter]

impresora de rodillo [f] barrel printer [ba'-rrel prin-ter]

impresora de rueda de mariposa [f] daisy-wheel printer [dei-si ju'-il prin-ter]

impresora de ruedas [f] wheel printer [ju'-il prin-ter]

impresora electroestática [f] electrostatic printer [elec-tro-es-ta-tik prin-ter]

impresora en serie [f] serial printer [se'-rial prin-ter]

impresora gráfica [f] graphics printer [gra-fik'-s prin-ter]

impresora por puntos [f] dot printer [dat prin-ter]

impresora sin percusión [f] nonimpact printer [non-in-pak'-t prin-ter]

impresora xerográfica [f] xerographic printer [se-ro-gra-fik prin-ter]

imprimir [v] printout [prin'-ta-ut]

impulsar [v] drive [dra-ib]

impulso [m] pulse [pul'-s]

impulso de activación [m] enable pulse [i-nei-bel pul'-s]

impulso de bloqueo [m] inhibit pulse [in-ji-bit pul'-s]

impulso de reposición [m] reset pulse [ri-set pul'-s]

impulso de sincronización [m] sprocket pulse [es-pro-ket pul'-s]

impulsor [m] actuator [ak-tu-ei-tor]

impulsor de cinta [m] tape drive [teip dra-ib]

impulsos del reloj [m] clock pulses [clok pul-ses]

inactivo [adj] inactive [i-nak-tib]

inclinación central [f] central tendency [sen-tral ten-den-si]

incrustación [f] embedding [em-be-din'-g]

independiente de la máquina [f] machine independent [ma-chin in-di-pen-den'-t]

independiente del margen [m] range independent [ra-in'-ch in-di-pen-den'-t]

indicación [f] designation [de-sig-nei'-sion]

indicador [m] pointer [po-in-ter]

indicador de prioridad [m] priority indicator [pra-io-ri-ti in-di-kei-tor]

indicador de verificación [m] check indicator [chek in-di-kei-tor]

indicador del signo de verificación [m] sign check indicator [sain chek in-di-kei-tor]

índice [m] index [in'-dex]

índice de pie [m] footer [fu-ter]

índice de transferencia [m] transfer rate [tran'-s-fer reit]

industria de conocimiento [f] knowledge industries [nou-le-ich in-dus-tris]

información [f] information [in-for-mei-sion]

información de salida [f] read out [rid aut]

información parásita [f] garbage [gar-ba'-ich]

informe de errores [f] error report [error re-por'-t]

ingeniería de conocimiento [f] knowledge engineering [nou-le-ich en-ji-nii-rin'-g]

ingeniería de soporte lógicos [f] software engineering [sof-gue-ar en-ji-nii-rin'-g]

inhibir [v] inhibit [in-ji-bit]

inicialización [f] initialization [ini-si-a-lisa-sion]

inicializador [m] startup [es-tar-ap]

inicializar [v] initialize [ini-si-a-lais]

iniciar el arranque [m] cold start [col es-tar'-t]

inscribirse [adj] signing-on [sai-nin'-g on]

insertar [v] insert [in-ser'-t]

instalación de emergencia [f] hot site [jat sait]

instalación de sistema [f] system installation [sis-tem in'-s-ta-lei-sion]

instalar [v] install [in'-s-tal]

instrucción [f] instruction [in'-s-trak-sion]

instrucción administrada en computador [f] computer-managed instruction (CMI) [com-piu'-ter ma-na-ich in'-s-trak-sion (CMI)]

instrucción administrada en computador [f] CMI computer-managed instruction [CMI com-piu'-ter ma-na-ich in'-s-trak-sion]

instrucción aritmética [f] arithmetic instruction [ar-rik-me-tik in'-s-trak-sion]

instrucción con ayuda del computador [f] computer-assisted instruction (CAI) [com-piu'-ter asis-ted in'-s-trak-sion (CAI)]

instrucción con ayuda del computador [f] CAI computer-assisted instruction [CAI com-piu'-ter asis-ted in'-s-trak-sion]

instrucción con dos direcciones [f] two-address instruction [tu ad-dres in'-s-trak-sion]

instrucción de bifurcación [f] branch instruction [bran'-ch in'-s-trak-sion]

instrucción de bifurcación condicional [f] conditional branch instruction [con-di-sio-nal bran'-ch in'-s-trak-sion]

instrucción de bifurcación incondicional [f] unconditional branch instruction [an-con-di-sio-nal bran'-ch in'-s-trak-sion]

instrucción de dirección cero [f] zero-address instruction [siro ad-dres in'-s-trak-sion]

instrucción de direcciones múltiples [f] multiple-address instruction [multi-ple ad-dres in'-s-trak-sion]

instrucción de llamada [f] call instruction [cal in'-s-trak-sion]

instrucción de repetición [f] repetition instruction [re-pe-ti-sion in'-s-trak-sion]

instrucción de retorno [f] return instruction [re-tur'-n in'-s-trak-sion]

instrucción de salto condicional [f] conditional jump instruction [con-di-sio-nal llam'-p in'-s-trak-sion]

instrucción de transferencia [f] transfer instruction [tran'-s-fer in'-s-trak-sion]

instrucción de tres-direcciones [f] three-address intruction [tri ad-dres in'-s-trak-sion]

instrucción de una sola dirección [f] single address instruction [sin-guel ad-dres in'-s-trak-sion]

instrucción del punto de interrupción [f] breakpoint instruction [bre-ik po-in'-t in'-s-trak-sion]

instrucción ficticia [f] dummy instruction [da-mi in'-s-trak-sion]

instrucción mnemotécnica [f] instruction mnemonic [in'-s-trak-sion ne-mo-nik]

instrucción sin dirección [f] no-address instruction [no-ad-dres in'-s-trak-sion]

integración en gran escala [f] large scale integration (LSI) [lar-ich es-keil in-te-grei-sion (LSI)]

integración en gran escala [f] LSI large scale integration [LSI lar-ich es-keil in-te-grei-sion]

integrador [m] integrator [in-te-grei-tor]

integridad [f] integrity [in-te-gri-ti]

inteligencia artificial [f] AI artificial intelligence [AI arti-fi-sial in-te-li-jen'-s]

inteligencia artificial [f] artificial intelligence (AI) [arti-fi-sial in-te-li-jen'-s (AI)]

inteligencia de la máquina [f] machine intelligence [ma-chin in-te-li-jen'-s]

inteligente [adj] smart [es-mar'-t]

intensidad [f] intensity [in-ten-si-ti]

intensificación de imagen [f] image enhancement [ima-ich en-jan-s-men'-t]

intensificación del contraste [f] contrast enhancement [con-tras'-t en-jan-s-men'-t]

interacción conversacional [f] conversational interaction [con-ver-sei-sio-nal in-ter-ak-sion]

interacción hombre-máquina [f] man-machine interaction [man ma-chin in-ter-ak-sion]

interactivo [adj] interactive [in-ter-ak-tib]

interbloquear [v] interlock [in-ter-lak]

intercaladora [f] collator [co-lei-tor]

intercalar [v] collate [co-lei'-t]

intercambiando [adj] swapping [sua-pin'-g]

intercambio [m] exchange [ex-chein]

interfase amiga [f] friendly interface [fri-en'-d-li in-ter-feis]

interfase de extensión [mf] expansion interface [es-pan-sion in-ter-feis]

interfase de transmisión [mf] transmission interface [tran'-s-mi-sion in-ter-feis]

interfase del computador [mf] computer interface [com-piu'-ter in-ter-feis]

interfase en paralelo [mf] parallel interface [para'-lel in-ter-feis]

interfase en series [mf] serial interface [se-ryal' in-ter-feis]

interfase entre humanos y máquinas [mf] human-machine interface [jiu-man ma-chin in-ter-feis]

interfase normalizada [mf] standard interface [es-tan-dar'-d in-ter-feis]

interfolición [f] interleaving [in-ter-li-vin'-g]

interpolación [f] interpolation [in-ter-po-lei-sion]

interpolador [m] interpolator [in-ter-po-lei-tor]

interpretadora [f] interpreter [in-ter-pre-ter]

interpretar [v] interpret [in-ter-pre'-t]

interrogación [f] query [kue-ri]

interrogación interactiva [f] interactive query [in-ter-ak-tib kue-ri]

interrumpir [v] interrupt [in-ter-rrup'-t]

interrupción [f] interrupt [in-ter-rrup'-t]

interrupción automática [f] automatic interrupt [auto-ma-tik in-ter-rrup'-t]

interruptor [m] trapping [tra-pin'-g]

intervalo [m] gap [gap]

intervalo del bloque [m] block gap [blok gap]

intervalo entre archivos [m] IRG interrecord gap [IRG in-ter-rre-kor'-d gap]

intervalo entre archivos [m] interrecord gap (IRG) [in-ter-rre-kor'-d gap (IRG)]

introducir [v] input [in-put]

inversión [f] inversion [in-ver-sion]

inversión de matriz [f] matrix inversion [mei-tris in-ver-sion]

inversor [m] inverter [in-ver-ter]

invertir [v] invert [in-ver'-t]

investigación operativa [f] operational research [ope-rei-sio-nal re-se-irch]

iteración [f] iteration [ai-te-rei-sion]

iterativo [adj] iterative [ai-te-ra-tib]

J

jalarlo [v] slew [es-liu]

jerarquía [f] hierarchy [jai-rar'-ki]

jerarquizar [v] nest [nes'-t]

jerga de computador [f] computer jargon [com-piu'-ter llar'-gon]

jerga informática [f] computerese [com-piu'-te-ris]

jornal electrónico [m] electronic journal [elek-tro-nik yo-ur-nal]

juego de galería [m] arcade game [ark-que-id ge-im]

juego de instrucciones [m] instruction set [in'-s-trak-sion set]

juego de video [m] video game [vi-deo ge-im]

juego inalterable [m] funware [fan-gue-ar]

juego por computador [m] computer game [com-piu'-ter ga-im]

justificado a la derecha [adj] right-justified [rait llus'-ti-faid]

justificado a la izquierda [adj] left-justified [lef'-t llus'-ti-faid]

justificar [v] justify [llus'-ti-fai]

K

kilobit [m] kilobit [kilo-bit]

kilonúcleo segundos [m] kilo core seconds (KCS) [kilo ko-ar se-con'-s (KCS)]

kilonúcleo segundos [m] KCS kilo core seconds [KCS kilo ko-ar se-con'-s]

kilo-octero [m] kilobyte [kilo-bait]

L

lado derecho roto [m] ragged right [ra'-gued ra-it]

lado izquierdo roto [m] ragged left [ra'-gued lef'-t]

lapicero electrónico [m] electronic pen [e-lek-tro-nik pen]

lápiz fotosensible [m] light pen [la-it pen]

largo de la palabra variable [m] variable word length [va-ria-bel gu-or'-d len'-t]

largo de las series [m] string length [es-trin'-g len'-t]

latencia [f] latency [la-ten-si]

lazo de comunicación [m] communications link [com-mu-ni-kei-sion'-s lin'-k]

lazo enninado [m] nested loop [nes-ted lup]

lea disperso-escriba junto [f] scatter read-gather write [es-ka-ter ri-id ga-der bra'-it]

lectura [f] read [ri-id]

lectura de marcas [f] mark sensing [mark sen-sin'-g]

lectura de salida [f] read out [ri-id aut]

lectura ilegible [f] disrupted read-out [dis-rrup-ted ri-id aut]

lectura inmediata [f] demand reading [di-man'-d ri-i-din'-g]

lectura no destructiva [f] nondestructive read [non-des-truk-tib ri-id]

lectura regenerativa [f] regenerative read [re-ge-ne-ra-tib ri-id]

leedor [m] reader [rri-der]

leedor de películas [m] film reader [fil'-m rri-der]

leedor de placa [m] badge reader [bad'-ch]

leedor óptico de páginas [m] optical page reader [op-ti-cal pe-ich rri-der]

leedora de carácteres [f] character reader [ca-rak'-ter rri-der]

leedora de cinta [f] tape reader [te'-ip rri-der]

leedora de cinta de papel [f] paper-tape reader [pei-per te'-ip rri-der]

leedora de tarjetas [f] card reader [car'-d rri-der]

leedora óptica de carácteres [f] optical character reader [op-ti-cal ca-rak'-ter rri-der]

leer [v] read [ri-id]

legible por la máquina [adj] machine-readable [ma-chin rri-da'-bel]

legible por la máquina [adj] machine-sensible [ma-chin sen-si-bel]

lenguaje [m] language [lan-gu'-ich]

lenguaje artificial [m] artificial language [ar-ti-fi-sial lan-gu'-ich]

lenguaje asestado [m] target language [tar-get lan-gu'-ich]

lenguaje conversacional [m] conversational language [con-ver-sei-sio-nal lan-gu'-ich]

lenguaje de alto nivel [m] high-level language [jai le-vel lan-gu'-ich]

lenguaje de bajo nivel [m] low-level language [lo le-vel lan-gu'-ich]

lenguaje de componer [m] author language [au'-tor lan-gu'-ich]

lenguaje de control [m] control language [con-trol lan-gu'-ich]

lenguaje de control de trabajos [m] job control language (JCL) [llob con-trol lan-gu'-ich (JCL)]

lenguaje de control de trabajos [m] JCL job control language [JCL llob con-trol lan-gu'-ich]

lenguaje de definición de datos [m] data definition language (DDL) [da'-ta di-fi-ni-sion lan-gu'-ich (DDL)]

lenguaje de definición de datos [m] DDL data definition language [DDL da'-ta di-fi-ni-sion lan-gu'-ich]

lenguaje de descripción de datos [m] DDL data description language [DDL da'-ta des-crip-sion lan-gu'-ich]

lenguaje de descripción de datos [m] data description language (DDL) [da'-ta des-crip-sion lan-gu'-ich (DDL)]

lenguaje de interrogación [m] query language [ku-eri lan-gu'-ich]

lenguaje de la máquina [m] machine language [ma-chin lan-gu'-ich]

lenguaje de orden [m] command language [co-man'-d la-gu'-ich]

lenguaje de programación [m] programming language [pro-gra-min'-g lan-gu'-ich]

lenguaje ensamblador [m] assembly language [a-sem-bli lan-gu'-ich]

lenguaje extensible [m] extensible language [es-ten'-si-bel lan-gu'-ich]

lenguaje fuente [m] source language [so-ur-se lan-gu'-ich]

lenguaje inteligente [m] intelligent language [in-te-li-llen'-t lan-gu'-ich]

lenguaje manipulativo de datos [m] data manipulating language (DML) [da'-ta ma-ni-pu-lei-tin'-g lan-gu'-ich (DML)]

lenguaje manipulativo de datos [m] DML data manipulating language [DML da'-ta ma-ni-pu-lei-tin'-g lan-gu'-ich]

lenguaje musical [m] musical language [miu-si-kal lan-gu'-ich]

lenguaje natal [m] native language [nei-tib lan-gu'-ich]

lenguaje objeto [m] object language [ob-llek'-t lan-gu'-ich]

lenguaje orientado a los problemas [m] problem-oriented language [pro-blem ori-en-ted lan-gu'-ich]

lenguaje orientado a los procedimientos [m] procedure-oriented language [pro-se-dur ori-en-ted lan-gu'-ich]

lenguaje simbólico [m] symbolic language [sin'-bo-lik lan-gu'-ich]

lenguaje sintético [m] synthetic language [sin'-te-tik lan-gu'-ich]

lenguaje tabular [m] tabular language [ta-biu-lar lan-gu'-ich]

letras mayúsculas [f] caps [kap'-s]

levante falso [m] false retrieval [fol-ul'-s re-tri-e-bal]

léxico [m] lexicon [lex-si-con]

libertar [v] release [re-lis]

limitado por los periféricos [adj] peripheral-limited [peri-fe-ral li-mi-ted]

límite gráfico [m] graphic limits [gra'-fik li-mit'-s]

limpieza de datos [f] data cleaning [da'-ta kli-nin'-g]

línea conectada [f] line plot [lain plot]

línea conmutada [f] switched line [sui-ched lain]

línea de edición [f] edit line [e-dit lain]

línea de flujo [f] flowline [flo-lain]

línea de retardo [f] delay line [di-ley lain]

línea oculta [f] hidden line [ji-den lain]

línea telefónica [f] trunk [tran'-k]

líneal [adj] in-line [in lain]

líneas-por-minuto [f] lines per minute (LPM) [lain'-s per mi'-nut (LPM)]

líneas-por-minuto [f] LPM lines per minute [LPM lain'-s per mi'-nut]

lista [f] list [lis'-t]

lista con punteros [f] linear list [li-near lis'-t]

lista de abajo hacia arriba [f] push-down list [puch-da-on lis'-t]

lista de empuje al final [f] push-up list [puch ap lis'-t]

lista de referencias [f] reference listing [re-fe-ren'-s lis-tin'-g]

lista del ensamblador [f] assembly listing [a-sem-bli lis-tin'-g]

lista encadenada [f] chained list [che-i-ned lis'-t]

listar [v] list [lis'-t]

listo para ejecución [m] statitizing [es-ta-tai-sin'-g]

local central [m] central site [sen-tral sait]

localidad distante [f] remote site [re-mo-ut sait]

localización de errores [f] troubleshooting [tra-bel-chu-tin'-g]

lógica [f] logic [lo-llic]

lógica de duda [f] fuzzy logic [fa'-si lo-llic]

lógica de emisor acoplado [f] ECL emitter coupled logic [ECL e-mi-ter ka-pel lo-llic]

lógica de emisor acoplado [f] emitter coupled logic (ECL) [e-mi-ter ka-pel lo-llic (ECL)]

lógica de flúidos [f] fluid logic[f] [flu'-id lo-llic]

lógica de injección integrada [f] integrated injection logic [in-te-grei-ted in-llek-cion lo-llic]

lógica de modo amplificador [f] CML current mode logic [CML cu-rren'-t mo-ud lo-llic]

lógica de modo amplificador [f] current mode logic (CML) [cu-rren'-t mo-ud lo-llic (CML)]

lógica de resistencia transistor [f] resistor-transistor logic (RTL) [re-sis'-tor tran-sis'-tor lo-llic (RTL)]

lógica de resistencia-transistor [f] RTL resistor-transistor logic [RTL re-sis'-tor tran-sis'-tor lo-llic]

lógica de secuencia sequential [f] logic [se-ku-en-sial lo-llic]

lógica de transistor-transistor [f] transistor-transistor logic (TTL) [tran-sis'-tor tran-sis'-tor lo-llic (TTL)]

lógica de transistor-transistor [f] TTL transistor-transistor logic [TTL tran-sis'-tor tran-sis'-tor lo-llic]

lógica diodo-transistor [f] diode-transistor logic (DTL) [dai'-od tra-sis'-tor lo-llic (DTL)]

lógica diodo-transistor [f] DTL diode-transistor logic [DTL dai'-od tra-sis'-tor lo-llic]

lógica predicativa del primer orden [f] first-order predicate logic [fir-s'-t or-der pre-di-kei'-t lo-llic]

lógica simbólica [f] symbolic logic [sim-bo-lik lo-llic]

longitud de bloque fijo [f] fixed-block length [fix'-d blok len'-t]

longitud de campo [f] field length [fi-el'-d len'-t]

longitud de palabra [f] word length [gu-or'-d len'-t]

longitud de registro [f] record length [re-cord len'-t]

luminiscente [mf] luminance [lu-mi-nan'-s]

luminosidad [f] luminosity [lu-mi-no-si-ti]

LL

llamada [f] call [kol]

llamar [v] call [kol]

llave de bloque [f] storage key [es-to-ra-ich ki]

llave del equipo físico [f] hardware key [jar-gue-ar ki]

llave mayor de clasificar [f] major sort key [ma-llor sor'-t ki]

llave secundaria [f] secondary key [se-con-da-ri ki]

llenado entre líneas [f] raster fill [ras-ter fi'-il]

llenando de ceros [adj] zeroize [si-ro-ais]

llevar [v] carry [ca-rri]

llevar arrastrado [m] dragging [drag-gin'-g]

M

macro- [pre] macro- [macro-]

macro ensamblador [m] macro assembler [macro a-sen-bler]

macro instrucción [f] macro instruction [macro ins-truk-sion]

macroprogramación [f] macroprogramming [macro-pro-gra-min'-g]

magnetoestricción [f] magnetostriction [mag-ni-to-es-trik-sion]

malla neural [f] neural net [ne-u-ral net]

manejo de series [m] string handling [es-trin'-g jan-dlin'-g]

manipulación de datos [f] data manipulation [da'-ta ma-ni-pu-lei-sion]

manipulación en series [f] string manipulation [es-trin'-g ma-ni-pu-lei-sion]

mantener [v] hold [jol'-d]

mantenimiento [m] maintenance [me-in-te-nan'-s]

mantenimiento correctivo [m] corrective maintenance [co-rrec-tib ma-in-te-nan'-s]

mantenimiento de fichero [m] file maintenance [fa-il' ma-in-te-nan'-s]

mantenimiento de rutina [m] routine maintenance [ru-tin ma-in-te-nan'-s]

mantenimiento planeado [m] scheduled maintenance [es-kei-dul ma-in-te-nan'-s]

mantenimiento preventivo [m] PM preventive maintenance [PM pre-ven-tib ma-in-te-nan'-s]

mantenimiento preventivo [m] preventive maintenance (PM) [pre-ven-tib ma-in-te-nan'-s (PM)]

mantenimiento programado [m] scheduled maintenance [es-kei-dul ma-in-te-nan'-s]

mantenimiento suplementario [m] supplementary maintenance [su-ple-men-ta-ri ma-in-te-nan'-s]

manufaturero integrado de computador [m] CIM computer integrated manufacturing [CIM com-piu'-ter in-te-grei-ted ma-nu-fak-chu-rin'-g]

manufaturero integrado de computador [m] computer integrated manufacturing (CIM) [com-piu'-ter in-te-grei-ted ma-nu-fak-chu-rin'-g (CIM)

mapa [m] map [map]

mapa de carácteres [m] character map [ka-rac'-ter map]

mapa de la memoria [m] memory map [me-mo-ri map]

mapeando [m] mapping [ma-pin'-g]

máquina cajera automática [f] automatic teller machine [auto-ma-tik te-ler ma-chin]

máquina de escribir [f] typewriter [ta'-ip-brai-ter]

máquina de escribir de consola [f] console typewriter [con-sol ta'-ip-brai-ter]

máquina de Turing universal [f] universal Turing machine [llu-ni-ver-sal tu-rin'-g ma-chin]

máquina inteligente [f] smart machines [es-mar'-t ma-chin'-s]

máquina virtual [f] virtual machine [vir-chu-al ma-chin]

marca [f] mark [mar'-k]

marca apuntadora [f] tick mark [tik mar'-k]

marca de cinta [f] tape mark [te'-ip mar'-k]

marca de grupo [f] group mark [grup mar'-k]

marca de segmento [f] segment mark [seg'-ment mar'-k]

marca final [f] end mark [en'-d mar'-k]

marcador [m] timer [tai-mer]

marcador [m] marker [mar-ker]

marcar [v] inscribe [ins-cra-ib]

margen [m] edge [eg-ich]

margen [m] range [rre-inch]

margen de alineación [m] aligning edge [ei-lin'-g eg-ich]

más grande que [adj] greater than [grei-ter dan]

máscara [f] mask [mas'-k]

matiz [m] tone [ton]

matizador de dimensiones [m] depth queuing [dep'-t kiu-in'-g]

matriz [f] matrix [mei-tris]

matriz de extensión [f] incidence matrix [in-si-den'-s mei-tris]

matriz de punto [f] dot matrix [dot mei-tris]

mayúscula [f] upper case [a-per keis]

mecanismo de acceso [m] access mechanism [ak-ses me-ka-nis'-m]

media palabra [f] half-word [haf gu-or'-d]

medio [m] medium [mi-dium]

medio tono [m] halftoning [haf to-nin'-g]

medios de salida [m] output media [aut-put mi-dia]

medios magnéticos [m] magnetic media [mag-ne-tik mi-dia]

megabit [m] megabit [mega-bit]

megabyte [m] megabyte [mega-ba'-it]

memoria [f] memory [me'-mo-ri]

memoria a rayos [f] beam store [bim es-tor-aich]

memoria asociativa [f] associative memory [aso-si-a-tib me'-mo-ri]

memoria asociativa ampliada [f] augmented content-addressed memory (ACAM) [ag-men-ted con-ten'-t ad-dres'-d me'-mo-ri (ACAM)]

memoria asociativa ampliada [f] ACAM augmented content-addressed memory [ACAM ag-men-ted con-ten'-t ad-dres'-d me'-mo-ri]

memoria auxiliar [f] auxiliary memory [au-si-li'-a-ri me'-mo-ri]

memoria auxiliar [f] backing store [ba-kin'-g es-to-ar]

memoria bidimensional [f] two-dimensional storage [tu di-men-sio-nal es-tor-aich]

memoria borrable [f] erasable memory [i-rrei-sa-bel me'-mo-ri]

memoria criogénica [f] cryogenic memory [crio-lle-nik me'-mo-ri]

memoria de acceso casual [f] RAM random-access memory [RAM rran-dom ak'-ses me'-mo-ri]

memoria de acceso casual [f] random-access memory (RAM) [rran-dom ak'-ses me'-mo-ri (RAM)]

memoria de burbuja [f] bubble memory [ba-bel me'-mo-ri]

memoria de burbuja magnética [f] magnetic bubble memory [mag-ne-tik ba-bel me'-mo-ri]

memoria de estado sólido [f] solid-state memory [so-lid es-tei'-t me'-mo-ri]

memoria de gran capacidad [f] mass storage [mas es-tor-aich]

memoria de gran capacidad [f] bulk storage [bul'-k es-tor-aich]

memoria de lectura fija [f] read-only memory (ROM) [ri-id on-li me'-mo-ri (ROM)]

memoria de lectura fija [f] ROM read-only memory [ROM ri-id on-li me'-mo-ri]

memoria de matriz [f] matrix storage [mei-tris es-tor-aich]

memoria de núcleos [f] storage memory [es-tor-aich me'-mo-ri]

memoria de núcleos [f] core memory [ko-ar me'-mo-ri]

memoria de película delgada [f] thin-film memory [tin-fil'-m me'-mo-ri]

memoria de semiconductores [f] semiconductor memory [semi-con-duk-tor me'-mo-ri]

memoria de un solo nivel [f] one level storage [u-an le-vel es-tor-aich]

memoria dinámica [f] dynamic memory [dai-na-mik me'-mo-ri]

memoria estática [f] static storage [es-ta-tik es-tor-aich]

memoria externa [f] external storage [es-ter-nal es-tor-aich]

memoria fija programable [f] PROM programmable read-only memory [PROM pro-gra-ma-bel ri-id on-li me'-mo-ri]

memoria fija programable [f] programmable read-only memory (PROM) [pro-gra-ma-bel ri-id on-li me'-mo-ri (PROM)]

memoria fotográfica óptica [f] photo-optic memory [fo-to op-tik me'-mo-ri]

memoria holográfica [f] holographic memory [jo-lo-gra'-fik me'-mo-ri]

memoria imborrable [f] nonerasable storage [non-e-rei-sa-bel es-tor-aich]

memoria integral [f] integral memory [in-te-gral me'-mo-ri]

memoria intermedia [f] intermediate storage [inter-mi-di-ate es-tor-aich]

memoria intermedia de entrada [f] input buffer [in-put ba-fer]

memoria intermedia de entrada/salida [f] input/output buffer [in-put/au-put ba-fer]

memoria intermedia de salida [f] output buffer [au-put ba-fer]

memoria magnética [f] magnetic memory [mag-ne-tik me'-mo-ri]

memoria nonvolátil [f] nonvolatile memory [non-vo-la-til me'-mo-ri]

memoria organizada en páginas [f] paged memory [pe-ich me'-mo-ri]

memoria permanente [f] permanent memory [per-ma-nen'-t me'-mo-ri]

memoria principal [f] primary storage [prai-ma-ri es-tor-aich]

memoria principal [f] main memory [me-in me'-mo-ri]

memoria real [f] real storage [rri-al es-tor-aich]

memoria regenerativa [f] regenerative storage [re-lle-ne-ra-tiv es-tor-aich]

memoria sin parte residente [f] slave storage [es-le-ib es-tor-aich]

memoria volátil [f] volatile memory [vo-la'-til me'-mo-ri]

menos que [adj] less than [les dan]

mensaje de error [m] error message [error me-saich]

menú de tirar [m] pull-down menu [pul-da-un me-niu]

menú de visualización [m] display menu [dis-plei me-niu]

método de acceso secuencial indicado [m] ISAM indexed sequential access method [ISAM in'-dex-ed se-ku-en-sial ak'-ses me-tod]

método de acceso secuencial indicado [m] indexed sequential access method (ISAM) [in'-dex-ed se-ku-en-sial ak'-ses me-tod (ISAM)]

método de combinaciones [m] combinatorics [con-bi-na-to-rik'-s]

método Montecarlo [m] Monte Carlo method [Mon-te Kar-lo me-tod]

mezclando [adj] dithering [di-te-rin'-g]

micro- [pre] micro- [mai-cro-]

microcódigo [m] microcode [mai-cro-co-ud]

microcomputador [m] microcomputer [mai-cro-com-piu'-ter]

microcontrolador [m] microcontroller [mai-cro-con-tro-ler]

microelectrónica [f] microelectronics [mai-cro-elek-tro-nik'-s]

microficha [f] microfiche [mai-cro-fich]

microfilm [m] microfilm [mai-cro-film]

microformas [f] microform [mai-cro-for'-m]

micrográfica [f] micrographics [mai-cro-gra-fik'-s]

microinstrucción [f] microinstruction [mai-cro-in'-s-trak-sion]

micropelícula [f] microfilm [mai-cro-film]

microplaqueta [f] microchip [mai-cro-chip]

microprocesador [m] microprocessor [mai-cro-pro-se-sor]

microprograma [m] microprogram [mai-cro-pro-gra'-m]

microprogramación [f] microprogramming [mai-cro-pro-gra-min'-g]

microsegundo [m] microsecond [mai-cro-se-con'-d]

microsistema [m] microsystem [mai-cro-sis-tem]

mili- [pre] milli- [mili-]

minicomputador [m] minicomputer [mini-com-piu'-ter]

minidisco [m] minidiskette [mini-dis-ket]

minidisco flexible [m] minifloppy disk [mini-fla-pi dis'-k]

minimáximo [adj] minimax [mini-max]

mirada rápida [f] peek [pik]

mnemotécnica [f] mnemonic [neu-mo-nik]

modelado [adj] modeling [mo-de-lin'-g]

modelar [v] model [mo-del]

modelo [m] model [mo-del]

modelo de relación [m] relational model [re-lei-sio-nal mo-del]

modelo del cerebro [m] homunculus [jo-mun-ku-lus]

modelo jerárquico [m] hierarchical model [ja-ie-rar-ki-cal mo-del]

modelo nivelado del archivo [m] file level model [fa-il' le-vel mo-del]

módem [m] modem [mo'-dem]

módem de enlace automático [m] auto dialing modem [auto dai-a-lin'-g mo'-dem]

módem interno [m] internal modem [in-ter-nal mo'-dem]

modernizar en el campo [m] field upgradable [fil'-d ap-grei-da-bel]

modificación [f] modification [mo-di-fi-ka-sion]

modificación del programa [f] program modification [pro-gram mo-di-fi-ka-sion]

modificador [m] modifier [mo-di-fai-ller]

modificador del direccional [m] address modification [ad-dres mo-di-fi-ka-sion]

modificar [v] modify [mo-di-fai]

modo [m] mode [mo-ud]

modo de diágolo [m] conversational mode [con-ver-sei-sio-nal mo-ud]

modo de edición [m] edit mode [edit mo-ud]

modo de presentación gráfica [m] graphic-display mode [gra-fik dis-plai mo-ud]

modo interactivo [m] interactive mode [inter-ak-tiv mo-ud]

modo ruidoso [m] noisy mode [noi-si mo-ud]

modulación [f] modulation [mo-du-lei-sion]

modulación de pulsación [f] pulse modulation [pul'-s mo-du-lei-sion]

modulador [m] modulator [mo-du-lei-tor]

modularisación [f] modularization [mo-du-la-ri-sei-sion]

módulo [m] module [ma-iul]

módulo de cargar [m] load module [lo-ud ma-iul]

monitor [m] monitor [mo-ni'-tor]

monitor de color [m] color monitor [color mo-ni'-tor]

monitor de ejecución [m] performance monitor [pre-for-man'-se mo-ni'-tor]

monitor de video [m] video monitor [vi-deo mo-ni'-tor]

monitor rojo-verde-azul [m] red-green-blue monitor (RGB) [rred-grin-blu mo-ni'-tor (RGB)]

monitor rojo-verde-azul [m] RGB red-green-blue monitor [RGB rred-grin-blu mo-ni'-tor]

monolítico [adj] monolithic [mono-li-tik]

montón de almacenamiento [m] heap [jip]

MOS-complementario [m] CMOS complementary MOS [CMOS com-ple-men-ta-ri MOS]

MOS-complementario [m] complementary MOS (CMOS) [com-ple-men-ta-ri MOS (CMOS)]

movimiento absoluto [m] absolute movement [ab-so-li-ut muf-men'-t]

movimiento de figura [m] figure shift [fi-giur chif'-t]

muestreo [m] sampling [sam-plin'-g]

múltiplex [m] multiplex [mul-ti-plex]

múltiplexado [m] multiplexing [mul-ti-plex-in'-g]

múltiplexado tiempo dividido [m] time-division multiplexing [ta-im di-vi-sion mul-ti-plex-in'-g]

multiplexar [m] multiplexer (MPX) [mul-ti-plex-er (MPX)]

multiplexar [m] multiplexor [mul-ti-plex-or]

multiplexar [m] MPX multiplexer [MPX mul-ti-plex-er]

multiplicador [m] multiplier [mul-ti-pla-ller]

multiprogramación [f] multiprogramming [mul-ti-pro-gra-min'-g]

N

nadando en la pantalla [adj] swim [su-im]

negación [f] negation [ne-gei-sion]

negación [f] disclaimer [dis-cle-i-mer]

negador [m] negator [ne-gei-tor]

nibble [m] nibble [ni-bel]

nido [m] nest [nes'-t]

nivel de entrada [m] access level [ak-ses' le-vel]

nivelación de recursos [f] resource leveling [rre-sour'-se le-ve-lin'-g]

nodo [m] node [no-ud]

nodo del árbol [m] leaf [lif]

nombre de datos [m] data name [da'-ta ne-im]

nombre de variable [m] variable name [va-ri-a'-bel ne-im]

nonconductivo [m] nonconductor [non-con-duk-tor]

normalización [f] standardization [es-tan-da-ri-sei-sion]

normalizar [v] standardize [es-tan-da-ra-is]

normalizar [v] normalize [nor-ma-lais]

notación binaria [f] binary notation [bai-na-ri no-tei-sion]

notación con base múltiple [f] mixed-base notation [mix'-d beis no-tei-sion]

notación de decimal a binario [f] decimal-to-binary notation [de-ci-mal tu bai-na-ri no-tei-sion]

notación decimal [f] decimal notation [de-ci-mal no-tei-sion]

notación hexadecimal [f] hexadecimal notation [jex-sa-de-si-mal no-tei-sion]

notación octal [f] octal notation [ok-tal no-tei-sion]

notación polaca [f] PN Polish notation [PN Po-lich no-tei-sion]

notación polaca [f] Polish notation (PN) [Po-lich no-tei-sion (PN)]

notación polaca inversa [f] reverse Polish notation [re-ver'-s Po-lich no-tei-sion]

notación por prefijos [f] prefix notation [pre-fix no-tei-sion]

notación posicional [f] positional notation [po-si-sio-nal no-tei-sion]

notar [m] remark [ri-mar'-k]

núcleo [m] core [ko-ar]

núcleo de ferria [m] ferrite core [fe-rrit ko-ar]

núcleo magnético [m] magnetic core [mag-ne-tik ko-ar]

núcleo primitivo [m] kernel [ker-nel]

núcleo primitivo asegurado [m] secure kernel [se-kiu-ar ker-nel]

núcleos [m] nucleus [nu-kle-as]

nuevo arranque [m] cold boot [kol'-d but]

nulo [m] null [nul]

numérico [adj] numeric [nu-me-rik]

número autoverificador [m] self-checking number [sel'-f che-kin'g nam-ber]

número de carrete [m] reel number [rri-il nam-ber]

número de llamada [m] call number [kol nam-ber]

número de longitud múltiple [m] multiple-length number [mul-ti-pel len-t nam-ber]

número de señales que entran [m] fan-in [fan-in]

número de señales que salen [m] fan-out [fan-aut]

O

oasis [m] oasis [oasis]

objeto de dirección/dimensión [m] gnomon [no-mon]

oblea [f] wafer [guei-fer]

oblea de silicio [f] silicon wafer [si-li-kon guei-fer]

obscurecer [v] overlay [over-lei]

observador de datos [m] data scope [da'-ta es-kop]

observar [v] monitor [mo'-ni-tor]

octal [m] octal [ok-tal]

oficina automatizada [f] automated office [auto-mei-ted ofis]

omitir [v] skip [es-kip]

opacidad [f] opacity [opa-si'-ti]

operación [f] operation [ope-rei-sion]

operación ambos ó uno [f] either-or operation [ei-der-or ope-rei-sion]

operación aritmética [f] arithmetic operation [arit-me-tik ope-rei-sion]

operación auxiliar [f] auxiliary operation [au-si'-lia-ri ope-rei-sion]

operación binaria [f] binary operation [bai-na-ri ope-rei-sion]

operación complementaria [f] complementary operation [com-ple-men'-ta-ri ope-rei-sion]

operación con llave en mano [f] turnkey operation [tur'-n-ki ope-rei-sion]

operación condicional [f] if-then operation [if-den ope-rei-sion]

operación condicional [f] conditional operation [con-di-sio-nal ope-rei-sion]

operación de disyunción [f] disjunction-operation [dis-llun-sion ope-rei-sion]

operación de equivalencia [f] equivalence operation [equi-va-len'-s ope-rei-sion]

operación de lectura no destructiva [f] NDRO non-destructive read operation [NDRO non-des-truk-tiv ri-id ope-rei-sion]

operación de lectura no destructiva [f] non-destructive read operation (NDRO) [non-des-truk-tiv ri-id ope-rei-sion (NDRO)]

operación de un paso [f] single-step operation [sin-gel es-tep ope-rei-sion]

operación destructiva [f] destructive operation [des-truk-tiv ope-rei-sion]

operacion diádica [f] dyadic operation [di-a-dik ope-rei-sion]

operación dual [f] dual operation [du-al' ope-rei-sion]

operación global [f] global operation [glo'-bal ope-rei-sion]

operación lógica [f] logical operation [lo-lli-kal ope-rei-sion]

operación lógica [f] logic operation [lo-llik ope-rei-sion]

operación NI [f] NOR-operation [NOR-ope-rei-sion]

operación ni-no [f] neither-nor operation [nei-der-nor ope-rei-sion]

operación NO [f] NOT-operation {NOT-ope-rei-sion]

operación NO-Y [f] NOT-AND operation {NOT-AN'-D ope-rei-sion]

operación NY [f] NAND-operation [NAN'-D-ope-rei-sion]

operación O [f] OR-operation [OR-ope-rei-sion]

operación O exclusivo [f] exclusive OR operation (XOR) [es-clu-siv OR ope-rei-sion (XOR)]

operación O exclusivo [f] XOR exclusive OR operation [XOR es-clu-siv OR ope-rei-sion]

operación O inclusivo [f] inclusive OR operation [in-clu-siv OR ope-rei-sion]

operación parcial [f] part operation [par'-t ope-rei-sion]

operación sin operando [adj] niladic [ni-la-dik]

operación sin personal [f] unattended operation [un-aten-ded ope-rei-sion]

operación síncrona [f] synchronous operation [sin-kro-nous ope-rei-tion]

operación unaria [f] unary operation [una-ri ope-rei-sion]

operación Y [f] AND-operation [AND'-D ope-rei-sion]

operador [m] operator [ope-rei-tor]

operador de asignación [m] assignment operator [a-sai-ment ope-rei-tor]

operador de entrada de datos [m] data entry operator [da'-ta en-tri ope-rei-tor]

operador de proceso del texto [m] word processing operator [gu-or'-d pro-se-sin'-g ope-rei-tor]

operador de relación [m] relational operator [re-lei-sio-nal ope-rei-tor]

operador del sistema [m] system operator (SYSOP) [sis-tem ope-rei-tor (SYSOP)]

operador del sistema [m] SYSOP system operator [(SYSOP) sis-tem ope-rei-tor]

operador lógico [m] logical operator [lo-lli-cal ope-rei-tor]

operador lógico [m] logic operator [lo-llik op-rei-tor]

óptica de las fibras [f] fibre optics [fai-ber op-tik'-s]

óptica de las fibras [f] fiber optics [fai-ber op-tik'-s]

óptica-electrónico [f] opto-electronics opto-elec-tro-nik'-s]

optimización [f] optimization [opti-mi-sei-sion]

optimizar [v] optimize [opti-mais]

orden [f] order [order]

orden [f] command [com-man'-d]

orden incrustado [m] embedded command [em-be-ded com-man'-d]

orden inferior [m] low order [lo order]

orden superior [m] high order [ji order]

ordenador [m] computer [com-piu'-ter]

ordenador digital [m] digital computer [di-lli-tal com-piu'-ter]

ordenar [v] order [order]

organización de páginas [f] paging [pei-llin]

organización y métodos [f] O&M organization and methods [O&M or-ga-ni-sei-sion an'-d me-tod'-s]

organización y métodos [f] organization and methods (O&M) [or-ga-ni-sei-sion an'-d me-tod'-s (O&M)]

orientado a el carácter [adj] character-oriented [ka-rac'-ter ori-en-ted]

orientado a la palabra [adj] word-oriented [gu-or'-d ori-en-ted]

orientado lenguaje de aplicación [m] application-oriented language [a-pli-kei'-sion ori-en-ted lan-gu'-ich]

origen [m] origin [ori-llin]

oscilando [adj] blinking [blin-kin'-g]

oscilográfica [f] oscillography [osci-lo'-gra-fi]

oscuro [adj] obscure [os-kiu'-ar]

P

página [f] page [pe-ich]

página de visualización [f] visual page [vi-su'-al pe-ich]

página visual completa [f] full-page display [ful pe-ich dis-plei]

paginación [f] pagination [pa-lli-nei-sion]

paginación condicional [f] conditional paging [con-di-sio-nal pei-llin]

palabra [f] word [gu-or'-d]

palabra clave [f] keyword [ki-gu-or'-d]

palabra de control [f] control word [con-trol gu-or'-d]

palabra de estado [f] status word [es-ta-tus gu-or'-d]

palabra de la instrucción [f] instruction word [ins-truc-cion' gu-or'-d]

palabra de máquina [f] machine word [ma-chin gu-or'-d]

palabras-por-minuto [f] WPM words-per-minute [WPM gu-or'-d-s per- mi-nut]

palabras-por-minuto [f] words-per-minute (WPM) [gu-or'-d-s per- mi-nut (WPM)]

palanca de juego [f] joy stick [yo-i es-tik]

palanca de juego [f] frob [frob]

palanca eléctrica [f] crowbar [cro-bar]

paleta [f] paddle [pa-del]

paleta [f] palette [pa'-let]

panel de control [m] control panel [control pa-nel]

panel de tocada sensitiva [m] touch-sensitive panel [tach sen-si-tiv pa-nel]

panel gráfico [m] graphic panel [gra-fik pa-nel]

panel posterior [m] back panel [bak pa-nel]

pantalla [f] screen [es-krin]

pantalla dividida [f] split screen [es-pli'-t es-krin]

pantalla gráfica [f] graphics screen [gra-fik'-s es-krin]

pantalla ladeadora [f] tilting screen [til-tin'-g es-krin]

pantalla llena [f] full-screen [ful es-krin]

papel [m] forms [form'-s]

papel continuo [m] continous stationery [con-ti-nous es-tei-sio-nei-ri]

papel continuo de muchas partes [m] multipart forms [mul-ti-par'-t form'-s]

papel de planeamiento [m] layout sheet [ley-aut chi-it]

paquete de datos [m] data packet [da'-ta pak-et]

paquete de gráficos diapositivos [m] slide show package [es-la-id cho pak-eich]

paquete de soporte lógico [m] software package [sof-gue-ar pak-eich]

parada [f] halt [jol'-t]

parada automática [f] automatic stop [auto-ma-tik es-tap]

parada de papel [f] form stop [for'-m es-tap]

parada del ciclo [f] cycle stealing [sai-kel es-ti-lin'-g]

parada terminal [f] dead halt [ded jol'-t]

paradigma [m[paradigm [para-dig'-m]

parámetrica [adj] parametric [para-me-trik]

parámetro [m] parameter [para'-me-ter]

parámetro de valor [m] value parameter [va-liu para'-me-ter]

parámetro definido previamente [m] preset parameter [pre-set para'-me-ter]

parámetro del programa [m] program parameter [pro-gram para'-me-ter]

parámetro superficial [m] passing parameters [pa-sin'-g para'-me-ter-s]

parche [m] patch [pach]

paridad par [f] even parity [iven pa-ri-ti]

parte de la palabra [f] slab [es-lab]

parte del direccional [f] address part [ad-dres par'-t]

parte elevada de las letras [f] ascender [as-sen-der]

partición del disco [f] disk partition [dis'-k par-ti-sion]

participación en los datos [f] data sharing [da'-ta chei-ring]

pasada [f] run [rran]

pasada de ensayo [f] test run [tes'-t rran]

pasada de máquina [adj] machine-run [ma-chin rran]

pasada de producción [f] production run [pro-dac-sion rran]

pasada del computador [f] computer run [com-piu'-ter rran]

pasada en seco [f] dry run [drai rran]

pasar [v] run [rran]

paso [m] path [pat'-s]

paso [m] step [es-tep]

paso entre filas [m] row pitch [rro pich]

pazo crítico [m] critical path [cri-ti-cal pat'-s]

pedestal [m] pedestal [pe'-des-tal]

pedestal de impresora [m] printer stand [pin-ter es-tan'-d]

pegar [v] paste [peis'-t]

película hecha en computador [f] computer flicks [com-piu'-ter flik'-s]

percepción de colisión [f] collision detection [co-li-sion di-tec-sion]

pérdida [f] loss [los]

perforaciones de alimentación [f] feed holes [fiid jol'-s]

perforaciones marginales [f] sprocket holes [es-pro-ket jol'-s]

perforado [m] chad [chad]

perforador [m] perforator [per-fo-rei-tor]

perforadora [f] punch [pan'-ch]

perforadora de cinta de papel [f] paper-tape punch [pei-per te'-ip pan'-ch]

perforadora de impresión [f] printing punch [prin-tin'-g pan'-ch]

perforadora de tarjetas [f] card punch [car'-d pan'-ch]

perforadora de tecla [f] key punch [ki pan'-ch]

perforar [v] punch [pan'-ch]

período de retención [m] retention period [rri-ten-sion pi-ri-od]

petición [f] inquiry [in-kui-ri]

petri nets [m] petri nets [pe-tri net'-s]

pica [m] pica [pica]

picado de tecla [m] key bounce [ki ba-un'-s]

pila [f] stack [es-tak]

pila de discos [f] disk pack [dis'-k pak]

pila de empuje y vaciado [f] push-pop stack [puch pap es-tak]

pila del programa [f] program stack [pro-gram es-tak]

pintura [f] painting [pe-in-tin'-g]

pista [f] track [trak]

pista de auditoría [f] audit trail [au-dit tre-il]

pista por pulgadas [f] TPI tracks per inch [TPI trak'-s per in'-ch]

pista por pulgadas [f] tracks per inch (TPI) [trak'-s per in'-ch (TPI)]

pixel [m] pixel [pic-sel]

placa madre [f] backplane [bak-ple-in]

placa madre [f] motherboard [mo-der-bo-ar'-d]

plan [m] layout [ley-aut]

plan de prueba [f] test plan [tes'-t plan]

planificación [f] scheduling [es-ke-llu-lin'-g]

planificador de trabajos [m] job scheduler [llob es-ke-llu-ler]

plantilla de carácteres [f] character template [ka-rac'-ter tem-ple-it]

plantilla de flujograma [f] flowchart template [flo-char'-t tem-ple-it]

plaqueta [f] chip [chip]

plaqueta de almacenamiento de memoria [f] memory chip [me-mo-ri chip]

plaqueta de silicio [f] silicon chip [si-li-con chip]

plaqueta microminiatura [f] microminiature chip [mai-cro-mini-a-chu-ar chip]

plaqueta plana [f] flat pack [flat pak]

platillo [m] platter [pla-ter]

polarización [f] bias [bai-as]

polarizar [v] bias [bai-as]

poner en un índice [v] index [in-dex]

poner rápido [v] poke [po-uk]

portador [m] carrier [ca-rri-er]

portilla [f] port [por'-t]

portilla [f] gateway [ge-it-buey]

portilla de series [f] serial port [si-ri-al port]

posición [f] location [lo-kei-sion]

posición de bit [f] bit location [bit lo-kei-sion]

posición de perforación [f] punching position [pan-chin po-si-sion]

posición en la pantalla [f] screen position [es-crin po-si-sion]

posición protegida [f] protected location [pro-tek-ted lo-kei-sion]

post-editar [v] post edit [pos'-t edit]

potencia de audio [f] audio output [au-dio aut-put]

pragmática [f] pragmatics [prag-ma-tik'-s]

precisión [f] precision [pre-si-sion]

preforadora de cinta [f] tape punch [te'-ip pan'-ch]

prender [v] power on [pou'-guer on]

preparación [f] setup [set-ap]

preparación de los datos [f] data preparation [da'-ta pre-pa-rei-sion]

preprocesador [m] preprocessor [pre-pro-se-sor]

presentacion de almacenamiento de memoria [f] storage display [es-to-ra-ich dis-plei]

presentación de líneas [f] raster [ras-ter]

presentación vectorial [f] vector display [vek-tor dis-plei]

presentación visual de líneas [f] raster display [ras-ter dis-plei]

presentar [v] display [dis-plei]

presición triple [f] triple precision [tri-pel pre-si-sion]

prevenir el salto [v] debounce [di-baun'-s]

pre-almacenar [v] pre-store [pre-es-to-ar]

pre-editar [v] pre-edit [pre-edit]

pre-separado [m] pre-sort [pre-sor'-t]

pre-separar [v] pre-sort [pre-sor'-t]

primera generación [adj] first-generation [fir-s ge-nei-rei-sion]

primero que llega-primero que sale [m] first in-first out (FIFO) [fir-s in fir-s aut (FIFO)]

primero que llega-primero que sale [m] FIFO first in-first out [FIFO fir-s in fir-s aut]

primitivo [adj] primitive [pri-mi-tiv]

prioridad de interrupción [f] interrupt priority [in-te-rrup'-t pra-io-ri-ti]

privado [m] privacy [prai-va-si]

probabilidad [f] probability [pro-ba-bi-li-ti]

probar [v] test [tes'-t]

problema de referencia [m] benchmark problem [ben'-ch mar'-k pro-ble'-m]

problema de verificación [m] check problem [chek pro-ble'-m]

procedimiento [m] procedure [pro-si-dur]

procedimiento estochastico [m] stochastic procedures [es-to-ka-is-tik pro-si-dur'-s]

procedimiento reentrante [m] re-entrant procedure [ri-en-tran'-t pro-si-dur]

procesador [m] processor [pro-se-sor]

procesador de arreglo [m] array processor [a-rey pro-se-sor]

procesador de comunicación [m] communications processor [co-miu-ni-kei-sion'-s pro-se-sor]

procesador de la palabra [m] word processor [gu-or'-d pro-se-sor]

procesador dual [m] dual processor [dual pro-se-sor]

procesador limitado [adj] processor-limited [pro-se-sor li-mi-ted]

procesador múltiple [m] multiprocessor [multi-pro-se-sor]

procesador periférico [m] peripheral processor [pe-ri-fe-ral pro-se-sor]

procesador vinculado [adj] processor-bound [pro-se-sor ba-un'-d]

procesamiento [m] processing [pro-se-sin'-g]

procesamiento centralizado de datos [m] centralized data processing [sen-tra-lai-sed da'-ta pro-se-sin'-g]

procesamiento de datos automatizados [m] automated data processing [auto-mei-ted da'-ta pro-se-sin'-g]

procesamiento de imagen [m] image processing [i-ma-ich pro-se-sin'-g]

procesamiento de la orden [m] command processing [co-man'-d pro-se-sin'-g]

procesamiento de señales digitales [m] digital signal processing [di-lli-tal sig-nal pro-se-sin'-g]

procesamiento de superposición [m] overlap processing [over-lap pro-se-sin'-g]

procesamiento de texto [m] text processing [tex'-t pro-se-sin'-g]

procesamiento interactivo [m] interactive processing [inter-ak-tiv pro-se-sin'-g]

procesamiento líneal [m] in-line processing [in la-in pro-se-sin'-g]

procesamiento remoto de lotes [m] remote batch processing [re-mot bat'-ch pro-se-sin'-g]

procesamiento simultáneo [m] simultaneous processing [si-mul-tei-ni-as pro-se-sin'-g]

procesamiento sin extenderse sobre [m] nonoverlap processing [non-over-lap pro-se-sin'-g]

procesar [v] process [pro-ses]

proceso [m] process [pro-ses]

proceso a distancia [m] remote processing [re-mot pro-se-sin'-g]

proceso automático de datos [m] automatic data processing [auto-ma-tik da'-ta pro-se-sin'-g]

proceso concurrente [m] concurrent processing [con-ku-rren'-t prose-sin'-g]

proceso de datos [m] DP data processing [DP da'-ta pro-se-sin'-g]

proceso de datos (PD) [m] data processing (DP) [da'-ta pro-se-sin'-g (DP)]

proceso de la información [m] information processing [in-for-mei-sion pro-se-sin'-g]

proceso de programas subordinados [m] background processing [bak-gra-un'-d pro-se-sin'-g]

proceso de texto [m] word processing (WP) [gu-or'-d pro-se-sin'g (WP)]

proceso de texto [m] WP word processing [WP gu-or'-d pro-se-sin'g]

proceso de transacciones [m] transaction processing [tra-sak-cion pro-se-sin'-g]

proceso distribuido [m] distributive processing [dis-tri-biu-tiv pro-se-sin'-g]

Proceso electrónico de datos [m] EDP electronic data processing [EDP elek-tro-nik da'-ta pro-se-sin'-g]

Proceso electrónico de datos [m] electronic data processing (EDP) [elek-tro-nik da'-ta pro-se-sin'-g (EDP)]

proceso en paralelo [m] parallel processing [para'-lel pro-se-sin'-g]

proceso en serie [m] serial processing [si-rial pro-se-sin'-g]

proceso en tiempo real [m] real-time processing [ri-al ta-im pro-se-sin'-g]

proceso integrado de datos [m] integrated data processing (IDP) [in-te-grei-ted da'-ta pro-se-sin'g (IDP)]

proceso integrado de datos [m] IDP integrated data processing [IDP in-te-grei-ted da'-ta pro-se-sin'g]

proceso por lista [m] list processing [lis'-t pro-se-sin'-g]

proceso por lotes [m] batch processing [bat'-ch pro-se-sin'-g]

proceso por prioridad [m] priority processing [pra-io-ri-ti pro-se-sin'-g]

proceso preferencial [m] foreground processing [fo-ar-gra-un'-d pro-se-sin'-g]

proceso secuencial [m] sequential processing [se-ku-en-sial pro-se-sin'-g]

proceso vectorial [m] vector processing [vek-tor pro-se-sin'-g]

producción en equilibrio [f] line balancing [la-in ba-lan-sin'-g]

programa [m] program [pro-gram]

programa activo [m] active program [ak-tiv pro-gram]

programa almacenado [m] stored program [es-to-ar'-d pro-gram]

programa de aplicación [m] application program [a-pli-kei'-cion pro-gram]

programa de componer [m] authorized program [auto-rai-sed pro-gram]

programa de edición [m] editor [e'-di-tor]

programa de edición simbólica [m] symbolic editor [sim-bo-lik e'-di-tor]

programa de ensayo [m] test program [tes'-t pro-gram]

programa de fuente [m] source program [so-ur'-s pro-gram]

programa de gráfica [m] graphics program [gra-fik'-s pro-gram]

programa de informes [m] report program [re-por'-t pro-gram]

programa de proceso de texto [m] word processing program [gu-or'-d pro-se-sin'-g pro-gram]

programa de servicio [m] service programs [ser-bis pro-gram'-s]

programa de supervisión [m] supervisory program [su-per-vai-so-ri pro-gram]

programa de utilidad [m] utility program [llu-ti-li-ti pro-gram]

programa de verificación [m] checking program [chek-in'-g pro-gram]

programa del computador [m] computer program [com-piu'-ter pro-gram]

programa ejecutivo [m] executive program [exe-kiu-tiv pro-gram]

programa enlazador [m] linker [lin-ker]

programa ensamblador [m] assembly program [asem-bli pro-gram]

programa estructurado [m] structured program [es-truk-chur'-d pro-gram]

programa heurístico [m] heuristic program [i-u-ris-tik pro-gram]

programa objeto [m] object program [ob-yet pro-gram]

programa preferencial [m] foreground program [fo-ar-gra-un'-d pro-gram]

programa segmentado [m] segmented program [seg-men-ted pro-gram]

programa subordinado [m] background program [bak-gra-un'-d pro-gram]

programa subordinado [m] background job [bak-gra-un'-d llob]

programa transitorio [m] transient program [tran-si-en'-t pro-gram]

programable [adj] programmable [pro-gra'-ma-bel]

programación [f] programming [pro-gra-min'-g]

programación automática [f] automatic programming [auto-ma-tik pro-gra-min'-g]

programación de aplicación [f] application programming [a-pli-kei'-cion pro-gra-min'-g]

programación de arriba-abajo [f] top-down programming [tap-da-un pro-gra-min'-g]

programación de sistemas [f] systems programming [sis-tem'-s pro-gra-min'-g]

programación líneal [f] LP linear programming [LP li-near pro-gra-min'-g]

programación líneal [f] linear programming (LP) [li-near pro-gra-min'-g (LP)]

programación matemática [f] mathematical programming [ma-te-ma-ti-cal pro-gra-min'-g]

programación modular [f] modular programming [mo'-du-lar pro-gra-min'-g]

programación no lineal [f] nonlinear programming [non-li-near pro-gra-min'-g]

programación óptima [f] optimum programming [opti-mum pro-gra-min'-g]

programación simbólica [f] symbolic programming [sim-bo-lik pro-gra-min'-g]

programación sin dueño [f] ego-less programming [igo-les pro-gra-min-g]

programado [m] programmed [pro-gram-med]

programador [m] programmer [pro-gra-mer]

programador de aplicación [m] application programmer [apli-kei'-cion pro-gra-mer]

programador de computador [m] computer programmer [com-piu'-ter pro-gra-mer]

programador de sistema [m] system programmer [sis-tem pro-gra-mer]

programar [v] program [pro-gram]

programas en cascada [m] cascade programs [cas-kei'-d pro-gram'-s]

PROM borrable [m] erasable PROM (EPROM) [e-rei-sa-bel PROM (EPROM)]

PROM borrable [m] EPROM erasable PROM [EPROM e-rei-sa-bel PROM]

proporción de llegada [f] arrival rate [arra-i-bal rre-it]

protección [f] protection [pro-tek-sion]

protección de escritura [f] write protect [bra'-it pro-tek]

protección de fichero [f] file protection [fa-il' pro-tek-sion]

protección de la memoria [f] memory protection [me-mo-ri pro-tek-sion]

protección de los datos [f] data protection [da'-ta pro-tek-sion]

protección estructural [f] architectural protection [ar-qui-tek'-chu-ral pro-tek-sion]

proteger [v] protect [pro-tek] protocolo [m] protocol [proto-col]

protocolo [m] protocol [proto-col]

protocolo de comunicación [m] communications protocol [co-mu-ni-kei-sion'-s proto-col]

proyectando [adj] projecting [pro-yet-tin'-g]

prueba [f] proof [pruf]

prueba [f] test [tes'-t]

prueba de aceptación [f] acceptance test [a-sep-tan'-s tes'-t]

prueba de aceptación por el cliente [f] customer-acceptance test [cas-tu-mer a-sep-tan'-s tes'-t]

prueba de referencia [f] benchmark tests [ben'-ch mar'-k tes'-t]

prueba de regresión [f] regression testing [re-gre-sion tes-tin'-g]

prueba de tensión [f] stress testing [es-tres tes-tin'-g]

prueba del sistema [f] system testing [sis-tem tes-tin'-g]

prueba marginal [f] marginal test [mar-lli-nal tes'-t]

pseudocódigo [m] pseudocode [su-do-coud]

pseudo-casual [f] pseudorandom [su-do-rran-dom]

pseudo-instrucción [f] pseudoinstruction [su-do-ins-truc-cion]

pseudo-operación [f] pseudooperation [su-do-ope-rei-sion]

puerta [f] gate [gei-it]

puerta de anticoincidencia [f] anticoincidence gate [an-tai-co-in-si-den'-s gei-it]

puerta de coincidencia [f] coincidence gate [co-in-si-den'-s gei-it]

puerta de entrada/salida [f] input/output port [in-put/aut-put por'-t]

puerta lógica [f] logic gate [lo-llik gei-it]

puerta NI [f] NOR-gate [NOR-gei-it]

puerta NO [f] NOT-gate [NOT-gei-it]

puerta NY [f] NAND-gate [NAN'-D-gei-it]

puerta O [f] OR-gate [OR-gei-it]

puerta Y [f] AND-gate [AN'-D-gei-it]

puesto de trabajo [m] workstation [gu-or'-k es-tei-sion]

punta delantera [f] leading edge [li-din'-g eich]

puntero de pila [m] stack pointer [es-tak po-in-ter]

punto de carga [m] load point [lo-ud po-in'-t]

punto de control [m] checkpoint [chek-po-in'-t]

punto de entrada [m] entry point [en-tri po-in'-t]

punto de inserción [m] insertion point [in-ser-sion po-in'-t]

punto de interrupción [m] breakpoint [bre-ik po-in'-t]

punto de la base [m] radix point [rei-dix po-in'-t]

punto de reanudación [m] restart point [ri-es-tar'-t po-in'-t]

punto de reanudación de pasada [m] rerun point [rri-rran po-in'-t]

punto de rotura [m] breakpoint [bre-ik po-in'-t]

punto del plano señalado [m] bit mapped screen [bit ma-ped es-krin]

punto del vaciado [m] dump point [dum'-p po-in'-t]

purga [f] purge [per-ich]

Q

quadrimillónes [pre] femto- [fem'-to]

quadrimillónes segundo [m] femtosecond [fem'-to se-con'-d]

qualidad de letra [f] letter quality [le-ter kua-li-ti]

quebrar [v] crash [cra'-ch]

quedó huérfano [m] orphan [or-fan]

quedó viudo [m] widow [gui-dob]

quinta-generación [adj] fifth-generation [fif ge-ne-rei-sion]

quinti-millónes [pre] atto- [at-to]

R

raíz [f] radix [rra-dix]

raíz del árbol [f] root [rrut]

rango [m] rank [rran'-k]

ranura de extensión [f] expansion slots [ex-pan-sion es-lot'-s]

rastreando [adj] tracking [tra-kin'-g]

ratón [m] mouse [maus]

razonamiento analógico [m] analogical reasoning [a-na'-lo-lli-cal re-so-nin'-g]

reajustar [v] reset [re-set]

reajuste del sistema [m] system reset [sis-tem re-set]

realimentación [f] feedback [fi'-id-bak]

realización [f] implementation [in-ple-men-tei-sion]

reanudación [f] restart [ri-es-tar'-t]

reanudación [f] reboot [rri-but]

reanudar [v] restart [ri-es-tar'-t]

rebobinar [v] rewind [ri-gua-in'-d]

recargar [v] reload [re-lo-ud]

recompilar [v] recompile [re-com-pa-il]

reconfiguración [f] reconfiguration [re-con-fi-gu-rei-sion]

reconocer el usuario [m] log-in name [log-in ne-im]

reconocimiento [m] acknowledgement [ak-nou-led-ye-men'-t]

reconocimiento de carácteres [m] character recognition [ka-rac'-ter re-cog-ni-sion]

reconocimiento de carácteres de tinta magnética [m] magnetic ink character recognition [mag-ne-tik in'-k ka-rac'-ter re-cog-ni-sion]

reconocimiento de configuración [m] pattern recognition [pa-ter'-n re-cog-ni-sion]

reconocimiento de vista [m] vision recognition [vi-sion re-cog-ni-sion]

reconocimiento de voz [m] voice recognition [vo-is re-cog-ni-sion]

reconocimiento del hablar [m] speech recognition [es-pich re-cog-ni-sion]

reconocimiento óptico de carácteres [m] OCR optical character recognition [OCR op-ti-kal ka-rac'-ter re-cog-ni-sion]

reconocimiento óptico de carácteres [m] optical character recognition (OCR) [op-ti-kal ka-rac'-ter re-cog-ni-sion (OCR)]

reconocimiento óptico de las marcas [m] optical mark recognition [op-ti-kal mar'-k re-cog-ni-sion]

reconstitución [f] reconstitution [re-con'-s-ti-tu-sion]

recopilación de datos [f] data collection [da'-ta co-lec'-sion]

recorrer [v] roam [rrom]

recorrido alternativo [m] alternate routing [al-ter-neit rrau-tin'-g]

recortando [adj] scissoring [si-so-rin'-g]

recortando [adj] clipping [cli-pin'-g]

recortar [v] chop [chap]

recorte polígonal [m] polygon clipping [poligon cli-pin'-g]

recuperación [f] recovery [ri-ka-ve-ri]

recuperación [f] retrieval [ri-trie-val]

recuperación de alto nivel [f] high-level recovery [jai-le-vel ri-ka-ve-ri]

recuperación de la información [f] information retrieval [in-for-mei-sion ri-trie-val]

recuperación de mensajes [f] message retrieval [me-sa-ich ri-trie-val]

recuperación del fallo [f] failure recovery [fei-liur ri-ka-ve-ri]

recursión [f] recursion [re-cur-sion]

recursivo [adj] recursive [re-cur-siv]

recurso [m] resource [re-so-ur'-se]

red [f] network [net-gu'-ork]

red de commutación de paquetes [f] packet-switched network [pa-ket sui-ched net-gu'-ork]

red de comunicación [f] communication network [com-mu-ni-kei-sion net-gu'-ork]

red de conmutación de mensajes [f] switched-message network [sui-ched me-sa-ich net-gu'-ork]

red de puntos múltiples [f] multipoint network [multi-po-in'-t net-gu'-ork]

red de video/audio [f] Ethernet [I-ter-net]

red del conductor común [f] bus network [bas net-gu'-ork]

red digital [f] digital network [di-lli-tal net-gu'-ork]

red jerárquica [f] hierarchical network [jai-rar'-ki-cal net-gu'-ork]

red neural [f] neural network [neu-ral net-gu'-ork]

red para la transmisión de datos [f] data network [da'-ta net-gu'-ork]

redes en círculo [f] ring network [rrin'-g net-gu'-ork]

redes en estrella [f] star network [es-tar net-gu'-ork]

redimensionar [m] resizing [ri-sai-sin'-g]

redondear [v] round off [ra-un'-d of]

reducción de datos [f] data reduction [da'-ta ri-dak-sion]

reducción de datos en línea [f] on-line data reduction [on-la-in da'-ta ri-dak-sion]

redundancia [f] redundancy [ri-dan-dan-ci]

reemisor [m] relay [rri-lei]

reemplazo [m] displacement [dis-plei-se-men'-t]

reencaminar [v] reroute [rri-rra-ut]

reentrada [f] reentrant [ri-en-tran'-t]

reescribir [v] rewrite [ri-bra'-it]

referencia [f] benchmark [ben'-ch mar'-k]

reflectora [f] reflectance [re-flek-tan'-s]

regeneración [f] regeneration [ri-ge-nei-rei-sion]

regeneración invisible [f] invisible refresh [in-vi-si'-bel ri-fre'-ch]

regenerador estático [m] static refresh [es-ta-tik ri-fre'-ch]

regenerar [v] refresh [ri-fre'-ch]

regenerarse [v] regenerate [ri-ge-nei-re-it]

régimen de perforación [m] perforation rate [per-fo-rei-sion rre-it]

región de búsqueda [f] area search [ei-rea se-ir'-ch]

registrador automático [m] logger [lo-ger]

registrador de películas [m] film recorder [film re-kor-der]

registrar [v] log [log]

registrar [v] record [re-kor'-d]

registro [m] record [re-kor'-d]

registro [m] log [log]

registro [m] register [rre-llis-ter]

registro adquirido [m] addition record [adi-cion re-kor'-d]

registro circulante [m] circulating register [sir-cu-lai-tin'-g rre-llis-ter]

registro de cambio [m] change record [cha-in'-ch re-kor'-d]

registro de cola [m] trailer record [tre-i-ler re-kor'-d]

registro de control [m] control register [con-trol re-llis-ter]

registro de datos [m] data logging [da'-ta lo-gin'-g]

registro de desplazamiento [m] shift register [chif'-t re-llis-ter]

registro de eliminación [m] deletion record [di-li-sion re-kor'-d]

registro de enlazo [m] link register [lin'-k re-llis-ter]

registro de instrucción-dirección [m] instruction-address register [ins-truk-sion ad-dres re-llis-ter]

registro de tamaño variable [m] variable-length record [va-ria-bel len'-t re-kor'-d]

registro del direccional [m] address register [ad-dres re-llis-ter]

registro en paralelo [m] dual recording [dual re-kor-din'-g]

registro encadenado [m] chained record [chei-ned re-kor'-d]

registro intermedio [m] buffer [ba-fer]

registro maestro [m] master record [mas-ter re-kor'-d]

registro por haz de electrónes [m] EBR electron beam recording [EBR e-lec'-tron bim re-kor-din'-g]

registro por haz de electrónes [m] electron beam recording (EBR) [e-lec'-tron bim re-kor-din'-g (EBR)]

registro primario [m] base register [be-is re-llis-ter]

registro protegido [m] protected record [pro-tek-ted re-kor'-d]

registro unitario [m] unit record [iu-nit re-kor'-d]

registro vertical [m] vertical recording [ver-ti-cal re-kor-din'-g]

regreso blando [m] soft return [sof'-t ri-tur'-n]

relación de actividad [f] activity ratio [ak-ti-vi-ti rei-chio]

relación de nombres [f] wild card [gu'-ail car'-d]

relación de plegado [f] folding ratio [fol-din'-g rei-chio]

relación de señal-ruido [f] signal-to-noise ratio [sig-nal tu no-is rei-chio]

relación de utilización [f] operating ratio [ope-rei-tin'-g rei-chio]

relación de utilización [f] utilization ratio [llu-ti-li-sei-cion rei-chio]

relé [m] relay [rri-lai]

relleno [m] padding [pad-din'-g]

reloj [m] clock [clak]

reloj automático de intervalos [m] interval timer [inter-val tai-mer]

reloj binario [m] real-time clock [rri-al ta-im clak]

reloj de tiempo real [m] real-time clock [rri-al ta-im clak]

reloj digital [m] digital clock [di-lli-tal clak]

reloj interno [m] internal clock [in-ter-nal clak]

reloj maestro [m] master clock [mas-ter clack]

reloj marcador [m] time-clock [ta-im clak]

remendar [v] patch [pach]

remoción de línea oculta [f] hidden-line removal [ji-den la-in re-mu-val]

removerlo [v] demount [di-ma-un'-t]

reorganizar [v] reorganize [ri-or-ga-nais]

repaginación [f] repagination [ri-pa-lli-nei-sion]

repertorio [m] repertoire [re-per-chu-ar]

repetición [f] looping [lu-pin'-g]

repetición de pasada [f] rerun [rri-rran]

repetir la pasada [v] rerun [rri-rran]

repintar [v] repaint [rri-pe-in'-t]

réplica [f] replication [rre-pli-kei-sion]

reporte de categoría [m] status report [es-ta-tus ri-por'-t]

reporte de una acción-orientada [m] action-oriented management report [ak-cion ori-en-ted ma-na-ich-men'-t ri-por'-t]

representación de conocimiento [f] knowledge representation [nou'-led-ye ri-pre-sen-tei-sion]

representación de modo puntual [f] point-mode display [po-in'-t mo-ud dis-plei]

representación en modo vectorial [f] vector-mode display [vec'-tor mo-ud dis-plei]

representación gráfica [f] graphics display [gra-fik'-s di-plei]

representación incremental [f] incremental representation [in-cre-men-tal ri-pre-sen-tei-sion]

representación interactiva [f] interactive display [in-ter-ak-tiv dis-plei]

representación regenerada [f] refresh display [ri-fre'-ch dis-plei]

representación tabular [f] tabular display [ta'-biu-lar dis-plei]

reproductor [m] reproducer [ri-pro-du-ser]

reserva [f] backup [bak-ap]

reservar [v] reserve [ri-ser'-b]

resguardador [adj] shielding [chi-el-din'-g]

residir [v] reside [ri-sa-id]

resiliencia [f] resilience [ri-si-li-en'-s]

resituado [m] relocate [ri-lo-ke-it]

resolución de gráfica [f] graphics resolution [gra-fik'-s rre-so-lu-sion]

resolución de orden superior [f] high resolution [jai rre-so-lu-sion]

resolución de presentación gráfica [f] graphic-display resolution [gra-fik dis-plei rre-so-lu-sion]

resolución inferior [f] low resolution [lo rre-so-lu-sion]

respondedor de voz [m] VAB voice answer back [VAB vo-is an'-s-guer bak]

respondedor de voz [m] voice answer back (VAB) [vo-is an'-s-guer bak (VAB)]

respuesta vocal [f] voice response [vo-is rris-po-un'-s]

restablecer [v] recover [ri-co-ver]

restablecido y corre [adj] up-and-running [ap an'-d rra-nin'-g]

restaurar [v] restore [rris-to-ar]

retardo de propagación [m] propagation delay [pro-pa-gei-sion di-lei]

retículo [m] reticle [re-ti-kel]

retornar [v] return [rri-tur'-n]

retorno [m] return [rri-tur'-n]

retorno automático [m] wraparound [rap a-rra-un'-d]

retorno automático de la palabra [m] word wrap [gu-or'-d rap]

retorno del carro [m] carriage return [ca-rri-aich rri-tur'-n]

retrasado [m] lag [lag]

retraso rotacional [m] rotational delay [ro-tei-sio-nal di-lei]

retroapto [m] retrofit [rre-tro-fit]

retroceder [v] backspace [bak es-pe-is]

retroceso de cinta [m] backspace tape [bak es-pe-is ta'-ip]

retrovisor [m] mirroring [mi-rro-in'-g]

reubicar [v] relocate [ri-lo'-kei-it]

revestimiento [m] cladding [cla-din'-g]

revisión [f] review [rre-viu]

revolverse [adj] thrashing [tras-chin'-g]

robótica [f] robotics [ro-bo-tik'-s]

rodando [m] rollover [rol-over]

rodando [m] roll out [rol aut]

rollo [m] platen [pla-ten']

romper [v] crash [kra'-ach]

rueda de impresión [f] print wheel [prin'-t ju-il]

ruido [m] noise [no-is']

ruido confuso [m] babble [ba'-bel]

ruptura bajo control [f] control break [con-trol bre-ik]

ruta [f] route [rra-ut]

rutina [f] routine [rru-tin]

rutina cerrada [f] closed routine [clo-se'-d rru-tin]

rutina de apertura [f] open routine [o-pen rru-tin]

rutina de carga [f] loading routine [lo-u-din'-g rru-tin]

rutina de clasificación [f] sorting routine [sor-tin'-g rru-tin]

rutina de diagnóstico [f] diagnostic routine [di-ag-nos-tik rru-tin]

rutina de errores [f] error routine [error rru-tin]

rutina de servicio [f] service routine [ser-bis rru-tin]

rutina póstuma [f] post mortem routine [pos'-t mor-tem rru-tin]

rutina residente [f] resident routine [re-si-den'-t rru-tin]

rutinas enlatadas [f] precanned routines [pri-can-ned rru-tin]

S

sacado [adj] extract [es-trak'-t]

sacar [v] extract [es-trak'-t]

sacar del bloque [m] deblocking [di-blo-kin'-g]

sala de máquinas [f] machine room [ma-chin rrum]

salida [f] output [aut'-put]

salida [f] exit [ex'-it]

salida de buena información [f] outputting [aut-pu-tin'-g]

salida de voz [f] voice output [vo-is aut'-put]

salida del computador en microfilm [f] COM computer output on microfilm [COM com-piu'-ter aut'-put on mai-cro-film]

salida del computador en microfilm [f] computer output on microfilm (COM) [com-piu'-ter aut'-put on mai-cro-film (COM)]

salida impresa [f] hard copy [jar'-d co-pi]

salida para más tarde [m] deferred exit [de-fe-rred ex'-it]

salir [v] exit [ex'-it]

salir [v] output [aut'-put]

saltar [v] jump [jam'-p]

salto [m] jump [jam'-p]

salto de microondas [m] microwave hop [mai-cro-gu-eib jap]

salto de papel [m] paper throw [pei-per tro-u]

salto pequeño [m] jitter [lli-ter]

sangrar [v] indent [in-den'-t]

sangría [f] indentation [in-den-tei-sion]

satélite de comunicaciones [m] communications satellites [co-mu-ni-kei-sion'-s sa-de-la-it'-s]

saturación de color [f] color saturation [co-lor sa-chu-rei-sion]

saturado [adj] saturated [sa-chu-rei-ted]

sección de control de datos [f] data control section [da'-ta con-trol sek-cion]

sector del disco [m] disk sector [dis'-k sek-tor]

sector duro [m] hard sector [jar'-d sek-tor]

sector malo [m] bad sector [bad sek-tor]

secuencia [f] sequence [si-cu-en'-s]

secuencia de control [f] control sequence [con-trol se-cu-en'-s]

secuencia de llamada [f] calling sequence [co-lin se-cu-en'-s]

secuenciar [v] sequence [se-cu-en'-s]

segmentar [v] segment [seg-men'-t]

segmento [m] segment [seg-men'-t]

segmento conectado [m] line segment [la-in seg-men'-t]

segmento no paginado [m] unpaged segment [an-pe-ich seg-men'-t]

segunda-generación [adj] second-generation [se-kon'-d lle-nei-rei-sion]

seguridad de computador [f] computer security [com-piu'-ter se-kiu-ri-ti]

seleccionar [v] select [se-lek'-t]

selector [m] selector [se-lek-tor]

semáforado [m] semaphores [se-ma-for'-s]

semántico [adj] semantic [se-man-tik]

semiautomático [adj] semiautomatic [semi-auto-ma-tik]

semiconductor [m] semiconductor [semi-con-duk-tor]

semiconductor de óxido metálico [m] MOS metal oxide semiconductor [MOS me'-tal ox-sa-id semi-con-duk-tor]

semiconductor de óxido metálico [m] metal oxide semiconductor (MOS) [me'-tal ox-sa-id semi-con-duk-tor (MOS)]

semi-duplex [mf] half-duplex [jaf du-plex]

semi-sumador [m] half-adder [jaf ad'-der]

semi-sustractor [m] half subtractor [jaf sub-trak-tor]

sensor [m] sensors [sen-sor'-s]

señal [f] token [tou-ken]

señal [f] signal [sig-nal]

señal de activación [f] enabling signal [i-nei-blin'-g sig-nal]

señal de salida cero [f] zero-output signal [si-ro aut'-put sig-nal]

señal de salida no cambiada [f] undisturbed output signal [an-dis-tur-bed aut'-put sig-nal]

señal inhibidora [f] inhibiting signal [in-ji-bi-tin'-g sig-nal]

señalador [m] flag [fla'-g]

señalador del signo [m] sign flag [sa-in fla'-g]

separación entre registros [f] inter-record gap [inter-re-cor'-d gap]

separador [m] separator [se-pa-rei-tor]

separador de documentos [m] document sorter [do-kiu-men'-t sor-ter]

separadora de páginas [f] burster [burr-s-ter]

serie [f] string [es-trin'-g]

serie alfabética [f] alphabetic string [al-fa-be-tik es-trin'-g]

serie con valor añadido [f] value-added network [va-liu ad'-ded net-gu'-ork]

serie nula [f] null string [nul es-trin'-g]

series de bit [f] bit string [bit es-trin'-g]

series de búsqueda [f] search string [se-ir'-ch es-trin'-g]

series de carácteres [f] character string [ka-rac'-ter es-trin'-g]

serviciador de comunicaciones [m] communications server [com-miu-ni-kei-sion'-s ser-ver]

sesgado [m] skew [es-kiu]

signo [m] sign [sa-in'-g]

signo de intercalación [m] caret [ca'-ret]

silicio [m] silicon [si'-li-con]

símbolo [m] symbol [sim-bol]

símbolo anotado [m] annotation symbol [a-no-tei-sion sim-bol]

símbolo de decisión [m] decision box [de-si-sion bax]

símbolo de rastreo [m] tracking symbol [tra-kin'-g sim-bol]

símbolo de sombreado [m] shading symbols [chei-din'-g sim-bol'-s]

símbolo lógico [m] logic symbol [lo-llik sim-bol]

símbolos de esquemáticos [m] schematic symbols [es-ke-ma-tik sim-bol'-s]

símbolos de flujogramas [m] flowcharting symbol [flo-char-tin'-g sim-bol]

simplex [mf] simplex [sim-plex]

simulación [f] simulation [si-miu-lei-sion]

simulador [m] simulator [si-miu-lei-tor]

sin espacio blanco entre letras [m] kerning [ker-nin'-g]

sin operación [m] no-op [no- ap]

sin riesgo de fallo [adj] fail-safe [fe-il sei-if]

sin serif [f] sans serif [san'-s se-rif]

sincronización [f] synchronization [sin-cro-ni-sei-sion]

síncronizador [m] synchronizer [sin-cro-nai-ser]

sintaxis [f] syntax [sin-tax']

sintetiza la voz [f] voice synthesis [vo-is sin-te'-sis]

sintetizador [m] synthesizer [sin-te-tai-ser]

sintetizador de música [m] music synthesizer [miu-sik sin-te-sai-ser]

sintetizador de voz [m] voder [vou-der]

sintetizador del hablar [m] speech synthesizer [es-pich sin-te-sai-ser]

sintetizador musical [m] musicomp [miu-sic-com'-p]

sintonización [m] tuning [tu-nin'-g]

sistema [m] system [sis-tem]

sistema compatible [m] upward compatible [ap-gu-ar'-d com-pa-ti-bel]

sistema de cálculo a distancia [m] remote computing system [ri-mo-ut com-piu-tin'-g sis-tem]

sistema de cintas operacional [m] TOS tape operating system [TOS te'-ip ope-rei-tin'-g sis-tem]

sistema de cintas operacional [m] tape operating system (TOS) [te'-ip ope-rei-tin'-g sis-tem (TOS)]

sistema de componer [m] authoring system [auto-rin'-g sis-tem]

sistema de comunicación [m] communication system [com-miu-ni-kei-sion sis-tem]

sistema de comunicación de datos [m] data communications system [da'-ta co-miu-ni-kei-sion'-s sis-tem]

sistema de conductores comúnes [m] bus system [bas sis-tem]

sistema de control adaptable [m] adaptive-control system [a-dap-tiv con-trol sis-tem]

sistema de control de trabajos [m] job control system [llob con-trol sis-tem]

sistema de gestión del banco de datos [m] data base management system (DBMS) [da'-ta be-is ma-na-ich-men'-t sis-tem (DBMS)]

sistema de gestión del banco de datos [m] DBMS data base management system [DBMS da'-ta be-is ma-na-ich-men'-t sis-tem]

sistema de información [m] information system [in-for-mei-sion sis-tem]

sistema de numeración [m] number system [nam-ber sis-tem]

sistema de redes [m] network system [net-gu'-ork sis-tem]

sistema del maestro-esclavo [m] master-slave system [mas-ter es-le-ib sis-tem]

sistema duplex [m] duplex system [du-plex sis-tem]

sistema en tándem [m] tandem system [tan-dem sis-tem]

sistema experto [m] expert system [es-per'-t sis-tem]

sistema gráfico sólo [m] stand-alone graphics system [es-tan'-d a-lon gra-fik'-s sis-tem]

sistema incrustado [m] embedded systems [em-be-ded sis-tem'-s]

sistema maduro [m] mature system [ma-chur sis-tem]

sistema modular [m] modular system [mo'-du-lar sis-tem]

sistema operativo [m] operating system (OS) [ope-rei-tin'-g sis-tem (OS)]

sistema operativo [m] OS operating system [OS ope-rei-tin'-g sis-tem]

sistema operativo de discos [m] DOS disk operating system [DOS dis'-k ope-rei-tin'-g sis-tem]

sistema operativo de discos [m] disk operating system (DOS) [dis'-k ope-rei-tin'-g sis-tem (DOS)]

sistema para usuarios múltiples [m] multiuser system [multi-llu-ser sis-tem]

sistema probado [m] proving [prou-vin'-g]

sistema sin riesgo de fallo [m] fail-safe system [fe-il sa-if sis-tem]

sistema sin riesgo de muchos fallos [m] fail-soft system [fe-il sof'-t sis-tem]

sistema tolerante de averías en línea [m] on-line fault tolerant system [on-la-in fa-ul'-t to-le-ran'-t sis-tem]

sobreescribir [v] overwrite [over-bra'-it]

sobreescritura [f] superscript [super-es-crip'-t]

sobreexplorar [v] overscan [over-es-can]

sobreimprimir [m] overstriking [over-es-trai-kin'-g]

sobretensión [f] surge [ser-ich]

sobretensión oleada [f] surging [ser-chin'-g]

sobretensión transitoria [f] spike [es-pa-ik]

sobretensión transitoria [f] line surge [la-in ser-ich]

soltar [v] release [rri-lis]

soltura [f] release [rri-lis]

solución del problema [f] problem solving [pro-blem sol-vin'-g]

solución del problema en línea [f] on-line problem solving [on-la-in pro-blem sol-vin'-g]

sombra [f] shade [che-id]

sombreado [m] crosshatching [cros-ja-chin'-g]

sonda de sentir [f] sense probe [sen'-s pro-ub]

sonido de atención [m] feep [fi-ip]

sonido de continuidad [m] white noise [ju-ait no-is]

soporte lógico [m] software [sof-gue-ar]

soporte lógico de aplicación [m] application software [a-pli-kei'-cion sof-gue-ar]

soporte lógico en dominio público [m] shareware [che-ar-gue-ar]

soporte lógico en dominio público [m] public domain software [pa-blik do-mein sof-gue-ar]

soporte lógico en multicapas [m] multilayered software [multi-lei-lle-red sof-gue-ar]

soporte lógico hecho en casa [m] home-grown software [jom-gron sof-gue-ar]

soporte lógico inalterable [m] firmware [fir'-m-gue-ar]

soporte lógico integrado [m] integrated software [inte-grei-ted sof-gue-ar]

soporte lógico que funciona con un menú [m] menu-driven software [me-niu dri-ven sof-gue-ar]

suavizador [m] spline [es-pla-in]

subárbol [m] subtree [sab-tri]

subdesbordamiento [m] underflow [un-der-flo]

subdirectorio [m] subdirectory [sab-di-rek'-to-ri]

subesquema [m] subschema [sab-es-kim]

subestrato [m] substrate [sab-es-tre-it]

subgrupo [m] subset [sab-set]

subgrupo de lenguaje [m] language subset [lan-gu'-ich sab-set]

subprograma [m] subprogram [sab-pro-gram]

subrayar [m] autoscore [auto-es-cor]

subrutina [f] subroutine [sab-rru-tin]

subrutina cerrada [f] closed subroutine [clo-us sab-rru-tin]

subrutina de reentrada [f] reentrant subroutine [rri-en-tran'-t sab-rru-tin]

subrutina estática [f] static subroutine [es-ta-tik sab-rru-tin]

subrutina normal [f] standard subroutine [es-tan-dar'-d sab-rru-tin]

subserie [f] substring [sab-es-trin'-g]

subsistema [m] subsystem [sab-sis-tem]

suite [mf] suite [su-it']

sujetadatos [m] clipboard [clip-bo-ar'-d]

suma de verificación [f] check sum [chek sam]

sumador [m] adder [ad-der]

sumador-sustractor [m] adder-subtracter [ad-der sab-trak-ter]

superficie de visualización [f] display surface [dis-plai ser-fa-is]

superposicionamiento [m] overlapping [over-la-pin'-g]

supervisor [m] supervisor [super-vai-sor]

supresión [f] suppression [su-pre-sion]

supresión de ceros [f] zero suppression [si-ro su-pre-sion]

suprimidor transitorio [m] transient suppressors [tra-si-en'-t su-pre-sor'-s]

suprimir [v] suppress [su-pres]

suprimir [v] zap [za-ap]

suprimir [v] delete [di-lit]

suspención [f] abort [a-bort]

suspender [v] suspend [sas-pen'-d]

sustractor [m] subtracter [sab-trak-ter]

systema virtual en operación [m] virtual storage operating system (VSOS) [vir-chu-al es-tor-aich ope-rei-tin'-g sis-tem (VSOS)]

systema virtual en operación [m] VSOS virtual storage operating system [VSOS vir-chu-al es-tor-aich ope-rei-tin'-g sis-tem]

T

tabla [f] table [tei-bol]

tabla de consulta [f] look-up table [luk-ap tei-bol]

tabla de decisión [f] decision table [de-si-cion tei-bol]

tabla de decisión lógica [f] truth table [tru'-t tei-bol]

tabla de información [f] grid chart [gri'-d char'-t]

tabla simbólica [f] symbolic table [sim-bo-lik tei-bol]

tablero de conectadores [m] patchboard [pach-bo-ar'-d]

tablero de control [m] control panel [con-trol pa-nel]

tablero de enchufe [m] plugboard [plug-bo-ar'-d]

tablero de estacas [m] pinboard [pin-bo-ar'-d]

tablero electrónico [m] board [bo-ar'-d]

tablero electrónico con trasera [m] piggyback board [pigi-bak bo-ar'-d]

tablero electronico desnudo [m] bare board [be-ar bo-ar'-d]

tableta [f] tablet [ta-ble'-t]

tableta de tocada sensitiva [f] touch-sensitive tablet [tach-sen-si-tiv ta-ble'-t]

tableta gráfica [f] graphics tablet [gra-fik'-s ta-ble'-t]

tablón de anuncios [m] bulletin board [bu-le-tin bo-ar'-d]

tablón electrónico de anuncios [m] electronic bulletin board [e-lec'-tro-nik bu-le-tin bo-ar'-d]

tabulación [f] tabulation [ta-biu-lei-sion]

tabuladora [f] tabulator [ta-biu-lei-tor]

tabular [v] tabulate [ta-biu-lei'-t]

tamaño de la pantalla [m] screen size [es-crin za-is]

tamaño de la unidad de palabra [m] data word size [da'-ta gu-or'-d za-is]

tamaño del bloque [m] block length [blok len'-t]

tamaño del tipo [m] typesize [ta'-ip-za-is]

tambor [m] drum [dra'-m]

tambor de tipos [m] type drum [ta'-ip dra'-m]

tambor de traza [m] drum plotter [dra'-m plo-ter]

tambor magnético [m] magnetic drum [mag-ne-tik dra'-m]

tapar [v] plug [pla'-g]

tapón [m] plug [pla'-g]

tarea [f] task [tas'-k]

tarjeta de ochenta columnas [f] eighty-column card [ei-ti-co-lum car'-d]

tarjeta de perforación [f] punch card [pan'-ch car'-d]

tarjeta Hollerith [f] card (paper) [car'-d (pei-per)]

tarjeta magnética [f] magnetic card [mag-ne-tik car'-d]

tarjeta perforada [f] punched card [pan-ched car'-d]

tasa en bit [f] bit rate [bit rre-it]

tecla [f] key [ki]

tecla de control [f] control key [con-trol ki]

tecla de desplazamiento [f] SHIFT key [chif'-t ki]

tecla de ENTRADA [f] ENTER key [en-ter ki]

tecla de escape [f] ESCAPE key [es-ke-ip ki]

tecla de espaciar [f] spacebar [es-pe-is-bar]

tecla de función [f] function key [fun-sion ki]

tecla de inicio [f] HOME key [jom ki]

tecla de mando [f] command key [co-man'-d ki]

tecla de opción [f] option key [op-sion ki]

tecla de REGRESO [f] RETURN key [re-tur'-n ki]

tecla de repetición [f] repeat key [rri-pit ki]

tecla definida por el usuario [f] user-defined key [llu-ser-di-fai-ned ki]

tecla funcional programable [f] programmable function key [pro-gram-ma-bel fan-sion ki]

tecla repetitiva [f] typematic [ta'-ip-ma-tik]

teclado [m] keyboard [ki-bo-ar'-d]

teclado cerrado [m] locked-up keyboard [lak-ed-ap ki-bo-ar'-d]

teclado de a diez [m] ten-key pad [ten-ki pad]

teclado de registro sobre cinta [m] key-to-tape [ki-tu-te'-ip]

teclado de registro sobre disco [m] key-to-disk [ki-tu-dis'-k]

teclas blandas [f] soft keys [sof'-t kis]

teclas de control del cursor [f] cursor control keys [cur-sor con-trol kis]

tecleando [m] keyboarding [ki-bor-din'-g]

teclear [v] keyboard [ki-bo-ar'-d]

técnica con fuerza bruta [f] brute-force technique [brut-for'-s tec-nik]

técnica dinámica de depuración [f] DDT dynamic debugging technique [DDT dai-na-mik di-bu-gin'-g tec-nik]

técnica dinámica de depuración [f] dynamic debugging technique (DDT) [dai-na-mik di-bu-gin'-g tec-nik (DDT)]

tecnología de las fibras ópticas [f] optical fibre technology [op-ti-cal fai-bre tek-no-lo-lli]

tecnología de las fibras ópticas [f] optical fiber technology [op-ti-cal fai-bre tek-no-lo-lli]

teleautomático [m] Telematics [Tele-ma-tik'-s]

telecomunicación [f] telecommunication [tele'-co-miu-ni-ca-sion]

teleconmutar [m] telecommuting [tele-com-miu-tin'-g]

teleimpresor [m] teleprinter [tele'-prin-ter]

telemedicina [f] telemedicine [tele'-me-di-sin]

telemetría [f] telemetry [tele'-me-tri]

teleproceso [m] teleprocessing [tele-pro-se-sin'-g]

teleproductor de imagenes [m] facsimile (FAX) [fak-si'-mi-le (FAX)]

teleproductor de imagenes [m] FAX facsimile [FAX fak-si'-mi-le]

teleseries [f] Telenet [Tele'-net]

teletexto [m] teletext [tele-tex'-t]

temperatura del medio ambiente [f] ambient temperature [am-bien'-t tem-pera-chur]

tener una avería [v] go down [go da-un]

teoría de control [f] control theory [con-trol ti-o-ri]

teoría de esperar [f] queuing theory [ki-u-in ti-o-ri]

teoría de la información [f] information theory [in-for-mei-sion te-o-ri]

tercera-generación [adj] third-generation [tir'-d lle-ne-rei-sion]

terminación [f] termination [ter-mi-nei-sion]

terminación anormal [f] abend [a-ben'-d]

terminación anormal [f] abnormal termination [ab-nor-mal ter-mi-nei-sion]

terminal [m] terminal [ter-mi-nal]

terminal clave [m] key stations [ki es-tei-sion'-s]

terminal con teclado [m] typewriter terminal [ta'-ip-brai-ter ter-mi-nal]

terminal de interrogación [m] inquiry terminal [in'-kui-ri ter-mi-nal]

terminal de presentación alfanumérica [m] alphanumeric display terminal [al-fa-nu-me-rik dis-plei ter-mi-nal]

terminal de presentación gráfica [m] graphic-display terminal [gra-fik-dis-plei ter-mi-nal]

terminal de representación de video [m] VDT video display terminal [VDT vi-deo dis-plei ter-mi-nal]

terminal de representación de video [m] video display terminal (VDT) [vi-deo dis-plei ter-mi-nal (VDT)]

terminal de video [m] video terminal [vi-deo ter-mi-nal]

terminal de visualización [m] display terminal [dis-plei ter-mi-nal]

terminal gráfico [m] graphics terminal [gra-fik'-s ter-mi-nal]

terminal inteligente [m] intelligent terminal [in-te-li-llen'-t ter-mi-nal]

terminal inteligente local [m] local intelligence [local in-te-li-llen'-s]

terminal interactivo [m] interactive terminal [inter-ak-tiv ter-mi-nal]

terminal sávido [m] smart terminal [es-mar'-t ter-mi-nal]

terminar el modo de diágolo [v] logging-off [lo-gin-of]

terminar la sesión [v] log out [log aut]

terminar teledirigido [m] remote terminal [re-mot ter-mi-nal]

texto [m] text [tex'-t]

texto [m] format [for-mat]

texto plano [m] plaintext [plein-tex'-t]

texto repetido [m] boilerplate [boi-ler-plei-it]

textura [f] texture [tex-chur]

tiempo compartido [m] time-sharing [ta-im-chei-rin'-g]

tiempo contable [m] accountable time [aka-un-ta-bel ta-im]

tiempo de aceleración [m] acceleration time [a-ce-le-rei-sion ta-im]

tiempo de actividades anexas [m] incidental time [in-si-den-tal ta-im]

tiempo de arranque [m] start time [es-tar'-t ta-im]

tiempo de arranque-espera [m] start-stop time [es-tar'-t es-tap ta-im]

tiempo de búsqueda [m] search time [rri-ser'-ch ta-im]

tiempo de calentura [m] warm-up time [gu-ar'-m ap ta-im]

tiempo de deceleración [m] deceleration time [di-se-le-rei-sion ta-im]

tiempo de desarreglo [m] downtime [da-un-ta-im]

tiempo de ejecución [m] execution time [exe-kiu-sion ta-im]

tiempo de ensayo [m] proving time [pro-vin'-g ta-im]

tiempo de entrada [m] access time [ak-ses ta-im]

tiempo de escritura [m] write time [rra'-it ta-im]

tiempo de espera [m] wait time [gu-ait ta-im]

tiempo de lectura [m] read time [ri-id ta-im]

tiempo de parada [m] downtime [da-un-ta-im]

tiempo de pasada [m] run time [rran ta-im]

tiempo de preparación [m] setup time [set-ap ta-im]

tiempo de producción [m] productive time [pro-duc-tiv ta-im]

tiempo de reparación [m] repair time [ri-pe-ar ta-im]

tiempo de respuesta [m] response time [ris-pon'-s ta-im]

tiempo de reviso [m] engineering time [en-lli-nie-rin'-g ta-im]

tiempo de suma-resta [m] add-subtract time [ad'-d sub-trak'-t ta-im]

tiempo de una instrucción [m] instruction time [ins-truc-cion' ta-im]

tiempo del ciclo [m] cycle time [sai-kel ta-im]

tiempo disponible [m] available time [a-vei-la-bel ta-im]

tiempo efectivo [m] effective time [e-fek-tiv ta-im]

tiempo flotante [m] slack time [es-lak ta-im]

tiempo ineficaz [m] ineffective time [i-nek-fek-tiv ta-im]

tiempo medio entre fallos [m] mean time between failures [min ta-im bit-tu-in fei-liur'-s]

tiempo medio para reparación [m] mean repair time [min ri-pe-ar ta-im]

tiempo muerto [m] dead time [ded ta-im]

tiempo no empleado [m] unused time [an-llu-sed ta-im]

tiempo obligatorio [m] binding time [ba-in-din'-g ta-im]

tiempo pasivo [m] idle time [ai-del ta-im]

tiempo productivo [m] uptime [ap-ta-im]

tiempo real [m] real time [rri-al ta-im]

tiempo sin personal [m] unattended time [an-aten-ded ta-im]

tiempo transcurrido [m] elapsed time [i-lap-sed ta-im]

tinta magnética [f] magnetic ink [mag-ne-tik in'-k]

tinta nonreflectora [f] nonreflective ink [non-re-flek-tiv in'-k]

tinta reflectora [f] reflectance ink [rri-flek-tan'-s in'-k]

tipo [m] type [ta'-ip]

tipógrafos [m] typeface [ta'-ip-fe-is]

tipógrafos incorporados [m] built-in fonts [bil'-t in fan-t'-s]

tirar los contenidos [v] flush [flu'-ch]

tolerante de averías [m] fault-tolerant [fa-ul'-t to-le-ran'-t]

tomografía informática [f] computerized tomography (CT) [com-piu'-te-rai-sed tomo-gra'-fi (CT)]

tomografía informática [f] CT computerized tomography [CT com-piu'-te-rai-sed tomo-gra'-fi]

tortuga automatizada [f] turtle [tur-tel]

tostando [m] burn-in [bur'-n in]

tostar [v] burn [bur'-n]

total de control [m] control total [con-trol tou-tal]

total de números [m] hash totals [jach tou-tal'-s]

trabajo [m] job [llob]

trabajo de conocimiento [m] knowledge work [nou'-led-ye gu-or'-k]

trabajo por lotes [m] batch job [bach llob]

tractor de arrastre de papel [m] forms tractor [form'-s trac-tor']

traducir [v] translate [trans-le-it]

traductor [m] translator [trans-lei-tor]

traductor del direccional [m] address translation [ad-dres trans-lei-sion]

trampa [f] trap [trap]

tranceptor de facsímile [m] facsimile transceiver [fak-si-mi'-le trans-sei-ver]

transacción [f] transaction [tran-sak-sion]

transceptor [m] tranceiver [tran-sei-ver]

transcribir [v] transcribe [trans-cra-ib]

transductor [m] transducer [tran'-s-du-ser]

transferencia [f] transfer [trans-fer]

transferencia condicional [f] conditional transfer [con-di-sio-nal trans-fer]

transferencia de bloque [f] block transfer [blok trans-fer]

transferencia de control [f] control transfer [con-trol trans-fer]

transferencia de control [f] transfer control [trans-fer con-trol]

transferencia en paralelo [f] parallel transfer [pa-ra-lel trans-fer]

transferencia en series [f] serial transfer [si-rial trans-fer]

transferencia incondicional [f] unconditional transfer [an-con-di-sio-nal trans-fer]

transferencia periférica [f] peripheral transfer [peri-fe-ral trans-fer]

transferir [v] transfer [trans-fer]

transformar [v] transform [trans-for'-m]

transfrontera [f] transborder [trans-bor-der]

transición [f] transition [tran-si-sion]

transistor [m] transistor [tran-sis-tor]

transistor de efecto de campo [m] field effect transistor (FET) [fil'-d e-fek'-t tran-sis-tor (FET)]

transistor de efecto de campo [m] FET field effect transistor [FET fil'-d e-fek'-t tran-sis-tor]

transistor MOS de efecto de campo [m] MOSFET MOS field-effect transistor [MOSFET MOS fil'-d e-fek'-t tran-sis-tor]

transistor MOS de efecto de campo [m] MOS field-effect transistor (MOSFET) [MOS fil'-d e-fek'-t tran-sis-tor (MOSFET)]

transitorio [adj] transient [tran-si-en'-t]

transliterar [v] transliterate [trans-li-te-reit]

transmisión [f] transmission [trans-mi-sion]

transmisión de banda baja [f] baseband transmission [be-is-ban'-d trans-mi-sion]

transmisión de datos [f] data transmission [da'-ta trans-mi-sion]

transmisión de luz [f] light guide [la-it ga-id]

transmisión digital [f] digital transmission [di-lli-tal trans-mi-sion]

transmisión en banda ancha [f] broadband transmission [bro-ud-ban'-d trans-mi-sion]

transmisión en series [f] serial transmission [si-ri-al trans-mi-sion]

transmisión síncrona [f] clocking [cla-kin'-g]

transmitir [v] transmit [trans-mit]

transparencia [f] transparency [trans-pa-ren-si]

transparente [adj] transparent [trans-pa-ren'-t]

transponder [m] transponder [trans-pon-der]

transportador de cinta [m] tape transport [te'-ip trans-port]

traslado de letra [m] letter shift [le-ter chif'-t]

trastornar [v] clobber [cla-ber]

tratamiento inmediato [m] demand processing [di-man'-d pro-se-sin'-g]

travesaño del árbol [m] tree traversal [tri tra-ver-sal]

traza [f] trace [tre-is]

trazador de base plana [m] flatbed plotter [flat-bed pla-ter]

trazador de curvas [m] graph plotter [graf pla-ter]

trazador incremental [m] incremental plotter [in-cre-men-tal pla-ter]

trazador X-Y [m] X-Y plotter [X-Y pla-ter]

trazadora [f] plotter [pla-ter]

trazadora digital [f] digital plotter [di-lli-tal pla-ter]

trazo [m] stroke [es-trok]

trazo de dispersión [m] scatter plot [es-ka-ter pla'-t]

trazo de verificación [m] check plot [chek pla'-t]

tren de impulsos [m] pulse train [pul'-s tre-in]

tres excedente [adj] excess-three [ek-ses tri]

tricolor [adj] trichromatic [tri-cro-ma-tik]

tridimensional [mf] 3-D three-dimensional [3-D tri-di-men-sio-nal]

tridimensional [mf] three-dimensional (3-D) [tri-di-men-sio-nal (3-D)]

truncar [v] truncate [tran-kei'-t]

tubo [m] tube [tub]

tubo de almacenamiento de memoria [m] storage tube [es-tor-aich tub]

tubo de rayos catódicos [m] cathode-ray tube (CRT) [ka-tod rey tub (CRT)]

tubo de rayos catódicos [m] CRT cathode-ray tube [CRT ka-tod rey tub]

tubo de representación visual [m] display tube [dis-plei tub]

turno en espera del trabajo [m] job queue [llob ki'-u]

typo de caligrafía [m] font [fon'-t]

typo de datos primitivos [m] primitive data type [pri-mi-tiv da'-ta ta'-ip]

U

ultraficha [f] ultrafiche [ultra-fich]

un billón de puntos por segundo [m] G flops [G flop'-s]

un conductor común [m] unibus [llu-ni-bas]

un trago de bit [m] gulp [gal'-p]

una interrupción [f] glitch [gli'-ch]

unidad [f] unit [llu-nit]

unidad aritmética [f] AU arithmetic unit [AU arit-me-tik llu-nit]

unidad aritmética [f] arithmetic unit (AU) [arit-me-tik llu-nit (AU)]

unidad aritmética y lógica [f] ALU arithmetic and logic unit [ALU arit-me-tik an'-d lo-llic llu-nit]

unidad aritmética y lógica [f] arithmetic and logic unit (ALU) [arit-me-tik an'-d lo-llic llu-nit (ALU)]

unidad central de proceso [f] CPU central processing unit [CPU sen-tral pro-se-sin'-g llu-nit]

unidad central de proceso [f] central processing unit (CPU) [sen-tral pro-se-sin'-g llu-nit (CPU)]

unidad de cinta [f] tape unit [te'-ip llu-nit]

unidad de control [f] control unit [con-trol llu-nit]

unidad de datos [f] datum [dei-tum]

unidad de disco flexible [f] floppy-disk drive [fla-pi dis'-k dra-ib]

unidad de discos [f] disk drive [dis'-k dra-ib]

unidad de discos movibles [f] EDS exchangable disk storage [EDS ex-che-in-lla-bel dis'-k es-tor-aich]

unidad de discos movibles [f] exchangable disk storage (EDS) [ex-che-in-lla-bel dis'-k es-tor-aich (EDS)]

unidad de doble acceso [f] dual-access drive [du-al ak-ses dra-ib]

unidad de expansión [f] expansion unit [ex-pan-sion llu-nit]

unidad de identidad [f] identity unit [ai-den-ti-ti llu-nit]

unidad de igualdad [f] equality unit [i-cua-li-ti llu-nit]

unidad de información [f] data unit [da'-ta llu-nit]

unidad de palabra [f] data word [da'-ta gu-or'-d]

unidad de respuesta de audio [f] audio response unit [au-dio ris-pon'-s llu-nit]

unidad de tiempo [f] time slice [ta-im es-la-is]

unidad de visualización [f] visual display unit (VDU) [vi-su-al dis-plei llu-nit (VDU)]

unidad de visualización [f] VDU visual display unit [VDU vi-su-al dis-plei llu-nit]

unidad del control de comunicación [f] communications control unit [co-mu-ni-kei-sion'-s con-trol llu-nit]

unidad lógica [f] LU logic unit [LU lo-llik llu-nit]

unidad lógica [f] LU logical unit [LU lo-lli-cal llu-nit]

unidad lógica [f] logical unit (LU) [lo-lli-cal llu-nit (LU)]

unidad lógica [f] logic unit (LU) [lo-llik llu-nit (LU)]

unidad periférica [f] peripheral unit [pe-ri-fe-ral llu-nit]

unipolar [adj] unipolar [llu-ni-po-lar]

unir [v] join [llo-in]

unirlo [v] attach [a-tach]

uno por uno [adj] one-for-one [uan-for-uan]

usuario [m] user [llu-ser]

usuario candido [m] naive user [ne-ib llu-ser]

V

vaceo instantáneo [m] snapshot dump [es-nap-chot dam'-p]

vaciado de rescate [m] rescue dump [res-kiu dam'-p]

vaciado póstumo [m] post mortem dump [post mor-tem dam'-p]

vaciar [v] dump [dam'-p]

vacilar [v] flicker [fli-ker]

valor [m] value [va-liu]

valor residual [m] residual value [re-si-diu-al va-liu]

valores de trimatiz [m] tristimulus values [tri-es-ti-miu-lus va-lius]

variable [f] variable [va-ria-bel]

variable ficticia [f] dummy variable [da-mi va-ria-bel]

variable global [f] global variable [glo-bal va-ria-bel]

variable manipulada [f] manipulated variable [ma-ni-piu-lei-ted va-ria-bel]

varilla [f] wand [gu-an'-d]

velocidad de impulsos del reloj [f] clock rate [clok rre-it]

velocidad de lectura [f] read rate [ri-id rre-it]

velocidad de los datos [f] data rate [da'-ta rre-it]

velocidad de perforación [f] punching rate [pan-chin'-g rre-it]

velocidad de regeneración [f] refresh rate [ri-fre'-ch rre-it]

velocidad de transferencia [f] line speed [la-in es-pid]

velocidad de transmisión [f] transmission speed [trans-mi-sion es-pid]

velocidad de transmisión de señal [f] signaling rate [sig-na-lin'-g rre-it]

velocidad en baudios [f] baud rate [ba-ud rre-it]

ventana [f] window [gu-in-dob]

ventana de texto [f] text window [tex'-t gu-in-dob]

ventana dividida [f] split window [es-pli'-t gu-in-dob]

ventana en el disco flexible [f] head slot [jed es-lat]

ventana en separación [f] splitting a window [es-pli-tin'-g ei gu-in-dob]

ventana inactiva [f] inactive window [i-nac-tiv gu-in-dob]

ventaneando [adj] windowing [gu-in-do-bu-in'-g]

ventanilla que proteje escritura [f] write-protect notch [bra'-it pro-tek'-t nach]

ventanita [f] puck [pak]

verificación [f] verification [veri-fi-kei-sion]

verificación [f] check [chek]

verificación automática [f] automatic check [auto-ma-tik chek]

verificación cruzada [f] cross-check [cros chek]

verificación de integridad [f] completeness check [com-plet-nes chek]

verificación de la codificación [f] coding check [cou-din'-g chek]

verificación de límites [f] limit check [li-mit chek]

verificación de modulo-N [f] modulo-N check [mo-llu-lo-N chek]

verificación de secuencia [f] sequence check [si-cu-en'-s chek]

verificación de tarjetas [f] card verifying [car'-d ve-ri-fa-llin'-g]

verificación de tolerancia [f] reasonableness check [rri-so-nei-bla-nes chek]

verificación de transferencia [f] transfer check [trans-fer chek]

verificación de uniformidad [f] consistency check [con-sis-ten-si chek]

verificación de validez [f] validity check [va-li-di-ti chek]

verificación incorporada [f] built-in check [bil'-t in chek]

verificación por eco [f] echo check [eco chek]

verificación por redundancia [f] redundancy check [rri-dan-dan-si chek]

verificación por residuo [f] residue check [re-si-du chek]

verificador [m] checker [chek-er]

verificador de perforación [m] punch verifier [pan'-ch ve-ri-fa-ller]

verificadora de cinta [f] tape verifier [te'-ip ve-ri-fa-ller]

verificar [v] check [chek]

verificar [v] verify [ve-ri-fai]

verificar por comparación [v] cross-check [cros-chek]

video [m] video [vi-deo]

video composición [m] composite video [com-po-sit vi-deo]

video inverso [m] inverse video [in-ver'-s vi-deo]

video invertido [m] reverse video [re-ver'-s vi-deo]

videodisco [m] videodisk [vi-deo-dis'-k]

vidicon [m] vidicon [vidi-con]

virtual [adj] virtual [vir-chu-al]

vista del campo [f] field of view [fil'-d of viu]

vista estallada [f] exploded view [ex-plo-ded viu]

vistaportador [m] viewport [viu-por'-t]

visual [mf] display [dis-plei]

visual menú [m] menu-display [me-niu-dis-plei]

visual regenerado [m] refreshed display [re-fre-cher dis-plei]

visualización de encima [f] display foreground [dis-plei foar-gro-un'-d]

visualización de la imagen [f] display image [dis-plei ima-ich]

vocabulario [m] vocabulary [vo-ca-bu-la-ri]

volcado del almacenamiento de memoria [m] storage dump [es-tor-aich dam'-p]

volcar [v] dump [dam'-p]

volteador de páginas [m] page turning [pe-ich tur-nin'-g]

volumen [m] volume [vo-li-um]

vuelco de la memoria [m] dump [dam'-p]

vuelco de la memoria [m] memory dump [me-mo-ri dam'-p]

vuelco de pantalla [m] screen dump [es-crin dam'-p]

vuelco estático de la memoria [m] static dump [es-ta-tik dam'-p]

W

wetzel [m] wetzel [gu-et-sel]

Z

zona [f] zone [zon]

zona caliente [f] hot zone [jot zon]

zona de trabajo [f] work area [gu-ork e-ria]

zona negativa [f] minus zone [mai-nus zon]

zona positiva [f] plus zone [plas zon]

ENGLISH-SPANISH

A

abbreviated addressing [np] direccionamiento abreviado [dee-rek-syo-na-myen'-to a-bre-bya'-do]

abend [n] terminación anormal [ter-meen-a-syon' a-nor-mal']

abnormal termination [np] terminación anormal [ter-meen-a-syon' a-nor-mal']

abort [v] abortar [a-bor-tar']

abort [n] suspención [soos-pen-syon']

absolute address [np] direccional absoluto [dee-rek-syo-nal' ab-so-loo'-to]

absolute code [np] código absoluto [ko'-dee-go ab-so-loo'-to]

absolute movement [np] movimiento absoluto [mo-bee-myen'-to ab-so-loo'-to]

ACAM augmented content-addressed memory [np] memoria asociativa ampliada [me-mo-rya a-so-sya-tee'-ba am-plya'-da]

acceleration time [np] tiempo de aceleración [tyem'-po day a-se-le-ra-syon']

acceptance test [np] prueba de aceptación [prwe'-ba day a-sep-ta-syon']

access [v] entrar [en-trar']

access [n] entrada [en-tra'-da]

access arm [np] brazo de acceso [bra'-so day ak-se'-so]

access code [np] código de entrada [ko'-dee-go day en-tra'-da]

access level [np] nivel de entrada [nee-bel' day en-tra'-da]

access mechanism [np] mecanismo de acceso [me-ka-nees'-mo day ak-se'-so]

access time [np] tiempo de entrada [tyem'-po day en-tra'-da]

accessory [n] accesorio [ak-se-so'-ryo]

accountable time [np] tiempo contable [tyem'-po kon-ta'-blay]

accumulator [n] acumulador [a-koom-u-la-dor']

accuracy [n] exactitud [ek-sak-tee-tood']

acknowledgement [n] reconocimiento [re-kon-o-see-myent'-to]

acoustic coupler [np] acoplador acústico [a-ko-pla-dor' a-koo'-stee-ko]

acoustical sound enclosure [np] cerco de sonido acústico [ser'-ko day so-nee'-do a-koo'-stee-ko]

action statement [np] declaración de acción [de-kla-ra-syon' day ak-syon']

action-oriented management report [np] reporte de una acción-orientada [re-por'-tay day oo'-na ak-syon' o-ryen-ta'-da]

active cell [np] célula activa [se'-loo-la ak-tee'-ba]

active file [np] fichero activo [fee-che'-ro ak-tee'-bo]

active program [np] programa activo [pro-gra'-ma ak-tee'-bo]

activity [n] actividad [ak-tee-bee-dad']

activity ratio [np] relación de actividad [re-la-syon' day ak-tee-bee-dad']

actual address [np] direccional verdadero [dee-rek-syon-al' ber-da-de'-ro]

actuator [n] impulsor [eem-pool-sor']

ADA automatic data acquisition [np] adquisición automática de datos [ad-kee-see-syon' ow-to-ma'-tee-ka day da'-tos]

adapter [n] adaptador [a-dap-ta-dor']

adapter boards [np] adaptador de circuitos estampados [a-dap-ta-dor' day seer-kwee'-tos es-tam-pa'-dos]

adaptive-control system [np] sistema de control adaptable [sees-te'-ma day kon-trol' a-dap-ta'-blay]

adder [n] sumador [soo-ma-dor']

adder-subtracter [np] sumador-sustractor [so-ma-dor' soos-trak-tor']

addition record [np] registro adquirido [rre-hees'-tro ad-kee-ree'-do]

address [v] direccionar [dee-rek-syo-nar']

address [n] direccional [dee-rek-syo-nal']

address bus [np] conductor común del direccional [kon-dook-tor' ko-moon' del dee-rek-syo-nal']

address decoder [np] decodificador del direccional [de-ko-dee-fee-ka-dor' del dee-rek-syo-nal']

address modification [np] modificador del direccional [mo-dee-fee-ka-dor' del dee-rek-syo-nal']

address part [np] parte del direccional [par'-tay del dee-rek-syo-nal']

address register [np] registro del direccional [rre-hees'-tro del dee-rek-syo-nal']

address space [np] espacio del direccional [es-pa'-syo del dee-rek-syo-nal']

address translation [np] traductor del direccional [tra-dook-tor' del dee-rek-syo-nal']

addressing [n] direccionamiento [dee-rek-syo-na-myen'-to]

add-in [n] añadir un circuito [a-nya-deer' oon seer-kwee'-to]

add-on [n] añadir memoria [a-nya-deer' me-mo'-rya]

add-subtract time [np] tiempo de suma-resta [tyem'-po day soo'-ma res'-ta]

advance-feed tape [np] cinta de alimentación por arrastre [seen'-ta day a-lee-men-ta-syon' por a-rras'-tray]

AED automated engineering design [np] diseño técnico automatizado [dee-say'-nyo tek'nee-ko ow-to-ma-tee-sa'-do]

affective address [np] direccional afectivo [dee-rek-syo-nal' a-fek-tee'-bo]

agenda [n] agenda [a-hen'-da]

AI artificial intelligence [np] inteligencia artificial [een-tel-ee-hen'-sya ar-tee-fee-syal']

algorithm [n] algoritmo [al-go-reet'-mo]

aliasing [n] escalera visual [es-ka-le'-ra bee-sual']

aligning edge [np] margen de alineación [mar'-hen day a-lee-ne-a-syon']

alignment [n] alineación [a-lee-ne-a-syon']

allocate [v] asignar [a-seeg-nar']

allocation [n] asignación [a-seeg-na-syon']

alphabet [n] alfabeto [al-fa-be'-to]

alphabetic string [np] serie alfabética [se'-rye al-fa-be'-tee-ka]

alphameric [adj] alfanumérico [al-fa-noo-me'-ree-ko]

alphanumeric [adj] alfanumérico [al-fa-noo-me'-ree-ko]

alphanumeric display terminal [np] terminal de presentación alfanumérica [ter-mee-nal' day pre-sen-ta-syon' al-fa-noo-me'-ree-ka]

alphanumeric sort [np] clasificador alfanumérico [kla-see-fee-ka-dor' al-fa-noo-me'ree-ko]

alternate routing [np] recorrido alternativo [re-kor-ree'-do al-ter-na-tee'-bo]

alternation [n] alternación [al-ter-na-syon']

ALU arithmetic and logic unit [np] unidad aritmética y lógica [oo-nee-dad' a-reet-me'-tee-ka ee lo'-hee-ka]

ambient conditions [np] condición del medio ambiente [kon-dee-syon' del me'-dyo am-byen'-tay]

ambient temperature [np] temperatura del medio ambiente [tem-pe-ra-too'-ra del me'-dyo am-byen'-tay]

ambiguity error [np] error de ambigüedad [air-ror' day am-bee-gway-dad']

analog [adj] analógico [a-na-lo'-hee-ko]

analog computer [np] computador analógico [kom-poo-ta-dor' a-na-lo'-hee-ko]

analog data [np] datos analógicos [da'-tos a-na-lo'-hee-kos]

analogical reasoning [np] razonamiento analógico [ra-so-na-myen'-to a-na-lo'-hee-ko]

analog-digital converter [np] convertidor analógico-digital [kon-ber-tee-dor' a-na-lo'-hee-ko dee-hee-tal']

analyser [n] analizador [a-na-lee-sa-dor']

analysis graphics [np] análisis de dibujos [a-na'-lee-sees day dee-boo'-hos]

analyst [n] analista [a-na-lees'-ta]

analyzer [n] analizador [a-na-lee-sa-dor']

ancillary equipment [np] equipo subordinado [e-kee'-po soo-bor-dee-na'-do]

android [n] androide [an-droy'-day]

AND-gate [n] puerta Y [pwer'-ta ee]

AND-operation [n] operación Y [o-pe-ra-syon' ee]

animation [n] animación [a-nee-ma-syon']

annotation [n] anotación [a-no-ta-syon']

annotation symbol [np] símbolo anotado [seem'-bo-lo a-no-ta'-do]

answer code [np] código de respuesta [ko'-dee-go day res-pwes'-ta]

answer/originate [n] despacho/captor [des-pa'-cho/kap-tor']

anticoincidence gate [np] puerta de anticoincidencia [pwer'-ta day an-tee-ko-een-see-den'-sya]

antistatic mat [np] estera contra la estática [es-te'ra kon'-tra la es-ta'-tee-ka]

anti-aliasing [adj] contra la escalera visual [kon'-tra la es-ka-le'-ra bee-swal']

APL application programs library [np] biblioteca de programas de aplicación [bee-blyo-te'-ka day pro-gra'-mas day ap-lee-ka-syon']

append [v] adjuntar [ad-hoon-tar']

application [n] aplicación [ap-lee-ka-syon']

application program [np] programa de aplicación [pro-gra'-ma day ap-lee-ka-syon']

application programmer [np] programador de aplicación [pro-gra-ma-dor' day ap-lee-ka-syon']

application programming [np] programación de aplicación [pro-gra-ma-syon' day ap-lee-ka-syon']

application programs library (APL) [np] biblioteca de programas de aplicación [bee-blyo-te'-ka day pro-gra'-mas day ap-lee-ka-syon']

application software [np] soporte lógico de aplicación [so-por'-tay lo'-hee-ko day ap-lee-ka-syon']

application-oriented language [np] orientado lenguaje de aplicación [o-ryen-ta'-do leng-gwa'-hay day ap-lee-ka-syon']

APT automatically programmed tools [np] herramientas programadas automaticamente [e-rra-myen'-tas pro-gra-ma'-das ow-to-ma-tee-ka-men'tay]

arcade game [np] juego de galería [hway'-go day ga-le-ree'-a]

architectural protection [np] protección estructural [pro-tek-syon' es-trook-too-ral']

architecture [n] arquitectura [ar-kee-tek-too'-ra]

archival [n] archivado [ar-chee-ba'-do]

archived file [np] fichero archivado [fee-che'-ro ar-chee-ba'-do]

archiving [adj] archivando [ar-chee-ban'-do]

area chart [np] gráfica acentuada [gra'-fee-ka a-sen-twa'-da]

area search [np] región de búsqueda [re-hyon' day boos'-kay-da]

argument n] argumento [ar-goo-men'-to]

arithmetic and logic unit (ALU) [np] unidad aritmética y lógica [oo-nee-dad' a-reet-me'-tee-ka ee lo'-hee-ka]

arithmetic instruction [np] instrucción aritmética [een-strook-syon' a-reet-me'-tee-ka]

arithmetic operation [np] operación aritmética [o-pe-ra-syon' a-reet-me'-tee-ka]

arithmetic shift [np] desplazamiento arimético [des-pla-sa-myen'-to a-reet-me'-tee-ko]

arithmetic unit (AU) [np] unidad aritmética [oo-nee-dad' a-reet-me'-tee-ka]

array [n] arreglo [a-rre'-glo]

array processor [np] procesador de arreglo [pro-se-sa-dor' day a-rre'-glo]

arrival rate [np] proporción de llegada [pro-por-syon' day yay-ga'-da]

artificial intelligence (AI) [np] inteligencia artificial [een-te-lee-hen'-sya ar-tee-fee-syal']

artificial language [np] lenguaje artificial [leng-gwa'-hay ar-tee-fee-syal']

ascender [n] parte elevada de las letras [par'tay e-le-ba'-da day las le'tras]

ascending order [np] en orden de subida [en or'-den day soo-bee'-da]

assemble [v] ensamblar [en-sam-blar']

assembler [n] ensamblador [en-sam-bla-dor']

assembling [n] ensamblándolo [en-sam-blan'-do-lo]

assembly [n] ensamblando [en-sam-blan'-do]

assembly language [np] lenguaje emsamblador [leng-gwa'-hay en-sam-bla-dor']

assembly listing [np] lista del ensamblador [lees'-ta del en-sam-bla-dor']

assembly program [np] programa ensamblador [pro-gra'-ma en-sam-bla-dor']

assignment operator [np] operador de asignación [o-pe-ra-dor' day a-seeg-na-syon']

assignment statement [np] declaración de asignación [dek-la-ra-syon' day a-seeg-na-syon']

associative memory [np] memoria asociativa [me-mo'-rya a-so-sya-tee'-ba]

asterisk [n] asterisco [as-te-rees'-ko]

asynchronous [adj] asíncrono [a-seen'-kro-no]

asynchronous communication [np] comunicación asíncrona [ko-moo-nee-ka-syon' a-seen'-kro-na]

asynchronous device [np] aparato asíncrono [a-pa-ra'-to a-seen-kro'-no]

at random [adv] al azar [al a-sar']

attach [v] unirlo [oo-neer'-lo]

attenuation [n] atenuación [a-te-nwa-syon']

atto [pre] quinti-millónes [keen'-tee mee-yon'-es]

attribute [n] atributo [a-tree-boo'-to]

AU arithmetic unit [np] unidad aritmética [oo-nee-dad' a-reet-me'-tee-ka]

audio device [np] aparato de audio [a-pa-ra'-to day ow'-dyo]

audio output [np] potencia de audio [po-ten'-sya day ow'-dyo]

audio response unit [np] unidad de respuesta de audio [oo-nee-dad' day res-pwes'-ta day ow'-dyo]

audio-visual [n] audiovisual [ow-dyo-bee-swal']

audit trail [np] pista de auditoría [pees'-ta day ow-dee-to'-rya]

augmented content-addressed memory (ACAM) [np] memoria asociativa ampliada [me-mo'-rya a-so-sya-tee'-ba am-plya'-da]

author language [np] lenguaje de componer [len-gwa'-hay day com-po-ner']

authoring system [np] sistema de componer [sees-te'-ma day kom-po-ner']

authorized program [np] programa de componer [pro-gra'-ma day kom-po-ner']

auto dialing modem [np] módem de enlace automático [mo'-dem day en-la'-say ow-to-ma'-tee-ko]

automated data processing [np] procesamiento de datos automatizados [pro-se-sa-myen'-to day da'-tos ow-to-ma-tee-sa'-dos]

automated engineering design (AED) [np] diseño técnico automatizado [dee-se-nyo tek'-nee-ko ow-to-ma-tee-sa'-do]

automated flowchart [np] flujograma automatizado [floo-ho-gra'-ma ow-to-ma-tee-sa'-do]

automated office [np] oficina automatizada [o-fee-see'-na ow-to-ma-tee-sa'-da]

automatic carriage [np] carro automático [kar'-ro ow-to-ma'-tee-ko]

automatic check [np] verificación automática [be-ree-fee-ka-syon' ow-to-ma'-tee-ka]

automatic coding [np] codificación automática [ko-dee-fee-ka-syon' ow-to-ma'-tee-ka]

automatic data acquisition (ADA) [np] adquisición automática de datos [ad-kee-see-syon' ow-to-ma'-tee-ka day da'-tos]

automatic data conversion [np] conversión automática de datos [kon-ber-syon' ow-to-ma'-tee-ka day da'-tos]

automatic data processing [np] proceso automático de datos [pro-se'-so ow-to-ma'-tee-ko day da'-tos]

automatic error correction [np] corrección automática de errores [ko-rek-syon' ow-to-ma'-tee-ka day air-ro'-res]

automatic interrupt [np] interrupción automática [een-ter-roop-syon' ow-to-ma'-tee-ka]

automatic loader [np] cargador automático [kar-ga-dor' ow-to-ma'-tee-ko]

automatic message switching [np] conmutación automática de mensajes [kon-moo-ta-syon' ow-to-ma'-tee-ka day men-sa'-hays]

automatic programming [np] programación automática [pro-gra-ma-syon' ow-to-ma'-tee-ka]

automatic quality control [np] control automático de calidad [kon-trol' ow-to-ma'-tee-ko day ka-lee-dad']

automatic scrolling [np] enrollamiento automatico [en-ro-ya-myen'-to ow-to-ma'-tee-ko]

automatic shutdown [np] cierre automático [sye'-rre ow-to-ma'-tee-ko]

automatic stop [np] parada automática [pa-ra'-da ow-to-ma'-tee-ka]

automatic system design [np] diseño automático de sistemas [dee-se'-nyo ow-to-ma'-tee-ko day sees-te'-mas]

automatic teller machine [np] máquina cajera automática [ma'-kee-na ka-he'-ra ow-to-ma'-tee-ka]

automatically programmed tools (APT) [np] herramientas programadas automaticamente [air-ra-myen'-tas pro-gra-ma'-das ow-to-ma-tee-ka-men'-tay]

automation [n] automación [ow-to-ma-syon']

automaton [n] autómata [ow-to'-ma-ta]

automonitor [n] automonitor [ow-to-mo-nee-tor']

autopolling [n] autoelección [ow-to-e-lek-syon']

autoscore [n] subrayar [soo-bra-yar']

auto-answer [n] auto-despacho [ow'-to des-pa'-cho]

auto-dial [n] auto-enlace [ow'-to en-la'-say]

auto-load [n] auto-cargador [ow'-to kar-ga-dor']

auto-repeat [n] auto-retransmisión [ow'-to re-trans-mee-syon']

auto-restart [n] auto-reanudarse [ow'to re-a-noo-dar'-say]

auxiliary equipment [np] equipo auxiliar [e-kee-po owk-see-lyar']

auxiliary memory [np] memoria auxiliar [me-mo'-rya owk-see-lyar']

auxiliary operation [np] operación auxiliar [o-pe-ra-syon' owk-see-lyar']

auxiliary storage [np] almacenamiento de memoria auxiliar [al-ma-se-na-myen'-to day me-mo'-rya owk-see-lyar']

available time [np] tiempo disponible [tyem'-po dees-po-nee'-blay]

B

babble [n] ruido confuso [rwee'-do kon-foo'-so]

back panel [np] panel posterior [pa-nel' pos-te-ryor']

background [n] fondo [fon'-do]

background job [np] programa subordinado [pro-gra'-ma soo-bor-dee-na'-do]

background processing [np] proceso de programas subordinados [pro-se'-so day pro-gra'-mas soo-bor-dee-na'-dos]

background program [np] programa subordinado [pro-gra'-ma soo-bor-dee-na'-do]

backing store [np] memoria auxiliar [me-mo'-rya owk-see-lyar']

backplane [n] placa madre [pla'-ka ma'-dray]

backspace [v] retroceder [re-tro-se-der']

backspace tape [np] retroceso de cinta [re-tro-se'-so day seen'-ta]

backtracking [n] explorar hacia atrás [eks-plo-rar' a'-sya a-tras']

backup copy [np] copia de reserva [ko'-pya day re-ser'-ba]

backward read [np] cinta que lee al revés [seen'-ta kay le'-e al re-bes']

bad sector [np] sector malo [sek-tor' ma'-lo]

badge reader [np] leedor de placa [le-e-dor' day pla'-ka]

ball printer [np] impresora de esfera [eem-pre-so'-ra day es-fe'-ra]

band [n] banda [ban'-da]

band printer [np] impresora de banda [eem-pre-so'-ra day ban'-da]

bandwidth [n] anchura de banda [an-choo'-ra day ban'-da]

bar code [np] código de trazos [ko'-dee-go day tra'-sos]

bar printer [np] impresora de barras [eem-pre-so'-ra day bar'-ras]

bare board [np] tablero electronico desnudo [ta-ble'-ro e-lek-tro'-nee-ko des-noo'-do]

barrel printer [np] impresora de rodillo [eem-pre-so'-ra day ro-dee'-yo]

bar-code [n] código de barras [ko'-dee-go day bar'-ras]

base [n] bajo de ley [ba'-ho day le'-ee]

base address [np] direccional explicito [dee-rek-syo-nal' eks-plee-see'-to]

base register [np] registro primario [re-hees'-tro pree-ma'-ryo]

baseband transmission [np] transmisión de banda baja [trans-mee-syon' day ban'-da ba'ha]

basic linkage [np] enlace básico [en-la'-say ba'-see-ko]

batch job [np] trabajo por lotes [tra-ba'-ho por lo'tes]

batch processing [np] proceso por lotes [pro-se'-so por lo'-tes]

baud [n] baudio [bow'-dyo]

baud rate [np] velocidad en baudios [be-lo-see-dad' en bow'-dyos]

BCD binary-coded decimal [np] decimal codificado en binario [de-see-mal' ko-dee-fee-ka'-do en bee-na'-ryo]

beam store [np] memoria a rayos [me-mo'-rya a ra'-yos]

beat frequency [np] frequencia de pulsación [fre-kwen'-sya day pool-sa-syon']

bells-and-whistles [n] campaneando [kam-pa-ne-an'-do]

benchmark [n] referencia [re-fe-ren'-sya]

benchmark problem [np] problema de referencia [pro-ble'-ma day re-fe-ren'-sya]

benchmark tests [np] prueba de referencia [prwe'-ba day re-fe-ren'-sya]

bias [v] polarizar [po-la-ree-sar']

bias [n] polarización [po-la-ree-sa-syon']

bifurcation [n] bifurcación [bee-foor-ka-syon']

binary [adj] binario [bee-na'-ryo]

binary code [np] código binario [ko'-dee-go bee-na'-ryo]

binary device [np] aparato binario [a-pa-ra'-to bee-na'-ryo]

binary notation [np] notación binaria [no-ta-syon' bee-na'-rya]

binary operation [np] operación binaria [o-pe-ra-syon' bee-na'-rya]

binary search [np] búsqueda binaria [boos'-ke-da bee-na'-rya]

binary-coded decimal (BCD) [np] decimal codificado en binario [de-see-mal' ko-dee-fee-ka'-do en bee-na'-ryo]

binary-to-decimal conversion [np] conversión de binario a decimal [kon-ber-syon' day bee-na'-ryo a de-see-mal']

binary-to-hexadecimal conversion [np] conversión de binario a hexádecimal [kon-ber-syon' day bee-na'-ryo a ecks-a'-de-see-mal]

binary-to-octal conversion [np] conversión de binario a octal [kon-ber-syon' day bee-na'-ryo a ok-tal']

binding time [np] tiempo obligatorio [tyem'-po ob-lee-ga-to'-ryo]

biochip [n] bióplaqueta [byo'-pla-ke-ta]

bionics [n] biónica [byo'-nee-ka]

bipolar [adj] bipolar [bee-po-lar']

biquinary code [np] código biquinario [ko'-dee-go bee-kee-na'-ryo]

bistable circuit [np] circuito biestable [seer-kwee'-to bye-sta'-blay]

bit [n] bit [beet]

bit density [np] densidad de bit [den-see-dad' day beet]

bit location [np] posición de bit [po-see-syon' day beet]

bit mapped screen [np] punto del plano señalado [poon'-to del pla'-no se-nya-la'-do]

bit pattern [np] configuración de bit [kon-fee-goo-ra-syon' day beet]

bit rate [np] tasa en bit [ta'-sa en beet]

bit stream [np] flujo de bit [floo'-ho day beet]

bit string [np] series de bit [se'-ryes day beet]

bit-per-second (BPS) [n] bit-por-segundo [beet por se-goon'-do]

bi-directional [adj] bidireccional [bee-dee-rek-syo-nal']

bi-directional printer [np] impresora bidireccional [eem-pre-so'-ra bee-dee-rek-syo-nal']

blank [n] blanco [blan'-ko]

blanking [n] en blanco [en blan'-ko]

blind search [np] buscando ciegamente [boos-kan'-do sye-ga-men'-tay]

blinking [adj] oscilando [os-see-lan'-do]

block [n] bloque [blo'-kay]

block diagram [np] diagrama por bloques [dya-gra'-ma por blo'-kays]

block gap [np] intervalo del bloque [een-ter-ba'-lo del blo'-kay]

block header [np] cabeza del bloque [ka-be'-sa del blo'-kay]

block length [np] tamaño del bloque [ta-ma'-nyo del blo'-kay]

block switching [np] conmutación del bloque [kon-moo-ta-syon' del blo'-kay]

block transfer [np] transferencia de bloque [trans-fe-ren'-sya day blo'-kay]

blocking factor [np] elementos del bloque [e-le-men'-tos del blo'-kay]

board [n] tablero electrónico [ta-ble'-ro e-lek-tro'-nee-ko]

boilerplate [n] texto repetido [tecks'-to re-pe-tee'-do]

Boolean algebra [np] álgebra de Boole [al'-he-bra day Bool]

boot [v] arrancar [ar-ran-kar']

bootstrap [n] autocargador [ow-to-kar-ga-dor']

bootstrapping [n] arrancar el autocargador [ar-ran-kar' el ow-to-kar-ga-dor']

bottom-up [adj] del fondo hacia arriba [del fon'-do a'-sya ar-reeb'-a]

BPS bit-per-second [n] bit-por-segundo [beet por se-goon'-do]

branch [v] bifurcar [bee-foor-kar']

branch [n] bifurcación [bee-foor-ka-syon']

branch instruction [np] instrucción de bifurcación [een-strook-syon' day bee-foor-ka-syon']

breakpoint [n] punto de rotura [poon'-to day ro-toor'-a]

breakpoint [n] punto de interrupción [poon'-to day een-ter-roop-syon']

breakpoint instruction [np] instrucción del punto de interrupción [een-strook-syon' del poon'-to day een-ter-roop-syon']

brightness [n] brillantez [bree-yan-tes']

broadband [n] banda ancha [ban'-da an'-cha]

broadband transmission [np] transmisión en banda ancha [trans-mee-syon' en ban'-da an'-cha]

browsing [n] curiosear [koo-ryo-se-ar']

brute-force technique [np] técnica con fuerza bruta [tek'-nee-ka kon fwer'-sa broo'-ta]

bubble memory [np] memoria de burbuja [me-mo'-rya day boor-boo'-ha]

bubble sort [np] clasificación en onda [kla-see-fee-ka-syon' en on'-da]

buffer [n] registro intermedio [re-hees'-tro een-ter-me'-dyo]

bug [n] defecto [de-fek'-to]

built-in check [np] verificación incorporada [be-ree-fee-ka-syon' een-kor-po-ra'-da]

built-in fonts [np] tipógrafos incorporados [tee-po'-gra-fos een-kor-po-ra'-dos]

bulk storage [np] memoria de gran capacidad [me-mo'-rya day gran ka-pa-see-dad']

bulletin board [np] tablón de anuncios [ta-blon' day a-noon'-syos]

burn [v] tostar [tos-tar']

burn-in [n] tostando [tos-tan'-do]

burster [n] separadora de páginas [se-pa-ra-do'-ra day pa'-hee-nas]

bus [n] conductor común [kon-dook-tor' ko-moon']

bus network [np] red del conductor común [red del kon-dook-tor' ko-moon']

bus system [np] sistema de conductores comúnes [sees-te'-ma day kon-dook-to'-res ko-moon'-es]

byte [n] byte [bee'-tay]

C

cable [n] cable [ka'-blay]

cabling diagram [np] diagrama de cables [dya-gra'-ma day ka'-blays]

cache memory [np] escondrijo de la memoria [es-kon-dree'-ho day la me-mo'-rya]

CAD computer-aided design [np] diseño con ayuda del computador [dee-se'nyo kon a-yoo'-da del kom-poo-ta-dor']

CADD computer-aided design and drafting [np] diseño y dibujo con ayuda del computador [dee-se'-nyo ee dee-boo'-ho kon a-yoo'-da del kom-poo-ta-dor']

cage [n] chasis [cha'-sees]

CAI computer-assisted instruction [np] instrucción con ayuda del computador [een-strook-syon' kon a-yoo'-da del kom-poo-ta-dor']

CAL computer-augmented learning [np] aprendizaje amplificado con ayuda del computador [a-pren-dee-sa'-hay am-plee-fee-ka'-do kon a-yoo'-da del kom-poo-ta-dor']

calculator [n] calculadora mecánica [kal-koo-la-do'-ra me-ka'-nee-ka]

calibration [n] calibracion [ka-lee-bra-syon']

call [v] llamar [ya-mar']

call [n] llamada [ya-ma'-da]

call instruction [np] instrucción de llamada [een-strook-syon' day ya-ma'-da]

call number [np] número de llamada [noo'-me-ro day ya-ma'-da]

calligraphic graphics [np] gráfica del caligráfico [gra'-fee-ka del ka-lee-gra'-fee-ko]

calling sequence [np] secuencia de llamada [se-kwen'-sya day ya-ma'-da]

CAM computer-aided manufacture [np] fabricación con ayuda del computador [fa-bree-ka-syon' kon a-yoo'-da del kom-poo-ta-dor']

cancel [v] cancela [kan-se'-la]

capacity [n] capacidad [ka-pa-see-dad']

caps [n] letras mayúsculas [let'-ras ma-yoo'-skoo-las]

capstan [n] cabrestante [kab-res-tan'-tay]

card [n] circuito estampado [seer-kwee'-to es-tam-pa'-do]

card cage [np] caja de circuitos estampados [ka'-ha day seer-kwee'-tos es-tam-pa'-dos]

card column [np] columna de circuitos estampados [ko-loom'-na day seer-kwee'-tos es-tam-pa'-dos]

card punch [np] perforadora de tarjetas [per-fo-ra-do'-ra day tar-he'-tas]

card reader [np] leedora de tarjetas [le-e-do'-ra day tar-he'-tas]

card verifying [np] verificación de tarjetas [be-ree-fee-ka-syon' day tar-he'-tas]

card (paper) [n] tarjeta Hollerith [tar-he'-ta Hollerith]

caret [n] signo de intercalación [seeg'no day een-ter-ka-la-syon']

carriage control tape [np] cinta de control del carro [seen'-ta day kon-trol' del kar'-ro]

carriage return [np] retorno del carro [re-tor'-no del kar'-ro]

carrier [n] portador [por-ta-dor']

carrier frequency [np] frequencia del portador [fre-kwen'-sya del por-ta-dor']

carry [v] llevar [ye-bar']

cartridge [n] cartucho [kar-too'-cho]

cartridge disk [np] disco de cartucho [dees'-ko day kar-too'-cho]

cascade programs [np] programas en cascada [pro-gra'-mas en kas-ka'-da]

cassette [n] casete [ka-se'-tay]

cassette recorder [np] grabadora de casete [gra-ba-do'-ra day ka-se'-tay]

cathode-ray tube (CRT) [np] tubo de rayos catódicos [too'-bo day ra'-yos ka-to'-dee-kos]

CBL computer-based learning [np] aprendizaje automatizado [ap-ren-dee-sa'-hay ow-to-ma-tee-sa'-do]

CCD charge-coupled device [np] dispositivo aclopado con carga [dees-po-see-tee'-bo ak-lo-pa'-do kon kar'-ga]

cell [n] célula [se'-loo-la]

center-feed tape [np] cinta de alimentación central [seen'-ta day a-lee-men-ta-syon' sen-tral']

central information file [np] fichero central de información [fee-che'-ro sen-tral' day een-for-ma-syon']

central processing unit (CPU) [np] unidad central de proceso [oo-nee-dad' sen-tral' day pro-se'-so]

central site [np] local central [lo-kal' sen-tral']

central tendency [np] inclinación central [een-klee-na-syon' sen-tral']

centralized data processing [np] procesamiento centralizado de datos [pro-se-sa-myen'-to sen-tra-lee-sa'-do day da'-tos]

centralized design [np] diseño central [dee-se'-nyo sen-tral']

centralized network configuration [np] configuración de la central de redes [kon-fee-goo-ra-syon' day la sen-tral' day re'-des]

chad [n] perforado [per-fo-ra'-do]

chadded tape [np] cinta de perforación completa [seen'-ta day per-fo-ra-syon' kom-ple'-ta]

chadless tape [np] cinta sin perforación [seen'-ta seen per-fo-ra-syon']

chain [n] cadena puntera [ka-de'-na poon-te'-ra]

chain code [np] código de la cadena puntera [ko'-dee-go day la ka-de'-na poon-te'-ra]

chain field [np] campo de la cadena puntera [kam'-po day la ka-de'-na poon-te'-ra]

chain printer [np] impresora de cadena [eem-pre-so'-ra day ka-de'-na]

chained list [n] lista encadenada [lees'-ta en-ka-de-na'-da]

chained record [np] registro encadenada [re-hees'-tro en-ka-de-na'-do]

chaining search [np] búsqueda encadenada [boos'-ke-da en-ka-de-na'-da]

change record [np] registro de cambio [re-hees'-tro day kam'-byo]

channel [n] canal [ka-nal']

channel adapter [np] adaptador de canales [a-dap-ta-dor' day ka-na'-les]

chaos [n] caos [ka'-os]

chapter [n] capítulo [ka-pee'-too-lo]

character [n] carácter [ka-rak'-ter]

character code [np] código del carácter [ko'-dee-go del ka-rak'-ter]

character density [np] densidad de carácter [den-see-dad' day ka-rak'-ter]

character generator [np] generador de carácteres [he-ne-ra-dor' day ka-rak'-te-res]

character map [np] mapa de carácteres [ma'-pa day ka-rak'-te-res]

character pitch [np] grado de inclinación del carácter [gra'-do day een-klee-na-syon' del ka-rak'-ter]

character reader [np] leedora de carácteres [le-e-do'-ra day ka-rak'-te-res]

character recognition [np] reconocimiento de carácteres [re-ko-no-see-myen'-to day ka-rak'-te-res]

character set [np] grupo de carácteres [groo'-po day ka-rak'-te-res]

character string [np] series de carácteres [se'-ryes day ka-rak'-te-res]

character template [np] plantilla de carácteres [plan-tee'-ya day ka-rak'-te-res]

character-oriented [adj] orientado a el carácter [o-ryen-ta'-do a el ka-rak'-ter]

character-per-second (CPS) [n] carácter-por-segundo [ka-rak'-ter por se-goon'-do]

charge-coupled device (CCD) [np] dispositivo aclopado con carga [dees-po-see-tee'-bo ak-lo-pa'-do kon kar'-ga]

chassis [n] chasis [cha-sees']

check [v] verificar [be-ree-fee-kar']

check [v] examinar [ek-sa-mee-nar']

check [n] verificación [be-ree-fee-ka-syon']

check bit [np] bit de verificación [beet day be-ree-fee-ka-syon']

check digit [np] dígito de verificación [dee-hee'-to day be-ree-fee-ka-syon']

check indicator [np] indicador de verificación [een-dee-ka-dor' day be-ree-fee-ka-syon']

check plot [np] trazo de verificación [tra'-so day be-ree-fee-ka-syon']

check problem [np] problema de verificación [pro-ble'-ma day be-ree-fee-ka-syon']

check sum [np] suma de verificación [soo'-ma day be-ree-fee-ka-syon']

checker [n] verificador [be-ree-fee-ka-dor']

checking program [np] programa de verificación [pro-gra'-ma day be-ree-fee-ka-syon']

checkout [v] depurar [de-poo-rar']

checkpoint [n] punto de control [poon'-to day kon-trol']

chip [n] plaqueta [pla-ke'-ta]

chop [v] recortar [re-kor-tar']

chroma [n] cromático [kro-ma'-tee-ko]

CIM computer input microfilm [np] entrada de microfilm al computador [en-tra'-da day meek-ro-feelm' al kom-poo-ta-dor']

CIM computer integrated manufacturing [np] manufaturero integrado de computador [ma-noo-fa-too-re'-ro een-te-gra'-do day kom-poo-ta-dor']

cipher [n] cifra [see'fra]

circuit [n] circuito [seer-kwee'-to]

circulating register [np] registro circulante [re-hees'-tro seer-koo-lan'-tay]

cladding [n] revestimiento [y re-bes-tee-myen'-to]

clear [v] despejar [des-pe-har']

click [n] golpecito seco [gol-pe-see'-to se'-ko]

click art [np] dibujos artísticos preparados [dee-boo'-hos ar-tees'-tee-kos pre-pa-ra'-dos]

clicking [n] chasqueando [chas-ke-an'-do]

clip art [np] dibujos artísticos para cortar [dee-boo'-hos ar-tees'-tee-kos pa'-ra kor-tar']

clipboard [n] sujetadatos [soo-he-ta-da'-tos]

clipping [adj] recortando [re-kor-tan'-do]

clobber [v] trastornar [tras-tor-nar']

clock [n] reloj [re-lo']

clock pulses [np] impulsos del reloj [eem-pool'-sos del re-lo']

clock rate [np] velocidad de impulsos del reloj [be-lo-see-dad' day eem-pool'-sos del re-lo']

clocking [n] transmisión síncrona [trans-mee-syon' seen-kro'-na]

clone [n] clon [klon]

closed file [np] fichero cerrado [fee-che'-ro ser-ra'-do]

closed loop [np] circuito cerrado [seer-kwee'-to ser-ra'-do]

closed routine [np] rutina cerrada [roo-tee'-na ser-ra'-da]

closed subroutine [np] subrutina cerrada [soob-roo-tee'-na ser-ra'-da]

cluster controller [np] controlador de agrupación [kon-tro-la-dor day a-groo-pa-syon']

clustering [n] agrupación [a-groo-pa-syon']

CMI computer-managed instruction [np] instrucción administrada en computador [een-strook-syon' ad-mee-nee-stra'-da en kom-poo-ta-dor']

CML current mode logic [np] lógica de modo amplificador [lo'hee-ka day mo'-do am-plee-fee-ka-dor']

CMOS complementary MOS [np] MOS-complementario [MOS kom-ple-men-ta'-ryo]

code [v] codificar [ko-dee-fee-kar']

code [n] código [ko'-dee-go]

coding [n] codificación [ko-dee-fee-ka-syon']

coding check [np] verificación de la codificación [be-ree-fee-ka-syon' day la ko-dee-fee-ka-syon']

coercion [n] coerción [ko-er-syon']

coherence [n] coherencia [ko-e-ren'-sya]

cohesion [n] cohesión [ko-e-syon']

coincidence gate [np] puerta de coincidencia [pwer'-ta day ko-een-see-den'-sya]

cold boot [np] nuevo arranque [nwe'-bo ar-ran'-kay]

cold fault [np] falta de arranque [fal'-ta day ar-ran'-kay]

cold start [np] iniciar el arranque [ee-nee-syar' el ar-ran'-kay]

collate [v] intercalar [een-ter-ka-lar']

collating sort [np] clasificar el intercalo [kla-see-fee-kar' el een-ter-ka'-lo]

collator [n] intercaladora [een-ter-ka-la-do'-ra]

collision detection [np] percepción de colisión [per-sep-syon' day ko-lee-syon']

color camera [np] cámara de color [ka'-ma-ra day ko-lor']

color graphics [np] dibujos de color [dee-boo'-hos day ko-lor']

color monitor [np] monitor de color [mo-nee-tor' day ko-lor']

color printer [np] impresora de color [eem-pre-so'-ra day ko-lor']

color saturation [np] saturación de color [sa-too-ra-syon' day ko-lor']

column [n] columna [ko-loom'-na]

COM computer output on microfilm [np] salida del computador en microfilm [sa-lee'-da del kom-poo-ta-dor' en meek-ro-feelm']

combinatorial explosion [np] explosión de combinaciones [ecks-plo-syon' day kom-bee-na-syo'-nes]

combinatorics [n] método de combinaciones [me'-to-do day kom-bee-na-syo'-nes]

command [n] orden [or'-den]

command key [np] tecla de mando [tek'-la day man'-do]

command language [np] lenguaje de orden [len-gwa'-hay day or'-den]

command processing [np] procesamiento de la orden [pro-se-sa-myen'-to day la or'-den]

comment [n] comentario [ko-men-ta'-ryo]

communication [n] comunicación [ko-moo-nee-ka-syon']

communication channel [np] canal de comunicación [ka-nal' day ko-moo-nee-ka-syon']

communication network [np] red de comunicación [red day ko-moo-nee-ka-syon']

communication system [np] sistema de comunicación [sees-te'-ma day ko-moo-nee-ka-syon']

communications control unit [np] unidad del control de comunicación [oo-nee-dad' del kon-trol' day ko-moo-nee-ka-syon']

communications link [np] lazo de comunicación [la'-so day ko-moo-nee-ka-syon']

communications processor [np] procesador de comunicación [pro-se-sa-dor' day ko-moo-nee-ka-syon']

communications protocol [np] protocolo de comunicación [pro-to-ko'-lo day ko-moo-nee-ka-syon']

communications satellites [np] satélite de comunicaciones [sa-te'-lee-tay day ko-moo-nee-ka-syo'-nes]

communications server [np] serviciador de comunicaciones [ser-bee-sya-dor' day ko-moo-nee-ka-syo'-nes]

comparator [n] comparador [kom-pa-ra-dor']

compare [v] comparar [kom-pa-rar']

compatibility [n] compatibilidad [kom-pa-tee-bee-lee-dad']

compile [v] compilar [kom-pee-lar']

compiler [n] compiladora [kom-pee-la-do'-ra]

compile-and-go [n] compila y marcha [kom-pee'-la ee mar'-cha]

complement [v] complementar [kom-ple-men-tar']

complement [n] complemento [kom-ple-men'-to]

complementary MOS (CMOS) [np] MOS-complementario [MOS kom-ple-men-ta'-ryo]

complementary operation [np] operación complementario [o-pe-ra-syon' kom-ple-men-ta'-rya]

completeness check [np] verificación de integridad [be-ree-fee-ka-syon' day een-te-gree-dad']

composite [n] compuesto de color [kom-pwes'-to day ko-lor']

composite video [np] video composición [bee-de'-o kom-po-see-syon']

compute [v] computar [kom-poo-tar']

computer [n] computador [kom-poo-ta-dor']

computer [n] calculador [kal-koo-la-dor']

computer [n] ordenador [or-de-na-dor']

computer design [np] diseño de computadores [dee-se'-nyo day kom-poo-ta-do'-res]

computer drawing [np] dibujo en computador [dee-boo'-ho en kom-poo-ta-dor']

computer enclosure [np] cerca de computadores [ser'-ka day kom-poo-ta-do'-res]

computer flicks [np] película hecha en computador [pe-lee'-koo-la e'-cha en kom-poo-ta-dor']

computer game [np] juego por computador [hwe'-go por kom-poo-ta-dor']

computer graphicist [np] gráfista de computadores [gra-fees'-ta day kom-poo-ta-do'-res]

computer graphics [np] gráfica de computadores [gra'-fee-ka day kom-poo-ta-do'-res]

computer input microfilm (CIM) [np] entrada de microfilm al computador [en-tra'-da day meek-ro-feelm'al kom-poo-ta-dor']

computer integrated manufacturing (CIM) [np] manufaturero integrado de computador [ma-noo-fa-too-re'-ro een-te-gra'-do day kom-poo-ta-dor']

computer interface [np] interfase del computador [een-ter-fa'-say dek kom-poo-ta-dor']

computer jargon [np] jerga de computador [her'-ga day kom-poo-ta-dor']

computer output on microfilm (COM) [np] salida del computador en microfilm [sa-lee'-da del kom-poo-ta-dor' en meek-ro-feelm']

computer processing cycle [np] ciclo de procesamiento del computador [seek'-lo day pro-se-sa-myen'-to del kom-poo-ta-dor']

computer program [np] programa del computador [pro-gra'-ma del kom-poo-ta-dor']

computer programmer [np] programador de computador [pro-gra-ma-dor' day kom-poo-ta-dor']

computer run [np] pasada del computador [pa-sa'-da del kom-poo-ta-dor']

computer science [np] ciencia del computador [syen'-sya del kom-poo-ta-dor']

computer security [np] seguridad de computador [se-goo-ree-dad' day kom-poo-ta-dor']

computer typesetting [np] composición tipográfica de computador [kom-po-see-syon' tee-po-gra'-fee-ka day kom-poo-ta-dor']

computerese [n] jerga informática [her'-ga een-for-ma'-tee-ka]

computerized mail [np] correo informático [kor-re'-o een-for-ma'-tee-ko]

computerized tomography (CT) [np] tomografía informática [to-mo-gra'-fya een-for-ma'-tee-ka]

computernik [n] aficionado de computador [a-fee-syo-na'-do day kom-poo-ta-dor']

computer-aided design and drafting (CADD) [np] diseño y dibujo con ayuda del computador [dee-se'-nyo ee dee-boo'-ho kon a-yoo'-da del kom-poo-ta-dor']

computer-aided design (CAD) [np] diseño con ayuda del computador [dee-se'-nyo kon a-yoo'-da del kom-poo-ta-dor']

computer-aided manufacture (CAM) [np] fabricación con ayuda del computador [fa-bree-ka-syon' kon a-yoo'-da del kom-poo-ta-dor']

computer-assisted instruction (CAI) [np] instrucción con ayuda del computador [een-strook-syon' kon a-yoo'-da del kom-poo-ta-dor']

computer-augmented learning (CAL) [np] aprendizaje amplificado con ayuda del computador [a-pren-dee-sa'-hay am-plee-fee-ka'-do kon a-yoo'-da del kom-poo-ta-dor']

computer-based learning [np] enseñanza automatizada [en-sen-yan'-sa ow-to-ma-tee-sa'-da]

computer-based learning (CBL) [np] aprendizaje automatizada [a-pren-dee-sa'-hay ow-to-ma-tee-sa'-do]

computer-managed instruction (CMI) [np] instrucción administrada en computador [een-strook-syon' ad-mee-nee-stra'-da en kom-poo-ta-dor']

computer-on-a-chip [n] computador en una plaqueta [kom-poo-ta-dor' en oo'-na pla-ke'-ta]

concatenate [v] concatenar [kon-ka-te-nar']

concatenated data set [np] grupos de datos concatenados [groo'-pos day da'-tos kon-ka-te-na'-dos]

concatenated key [np] clave concatenada [kla'-be kon-ka-te-na'-da]

concentrator [n] concetrador [kon-se-tra-dor']

conceptual tool [np] herramienta conceptual [air-ra-myen'-ta kon-sep-twal']

concurrent processing [np] proceso concurrente [pro-se'-so kon-koor-ren'-tay]

concurrent program execution [np] ejecución de programas concurrentes [e-he-koo-syon' day pro-gra'-mas kon-koor-ren'-tes]

conditional branch instruction [np] instrucción de bifurcación condicional [een-strook-syon' day bee-foor-ka-syon' kon-dee-syo-nal']

conditional implication [np] implicación condicional [eem-plee-ka-syon' kon-dee-syo-nal']

conditional jump instruction [np] instrucción de salto condicional [een-strook-syon' day sal'-to kon-dee-syo-nal']

conditional operation [np] operación condicional [o-pe-ra-syon' kon-dee-syo-nal']

conditional paging [np] paginación condicional [pa-hee-na-syon' kon-dee-syo-nal']

conditional transfer [np] transferencia condicional [trans-fe-ren'-sya kon-dee-syo-nal']

configuration [n] configuración [kon-fee-goo-ra-syon']

conjunction [n] conjunción [kon-hoon-syon']

connector [n] conector [ko-nek-tor']

consistency check [np] verificación de uniformidad [be-ree-fee-ka-syon' day oo-nee-for-mee-dad']

console [n] consol [kon-so'-la]

console typewriter [np] máquina de escribir de consola [ma'-kee-na day es-kree-bir' day kon-so'-la]

constant area [np] área constante [a'-re-a kon-stan'-tay]

constants [n] constantes [kon-stan'-tes]

content [n] contenido [kon-te-nee'-do]

content-addressable [adj] contenido direcionable [kon-te-nee'-do dee-rek-syo-na'-blay]

continous scrolling [np] enrollamiento continuo [en-ro-ya-myen'-to kon-tee'-nwo]

continous stationery [np] papel continuo [pa-pel' kon-tee'-nwo]

continous stationery [np] estacionario continuo [es-ta-syo-na'-ryo kon-tee'-nwo]

continuous tone image [np] imagen de matiz continuo [ee-ma'-hen day ma-tees' kon-tee'-nwo]

contour analysis [np] análisis de contorno [a-na'-lee-sees day kon-tor'-no]

contouring [n] contorneando [kon-tor-ne-an'-do]

contrast [n] contraste [kon-tras'-tay]

contrast enhancement [np] intensificación del contraste [een-ten-see-fee-ka-syon' del kon-tras'-tay]

control [v] controlar [kon-tro-lar']

control [n] control [kon-trol']

control break [np] ruptura bajo control [roop-too'-ra ba'-ho kon-trol']

control data [np] datos de control [da'-tos day kon-trol']

control field [np] campo de control [kam'-po day kon-trol']

control key [np] tecla de control [tek'-la day kon-trol']

control language [np] lenguaje de control [len-gwa'-hay day kon-trol']

control panel [np] tablero de control [tab-le'-ro day kon-trol']

control panel [np] panel de control [pa-nel' day kon-trol']

control register [np] registro de control [re-hees'-tro day kon-trol']

control sequence [np] secuencia de control [se-kwen'-sya day kon-trol']

control statement [np] frase de control [fra'-say day kon-trol']

control structures [np] estructuras de control [es-trook-too'-ras day kon-trol']

control theory [np] teoría de control [te-o-ree'-a day kon-trol']

control total [np] total de control [to-tal' day kon-trol']

control transfer [np] transferencia de control [trans-fe-ren'-sya day kon-trol']

control unit [np] unidad de control [oo-nee-dad' day kon-trol']

control word [np] palabra de control [pa-la'-bra day kon-trol']

conversational interaction [np] interacción conversacional [een-te-rak-syon' kon-ver-sa-syo-nal']

conversational language [np] lenguaje conversacional [len-gwa'-hay kon-ver-sa-syo-nal']

conversational mode [np] modo de diágolo [mo'-do day dee-a'-go-lo]

conversion [n] conversión [kon-ber-syon']

convert [v] convertir [kon-ber-teer']

converter [n] convertidor [kon-ber-tee-dor']

cookbook [adj] como cocinando [ko'-mo ko-see-nan'-do]

copy [v] copiar [ko-pyar']

core [n] núcleo [nook'-le-o]

core memory [np] memoria de núcleos [me-mo'-rya day nook'-le-os]

coroutine [n] corutina [ko-roo-tee'-na]

corrective maintenance [np] mantenimiento correctivo [man-te-nee-myen'-to kor-rek-tee'-bo]

counter [n] contador [kon-ta-dor']

CPS character-per-second [np] carácter-por-segundo [ka-rak'-ter por se-goon'-do]

CPU central processing unit [np] unidad central de proceso [oo-nee-dad' sen-tral' day pro-se'-so]

crash [v] quebrar [ke-brar']

crash [v] romper [rom-per']

crash [n] choque [cho'-kay]

creeping [adj] arrastrando [ar-ras-tran'-do]

critical path [np] pazo crítico [pa'-so kree-tee'-ko]

crosshatching [n] sombreado [som-bre-a'-do]

cross-check [v] verificar por comparación [be-ree-fee-kar' por kom-pa-ra-syon']

cross-check [n] verificación cruzada [ve-ree-fee-ka-syon' kroo-sa'-da]

cross-compiler [n] compilador cruzado [kom-pee-la-dor' kroo-sa'-do]

cross-talk [n] conversación cruzada [kon-ber-sa-syon' kroo-sa'-da]

crowbar [n] palanca eléctrica [pa-lan'-ka e-lek'-tree-ka]

CRT cathode-ray tube [np] tubo de rayos catódicos [too'-bo day ra'-yos ka-to'-dee-kos]

crunch [n] crujido [kroo-hee'-do]

cryogenic memory [np] memoria criogénica [me-mo'-rya kryo-he'-nee-ka]

CT computerized tomography [np] tomografía informática [to-mo-gra-fee'-a een-for-ma'-tee-ka]

current mode logic (CML) [np] lógica de modo amplificador [lo'-hee-ka day mo'-do am-plee-fee-ka-dor']

current-loop interface [np] acoplamiento mutuo de bucle-corriente [a-ko-pla-myen'-to moo'-two day book'-lay kor-ryen'-tay]

cursive scanning [np] escudriñar en cursivo [es-kood-ree-nyar'en koor-see'-bo]

cursor [n] cursor [koor-sor']

cursor control [np] control del cursor [kon-trol' del koor-sor']

cursor control keys [np] teclas de control del cursor [tek'-las day kon-trol' del koor-sor']

customer-acceptance test [np] prueba de aceptación por el cliente [prwe'-ba day a-sep-ta-syon' por el clyen'-tay]

cut-and-paste [v] cortar y pegar [kor-tar' ee pe-gar']

cybernetics [n] cibernética [see-ber-ne'-tee-ka]

cycle [n] ciclo [seek'-lo]

cycle count [np] cuenta de ciclos [kwen'-ta day seek'-los]

cycle stealing [np] parada del ciclo [pa-ra'-da del seek'-lo]

cycle time [np] tiempo del ciclo [tyem'-po del seek'-lo]

cyclic code [np] código cíclico [ko'-dee-go seek'-lee-ko]

cylinder [n] cilindro [see-leen'-dro]

D

daisy-wheel printer [np] impresora de rueda de mariposa [eem-pre-so'-ra day rwe'-da day ma-ree-po'-sa]

damping [adj] amortiguamiento [a-mor-tee-gwa-myen'-to]

DASD direct access storage device [np] dispositivo de almacenamiento de acceso directo [dees-po-see-tee'-bo day al-ma-se-na-myen'-to day ak-se'-so dee-rek'-to]

data [n] datos [da'-tos]

data aggregate [np] agregación de datos [a-gre-ga-syon' day da'-tos]

data bank [np] banco de datos [ban'-ko day da'-tos]

data base [np] base de datos [ba'-say day da'-tos]

data base management system (DBMS) [np] sistema de gestión del banco de datos [sees-te'-ma day hes-tyon' del ban'-ko day da'-tos]

data capturing [np] captura de datos [kap-too'-ra day da'-tos]

data cartridge [np] cartucho de datos [kar-too'-cho day da'-tos]

data catalog [np] catálogo de datos [ka-ta'-lo-go day da'-tos]

data chaining [np] encadenamiento de datos [en-ka-de-na-myen'-to day da'-tos]

data cleaning [np] limpieza de datos [leem-pye'-sa day da'-tos]

data collection [np] recopilación de datos [re-ko-pee-la-syon' day da'-tos]

data communications equipment [np] equipo de comunicación de datos [e-kee'-po day ko-moo-nee-ka-syon' day da'-tos]

data communications system [np] sistema de comunicación de datos [sees-te'-ma day ko-moo-nee-ka-syon' day da'-tos]

data compression [np] compresión de datos [kom-pre-syon' day da'-tos]

data concentration [np] concentración de datos [kon-sen-tra-syon' day da'-tos]

data control section [np] sección de control de datos [sek-syon' day kon-trol' day da'-tos]

data definition language (DDL) [np] lenguaje de definición de datos [len-gwa'-hay day de-fee-nee-syon' day da'-tos]

data description language (DDL) [np] lenguaje de descripción de datos [len-gwa'-hay day des-kreep-syon' day da'-tos]

data diddling [np] embaucar los datos [em-bow-kar' los da'-tos]

data encryption [np] encriptar los datos [en-kreep-tar' los da'-tos]

data entry [np] entrada de datos [en-tra'-da day da'-tos]

data entry operator [np] operador de entrada de datos [o-pe-ra-dor' day en-tra'-da day da'-tos]

data export [np] exportación de datos [ecks-por-ta-syon' day da'-tos]

data import [np] importación de datos [eem-por-ta-syon' day da'-tos]

data leakage [np] divulgación de datos [dee-bool-ga-syon' day da'-tos]

data link [np] enlace para transmisión de datos [en-la'-say pa'-ra trans-mee-syon' day da'-tos]

data logging [np] registro de datos [re-hees'-tro day da'-tos]

data manipulating language (DML) [np] lenguaje manipulativo de datos [len-gwa'-hay ma-nee-poo-la-tee'-bo day da'-tos]

data manipulation [np] manipulación de datos [ma-nee-poo-la-syon' day da'-tos]

data name [np] nombre de datos [nom'-bray day da'-tos]

data network [np] red para la transmisión de datos [red pa'-ra la trans-mee-syon' day da'-tos]

np] paquete de datos [pa-ke'-tay day da'-tos]

data preparation [np] preparación de los datos [pre-pa-ra-syon' day los da'-tos]

data processing (DP) [np] proceso de datos (PD) [pro-se'-so day da'-tos]

data protection [np] protección de los datos [pro-tek-syon' day los da'-tos]

data rate [np] velocidad de los datos [be-lo-see-dad' day los da'-tos]

data reduction [np] reducción de datos [re-dook-syon' day da'-tos]

data scope [np] observador de datos [ob-ser-ba-dor' day da'-tos]

data set [np] grupo de datos [groo'-po day da'-tos]

data sharing [np] participación en los datos [par-tee-see-pa-syon' en los da'-tos]

data stream [np] flujo de datos [floo'-ho day da'-tos]

data tablet [np] digitilizador [dee-hee-tee-lee-sa-dor']

data transmission [np] transmisión de datos [trans-mee-syon' day da'-tos]

data unit [np] unidad de información [oo-nee-dad' day een-for-ma-syon']

data word [np] unidad de palabra [oo-nee-dad' day pa-la'-bra]

data word size [np] tamaño de la unidad de palabra [ta-ma'-nyo day la oo-nee-dad' day pa-la'-bra]

dataflow [n] flujodatos [floo-ho-da'-tos]

datum [n] unidad de datos [oo-nee-dad' day da'-tos]

DBMS data base management system [np] sistema de gestión del banco de datos [sees-te'-ma day hes-tyon' del ban'-ko day da'-tos]

DDL data definition language [np] lenguaje de definición de datos [len-gwa'-hay day de-fee-nee-syon' day da'-tos]

DDL data description language [np] lenguaje de descripción de datos [len-gwa'-hay day des-kreep-syon' day da'-tos]

DDT dynamic debugging technique [np] técnica dinámica de depuración [tek'-nee-ka dee-na'-mee-ka day de-poo-ra-syon']

dead halt [np] parada terminal [pa-ra'-da ter-mee-nal']

dead letter box [np] archivo de mensajes sin sentido [ar-chee'-bo day men-sa'-hes seen sen-tee'-do]

dead time [np] tiempo muerto [tyem'-po mwer'-to]

deblocking [n] sacar del bloque [sa-kar' del blo'-kay]

debounce [v] prevenir el salto [pre-be-neer' el sal'-to]

debug [v] depurar [de-poo-rar']

debugging aid [np] ayuda a la depuración [a-yoo'-da a la de-poo-ra-syon']

decatenate [v] decatenar [de-ka-te-nar']

deceleration time [np] tiempo de deceleración [tyem'-po day de-se-le-ra-syon']

decimal [n] decimal [de-see-mal']

decimal notation [np] notación decimal [no-ta-syon' de-see-mal']

decimal-to-binary notation [np] notación de decimal a binario [no-ta-syon' day de-see-mal' a bee-na'-ryo]

decision box [np] símbolo de decisión [seem'-bo-lo day de-see-syon']

decision table [np] tabla de decisión [tab'-la day de-see-syon']

decision tree [np] árbol de decisión [ar'-bol day de-see-syon']

deck (paper cards) [n] baraja [ba-ra'-ha]

declarative statement [np] frase de declaración [fra'-say day dek-la-ra-syon']

decode [v] decodificar [de-ko-dee-fee-kar']

decoder [n] decodificador [de-ko-dee-fee-ka-dor']

decollator [n] deglosador [de-glo-sa-dor']

decrement [n] decremento [de-kre-men'-to]

decryption [n] decriptar los datos [des-kreep-tar' los da'-tos]

dedicated [adj] dedicado [de-dee-ka'-do]

deferred address [np] direccional para más tarde [dee-rek-syo-nal' pa'-ra mas tar'-day]

deferred entry [np] entrada para más tarde [en-tra'-da pa'-ra mas tar'-day]

deferred exit [np] salida para más tarde [sa-lee'-da pa'-ra mas tar'-day]

degausser [n] degausador [de-gow-sa-dor']

deinstall [v] deinstalar [de-een-sta-lar']

dejagging [n] desdesigualar [des-de-see-gwa-lar']

delay line [np] línea de retardo [lee'-ne-a day re-tar'-do]

delayed updating [np] actualización diferida [ak-twa-lee-sa-syon' dee-fe-ree'-da]

delete [v] suprimir [soo-pree-meer']

deletion [n] eliminación [e-lee-mee-na-syon']

deletion record [np] registro de eliminación [re-hees'-tro day e-lee-mee-na-syon']

delimit [v] delimitar [de-lee-mee-tar']

delimiter [n] delimitador [de-lee-mee-ta-dor']

demand processing [np] tratamiento inmediato [tra-ta-myen'-to een-me-dya'-to]

demand reading [np] lectura inmediata [lek-too'-ra een-me-dya'-ta]

demand writing [np] escritura inmediata [es-kree-too'-ra een-me-dya'-ta]

demodulator [n] demodulador [de-mo-doo-la-dor']

demount [v] removerlo [re-mo-ber'-lo]

dense binary code [np] código binario denso [ko'-dee-go bee-na'-ryo den'-so]

deposit [n] depósito [de-po'-see-to]

depth queuing [np] matizador de dimensiones [ma-tee-sa-dor' day dee-men-syo'-nes]

deque [v] decolarse [de-ko-lar'-say]

descriptor [n] descriptor [des-kreep-tor']

design aids [n] ayuda de programación [a-yoo'-da day pro-gra-ma-syon']

designation [n] indicación [een-dee-ka-syon']

desk top computer [np] computador de mesa [kom-poo-ta-dor' day me'-sa]

destructive operation [np] operación destructiva [o-pe-ra-syon' des-trook-tee'-ba]

detail diagram [np] esquema detallado [es-ke'-ma de-ta-ya'-do]

detail file [np] archivo detallado [ar-chee'-bo de-ta-ya'-do]

detail flowchart [np] flujograma detallado [floo-ho-gra'-ma de-ta-ya'-do]

detail printing [np] impresión detallada [eem-pre-syon' de-ta-ya'-do]

diagnosis [n] diagnosis [dyag-no'-sees]

diagnostic routine [np] rutina de diagnóstico [roo-tee'-na day dyag-nos'-tee-ko]

dibit [n] bit dual [beet dwal]

dichotomizing search [np] búsqueda dicotómica [boos'-ke-da dee-ko-to'-mee-ka]

dictionary [n] diccionario [deek-syo-na'-ryo]

differential analyzer [np] analizador diferencial [a-na-lee-sa-dor' dee-fe-ren-syal']

differential analyzer [np] analizador diferencial [a-na-lee-sa-dor' dee-fe-ren-syal']

differentiator [n] diferenciador [dee-fe-ren-sya-dor']

digit [n] dígito [dee'-hee-to]

digital [adj] digital [dee-hee-tal']

digital clock [np] reloj digital [re-lo' dee-hee-tal']

digital computer [np] computador digital [kom-poo-ta-dor' dee-hee-tal']

digital computer [np] ordenador digital [or-de-na-dor' dee-hee-tal']

digital link [np] enlace digital [en-la'-say dee-hee-tal']

digital network [np] red digital [red dee-hee-tal']

digital plotter [np] trazadora digital [tra-sa-do'-ra dee-hee-tal']

digital signal processing [np] procesamiento de señales digitales [pro-se-sa-myen'-to day se-nya'-les dee-hee-ta'-les]

digital switching [np] conmutación digital [kon-moo-ta-syon' dee-hee-tal']

digital transmission [np] transmisión digital [trans-mee-syon' dee-hee-tal']

digital-to-analog converter [np] convertidor digital-analógico [kon-ber-tee-dor' dee-hee-tal' a-na-lo'-hee-ko]

digitize [v] digitalizar [dee-hee-ta-lee-sar']

digitizer [n] digitalizador [dee-hee-ta-lee-sa-dor']

diode [n] diodo [dyo'-do]

diode-transistor logic (DTL) [np] lógica diodo-transistor [lo'-hee-ka dyo'-do tran-sees-tor']

direct access [np] acceso directo [ak-se'-so dee-rek'-to]

direct access storage device (DASD) [np] dispositivo de almacenamiento de acceso directo [dees-po-see-tee'-bo day al-ma-se-na-myen'-to day ak-se'-so dee-rek'-to]

direct addressing [np] direccionamiento directo [dee-rek-syo-na-myen'-to dee-rek'-to]

directive [n] directiva [dee-rek-tee'-ba]

directory [n] directorio [dee-rek-to'-ryo]

disc [n] disco [dees'-ko]

disclaimer [n] negación [ne-ga-syon']

discrete [adj] discreto [dees-kre'-to]

discrete component [np] componente discreto [kom-po-nen'-tay dees-kre'-to]

disjunction-operation [n] operación de disyunción [o-pe-ra-syon' day dees-yoon-syon']

disk [n] disco [dees'-ko]

disk buffer [np] disco intermedio [dees'-ko een-ter-me'-dyo]

disk drive [np] unidad de discos [oo-nee-dad' day dees'-kos]

disk file [np] fichero de discos [fee-che'-ro day dees'-kos]

disk operating system (DOS) [np] sistema operativo de discos [sees-te'-ma o-pe-ra-tee'-bo day dees'-kos]

disk pack [np] pila de discos [pee'-la day dees'-kos]

disk partition [np] partición del disco [par-tee-syon' del dees'-ko]

disk sector [np] sector del disco [sek-tor' del dees'-ko]

diskette [n] disco flexible [dees'-ko flek-see'-blay]

dispatch [n] despacho [des-pa'-cho]

dispersion [n] dispersión [dees-per-syon']

displacement [n] reemplazo [re-em-pla'-so]

display [v] presentar [pre-sen-tar']

display [n] visual [bee-swal']

display console [np] consola de visualización [kon-so'-la day bee-swa-lee-sa-syon']

display foreground [np] visualización de encima [bee-swa-lee-sa-syon' day en-see'-ma]

display image [np] visualización de la imagen [bee-swa-lee-sa-syon' day la ee-ma'-hen]

display menu [np] menú de visualización [me-noo' day bee-swa-lee-sa-syon']

display station [np] estación de visualización [es-ta-syon' day bee-swa-lee-sa-syon']

display surface [np] superficie de visualización [soo-per-fee'-syay day bee-swa-lee-sa-syon']

display terminal [np] terminal de visualización [ter-mee-nal' day bee-swa-lee-sa-syon']

display tube [np] tubo de representación visual [too'-bo day re-pre-sen-ta-syon' bee-swal']

disrupted read-out [np] lectura ilegible [lek-too'-ra ee-le-hee'-blay]

distortion [n] deformación [de-for-ma-syon']

distributive processing [np] proceso distribuido [pro-se'-so dees-tree-bwee'-do]

dithering [adj] mezclando [mes-klan'-do]

divider [n] divisor [dee-bee-sor']

DML data manipulating language [np] lenguaje manipulativo de datos [len-gwa'-hay ma-nee-poo-la-tee'-bo day da'-tos]

document [n] documento [do-koo-men'-to]

document sorter [np] clasificador de documentos [kla-see-fee-ka-dor' day do-koo-men'-tos]

document sorter [np] separador de documentos [se-pa-ra-dor' day do-koo-men'-tos]

documentation [n] documentación [do-koo-men-ta-syon']

domain [n] dominio [do-mee'-nyo]

DOS disk operating system [n] sistema operativo de discos [sees-te'-ma o-pe-ra-tee'-bo day dees'-kos]

dot matrix [np] matriz de punto [ma-trees' day poon'-to]

dot printer [np] impresora por puntos [eem-pre-so'-ra por poon'-tos]

double precision [n] doble precisión [do'-blay pre-see-syon']

double-length [adj] doble longitud [do'-blay lon-hee-tood']

download [n] descenso de archivos [des-sen'-so day ar-chee'-bos]

downtime [n] tiempo de parada [tyem'-po day pa-ra'-da]

downtime [n] tiempo de desarreglo [tyem'-po day de-sar-re'-glo]

DP data processing [n] proceso de datos [pro-se'-so day da'-tos]

drag [v] arrastrado [ar-ras-tra'-do]

dragging [v] llevar arrastrado [ye-bar' ar-ras-tra'-do]

drive [v] impulsar [eem-pool-sar']

drop-in [n] caerse [ka-er'-say]

drop-out [n] desaparece [de-sa-pa-re'-say]

drum [n] tambor [tam-bor']

drum plotter [np] tambor de traza [tam-bor' day tra'-sa]

drum printer [np] impresadora de tambor [eem-pre-sa-do'-ra day tam-bor']

dry run [np] pasada en seco [pa-sa'-da en se'-ko]

DTL diode-transistor logic [np] lógica diodo-transistor [lo'-hee-ka dyo'-do tran-sees-tor']

dual operation [np] operación dual [o-pe-ra-syon' dwal]

dual processor [np] procesador dual [pro-se-sa-dor' dwal]

dual processor [np] biprocesador [bee-pro-se-sa-dor']

dual recording [np] registro en paralelo [re-hees'-tro en pa-ra-le'-lo]

dual-access drive [np] unidad de doble acceso [oo-nee-dad' day do'-blay ak-se'-so]

dummy [adj] ficticio [feek-tee'-syo]

dummy instruction [np] instrucción ficticia [een-strook-syon' feek-tee'-sya]

dummy variable [np] variable ficticia [ba-rya'-blay feek-tee'-sya]

dump [v] vaciar [ba-syar']

dump [v] volcar [bol-kar']

dump [n] vuelco de la memoria [bwel'-ko day la me-mo'-rya]

dump check [np] examinar el vuelco [eck-sa-mee-nar' el bwel'-ko]

dump point [np] punto del vaciado [poon'-to del ba-sya'-do]

duplex [n] duplex [doo-plex']

duplex channel [np] canal de duplex [ka-nal' day doo-plex']

duplex system [np] sistema duplex [sees-te'-ma doo-plex']

duplicate [v] duplicar [doo-plee-kar']

duplication [n] duplicación [doo-plee-ka-syon']

dyadic operation [np] operacion diádica [o-pe-ra-syon' dya'-dee-ka]

dynamic allocation [np] asignación dinámica [a-seeg-na-syon' dee-na'-mee-ka]

dynamic debugging technique (DDT) [np] técnica dinámica de depuración [tek'-nee-ka dee-na'-mee-ka day de-poo-ra-syon']

dynamic memory [np] memoria dinámica [me-mo'-rya dee-na'-mee-ka]

E

EBR electron beam recording [np] registro por haz de electrónes [re-hees'-tro por as day e-lek-tro'-nes]

echo check [np] verificación por eco [be-ree-fee-ka-syon' por e'-ko]

ECL emitter coupled logic [np] lógica de emisor acoplado [lo'-hee-ka day e-mee-sor' a-ko-pla'-do]

econometrics [n] económetria [e-ko-no-me'-trya]

edge [n] margen [mar'-hen]

edit [v] editar [e-dee-tar']

edit line [np] línea de edición [lee'-ne- a day e-dee-syon']

edit mode [np] modo de edición [mo'-do day e-dee-syon']

editor [n] programa de edición [pro-gra'-ma day e-dee-syon']

EDP electronic data processing [np] Proceso electrónico de datos [pro-se'-so e-lek-tro'-nee-ko day da'-tos]

EDS exchangable disk storage [np] unidad de discos movibles [oo-nee-dad' day dees'-kos mo-bee'-bles]

effective address [np] direccional efectivo [dee-rek-syo-nal' e-fek-tee'-bo]

effective time [np] tiempo efectivo [tyem'-po e-fek-tee'-bo]

ego-less programming [np] programación sin dueño [pro-gra-ma-syon' seen dwe'-nyo]

eighty-column card [np] tarjeta de ochenta columnas [tar-he'-ta day o-chen'-ta ko-loom'-nas]

either-or operation [np] operación ambos ó uno [o-pe-ra-syon' am'-bos o oo'-no]

elapsed time [np] tiempo transcurrido [tyem'-po trans-koor-ree'-do]

electric [adj] eléctrico [e-lek'-tree-ko]

electrical [adj] eléctrisado [e-lek'-tree-sa-do]

electron beam recording (EBR) [np] registro por haz de electrónes [re-hees'-tro por as day e-lek-tro'-nes]

electronic [adj] electrónico [e-lek-tro'-nee-ko]

electronic bulletin board [np] tablón electrónico de anuncios [ta-blon' e-lek-tro'-nee-ko day a-noon'-syos]

electronic data processing (EDP) [np] Proceso electrónico de datos [pro-se'-so e-lek-tro'-nee-ko day da'-tos]

electronic journal [np] jornal electrónico [hor-nal' e-lek-tro'-nee-ko]

electronic mail [np] correo electrónico [kor-re'-o e-lek-tro'-nee-ko]

electronic pen [np] lapicero electrónico [la-pee-se'-ro e-lek-tro'-nee-ko]

electronic switch [np] conmutador electrónico [kon-moo-ta-dor' e-lek-tro'-nee-ko]

electrostatic printer [np] impresora electroestática [eem-pre-so'-ra e-lek-tro-es-ta'-tee-ka]

element [n] elemento [e-le-men'-to]

embedded command [np] orden incrustado [or'-den een-kroos-ta'-do]

embedded systems [np] sistema incrustado [sees-te'-ma een-kroos-ta'-do]

embedding [n] incrustación [een-kroos-ta-syon']

emitter coupled logic (ECL) [np] lógica de emisor acoplado [lo'-hee-ka day e-mee-sor' a-ko-pla'-do]

emulator [n] emulador [e-moo-la-dor']

enable pulse [np] impulso de activación [eem-pool'-so day ak-tee-ba-syon']

enabling signal [np] señal de activación [se-nyal' day ak-tee-ba-syon']

encipher [v] encriptar [en-kreep-tar']

encode [v] encodificar [en-ko-dee-fee-kar']

encoder [n] encodificador [en-ko-dee-fee-ka-dor']

end mark [np] marca final [mar'-ka fee-nal']

end-of-block (EOB) [n] fin de bloque [feen day blo'-kay]

end-of-file (EOF) [n] fin de fichero [feen day fee-che'-ro]

end-of-job (EOJ) [n] fin de trabajo [feen day tra-ba'-ho]

end-of-run (EOR) [n] fin de pasada [feen day pa-sa'-da]

end-of-tape (EOT) [n] fin de cinta [feen day seen'-ta]

engineering time [np] tiempo de reviso [tyem'-po day re-bee'-so]

ENTER key [n] tecla de ENTRADA [tek'-la day en-tra'-da]

entry [n] entrada [en-tra'-da]

entry point [np] punto de entrada [poon'-to day en-tra'-da]

enveloped file [np] archivo envuelto [ar-chee'-bo en-bwel'-to]

environment [n] ambiente [am-byen'-tay]

EOB end-of-block [n] fin de bloque [feen day blo'-kay]

EOF end-of-file [n] fin de fichero [feen day fee-che'-ro]

EOJ end-of-job [n] fin de trabajo [feen day tra-ba'-ho]

EOR end-of-run [n] fin de pasada [feen day pa-sa'-da]

EOT end-of-tape [n] fin de cinta [feen day seen'-ta]

EPROM erasable PROM [np] PROM borrable [PROM bor-rab'-blay]

EPS exception principle system [np] control por excepción [kon-trol' por eck-sep-syon']

equality unit [np] unidad de igualdad [oo-nee-dad' day ee-gwal-dad']

equipment compatibility [np] compatibilidad entre equipos [kom-pa-tee-bee-lee-dad' en'-tray e-kee'-pos]

equipment failure [np] fallo del equipo [fa'-yo del e-kee'-po]

equivalence [n] equivalencia [e-kee-ba-len'-sya]

equivalence element [np] elemento de equivalencia [e-le-men'-to day e-kee-ba-len'-sya]

equivalence operation [np] operación de equivalencia [o-pe-ra-syon' day e-kee-ba-len'-sya]

equivalent binary digits [np] dígitos binarios equivalentes [dee'-hee-tos bee-na'-ryos e-kee-ba-len'-tes]

erasable memory [np] memoria borrable [me-mo'-rya bor-ra'-blay]

erasable PROM (EPROM) [np] PROM borrable [PROM bor-ra'-blay]

erase [v] borrar [bor-rar']

erase head [np] cabeza de borrar [ka-be'-sa day bor-rar']

erased [adj] borrado [bor-ra'-do]

ergonomics [n] ergonomía [er-go-no-mee'-a]

error [n] error [air-ror']

error diagnostics [np] diagnosis de errores [dyag-no'-sees day air-ro'-res]

error message [np] mensaje de error [men-sa'-hay day air-ror']

error rate [np] coeficiente de errores [ko-e-fee-syen'-tay day air-ro'-res]

error report [np] informe de errores [een-for'-may day air-ro'-res]

error routine [np] rutina de errores [roo-tee'-na day air-ro'-res

error-correcting code [np] código de corrección de errores [ko'-dee-go day kor-rek-syon' day air-ro'-res]

error-detecting code [np] código de detección de errores [ko'-dee-go day de-tek-syon' day air-ro'-res]

ESCAPE key [n] tecla de escape [tek'-la day es-ka'-pay]

Ethernet [n] red de video/audio [red day bee'-de-o ow'-dyo]

even parity [np] paridad par [pa-ree-dad' par]

exception principle system (EPS) [np] control por excepción [kon-trol' por eck-sep-syon']

excess-fifty [adj] cincuenta-excedente [seen-kwen'-ta eck-se-den'-tay]

excess-three [adj] tres excedente [tres eck-se-den'-tay]

exchangable disk storage (EDS) [np] unidad de discos movibles [oo-nee-dad' day dees'-kos mo-bee'-bles]

exchange [v] cambiar [kam-byar']

exchange [n] intercambio [een-ter-cam'-byo]

exclusive OR operation (XOR) [np] operación O exclusivo [o-pe-ra-syon' O ecks-kloo-see'-bo]

execute [v] ejecutar [e-he-koo-tar']

execute phase [np] fase de ejecución [fa'-say day e-he-koo-syon']

execution time [np] tiempo de ejecución [tyem'-po day e-he-koo-syon']

executive program [np] programa ejecutivo [pro-gra'-ma e-he-koo-tee'-bo]

exit [v] salir [sa-leer']

exit [n] salida [sa-lee'-da]

expandability [n] expansión [ecks-pan-syon']

expansion card [np] circuito estampado de extensión [seer-kwee'-to es-tam-pa'-do day ecks-ten-syon']

expansion interface [np] interfase de extensión [een-ter-fa'-say day ecks-ten-syon']

expansion slots [np] ranura de extensión [ra-noo'-ra day ecks-ten-syon']

expansion unit [np] unidad de expansión [oo-nee-dad' day ecks-pan-syon']

expert system [np] sistema experto [sees-te'-ma ecks-per'-to]

explicit address [np] direccional explicito [dee-rek-syon-al' ecks-plee-see'-to]

exploded view [np] vista estallada [vees'-ta es-ta-ya'-da]

export [v] exportar [ecks-por-tar']

expression [n] expresión [ecks-pre-syon']

extended addressing [np] direccionamiento alargado [dee-rek-syo-na-myen'-to a-lar-ga'-do]

extensible language [np] lenguaje extensible [len-gwa'-hay ecks-ten-see'-blay]

extent [n] al alcance [al al-kan'-say]

external storage [np] memoria externa [me-mo'-rya ecks-ter'-na]

extract [v] sacar [sa-kar']

extracted [adj] sacado [sa-ka'-do]

E-mail [n] C-electrónico [n] facilidades [C e-lek-tro'-nee-ko]

F

facilities [n] facilidades [fa-see-lee-da'-des]

facsimile [n] facsímile [fak-see'-mee-lay]

facsimile transceiver [np] tranceptor de facsímile [tran-sep-tor' day fak-see'-mee-lay]

facsimile (FAX) [n] teleproductor de imagenes [te-le-pro-dook-tor' day ee-ma'-he-nes]

failure rate [np] frequencia de fallos [fre-kwen'-sya day fa'-yos]

failure recovery [np] recuperación del fallo [re-koo-pe-ra-syon' del fa'-yo]

fail-safe [adj] sin riesgo de fallo [seen ryes'-go day fa'-yo]

fail-safe system [np] sistema sin riesgo de fallo [sees-te'-ma seen ryes'-go day fa'-yo]

fail-soft system [np] sistema sin riesgo de muchos fallos [sees-te'-ma seen ryes'-go day moo'-chos fa'-yos]

fall-back [n] de reserva [day re-ser'-ba]

false retrieval [np] levante falso [le-ban'-tay fal'-so]

fan-in [n] número de señales que entran [noo'-me-ro day se-nya'-les kay en'-tran]

fan-out [n] número de señales que salen [noo'-me-ro day se-nya'-les kay sa'-len]

fat bits [np] aumento de bit [ow-men'-to day beet]

father file [n] archivo original [ar-chee'-bo o-ree-hee-nal']

father tape [np] cinta creadora [seen'-ta kre-a-do'-ra]

fault [n] fallo [fa'-yo]

fault-tolerant [n] tolerante de averías [to-le-ran'-tay day a-be-ree'-as]

FAX facsimile [n] teleproductor de imágenes [te-le-pro-dook-tor' day ee-ma'-he-nes]

feasibility study [np] estudio de las posibilidades [es-too'-dyo day las po-see-bee-lee-da'-des]

feature [n] característico [ka-rak-te-rees'-tee-ko]

feature extraction [np] extracción caracteristica [ecks-trak-syon' ka-rak-te-rees'-tee-ka]

feed [v] avanzar [a-ban-sar']

feed [v] alimentar [a-lee-men-tar']

feed [n] alimentación [a-lee-men-ta-syon']

feed holes [np] perforaciones de alimentación [per-fo-ra-syo'-nes day a-lee-men-ta-syon']

feedback [n] realimentación [re-a-lee-men-ta-syon']

feedback control [np] control de realimentación [kon-trol' day re-a-lee-men-ta-syon']

feed-in [n] avancé [a-ban-say']

feep [n] sonido de atención [so-nee'-do day a-ten-syon']

femto [pre] quadrimillónes [kwa-dree-mee-yo'-nes]

femtosecond [n] quadrimillónes segundo [kwa-dree-mee-yo'-nes se-goon'-do]

ferrite core [np] núcleo de ferria [noo'-kle-o day fer'-rya]

FET field effect transistor [np] transistor de efecto de campo [tran-sees-tor' day e-fek'-to day kam'-po]

fiber optics [np] óptica de las fibras [op'-tee-ka day las fee'-bras]

fibre optics [np] óptica de las fibras [op'-tee-ka day las fee'-bras]

field [n] campo [kam'-po]

field effect transistor (FET) [np] transistor de efecto de campo [tran-sees-tor' day e-fek'-to day kam'-po]

field length [np] longitud de campo [lon-hee-tood' day kam'-po]

field of view [np] vista del campo [bees'-ta del kam'-po]

field upgradable [np] modernizar en el campo [mo-der-nee-sar' en el kam'-po]

FIFO first in-first out [np] primero que llega-primero que sale [pree-me'-ro kay ye'-ga pree-me'-ro kay sa'-lay]

fifth-generation [adj] quinta-generación [keen'-ta he-ne-ra-syon']

figure shift [np] movimiento de figura [mo-bee-myen'-to day fee-goo'-ra]

file [n] fichero [fee-che'-ro]

file [n] archivo [ar-chee'-bo]

file backup [np] archivo de reserva [ar-chee'-bo day re-ser'-ba]

file conversion [np] conversión de ficheros [kon-ber-syon' day fee-che'-ros]

file gap [np] brecha de fichero [bre'-cha day fee-che'-ro]

file identification [np] identificación de archivos [ee-den-tee-fee-ka-syon' day ar-chee'-bos]

file label [np] etiqueta del fichero [e-tee-ke'-ta del fee-che'-ro]

file layout [np] arreglo del archivo [ar-reg'-lo del ar-chee'-bo]

file level model [np] modelo nivelado del archivo [mo-de'-lo nee-be-la'-do del ar-chee'-bo]

file maintenance [np] mantenimiento de fichero [man-te-nee-myen'-to day fee-che'-ro]

file protection [np] protección de fichero [pro-tek-syon' day fee-che'-ro]

file storage [np] fichero de almacenamiento de memoria [fee-che'-ro day al-ma-se-na-myen'-to day me-mo'-rya]

file-protect ring [np] anillo de protección del fichero [a-nee'-yo day pro-tek-syon' del fee-che'-ro]

filling [n] empaste [em-pas'-tay]

film reader [np] leedor de películas [le-e-dor' day pe-lee'-koo-las]

film recorder [np] registrador de películas [re-hees-tra-dor' day pe-lee'-koo-las]

FILO first in-last out [np] el primero entra-el último sale [el pree-me'-ro en'-tra — el ool'-tee-mo sa'-lay]

filter [n] filtro [feel'-tro]

find [v] descubrir [des-koo-breer']

find and replace [np] descubra y sustituya [des-koo'-bra ee soos-tee-too'-ya]

firmware [n] soporte lógico inalterable [so-por'-tay lo'-hee-ko ee-nal-te-ra'-blay]

first in-first out (FIFO) [np] primero que llega-primero que sale [pree-me'-ro kay ye'-ga — pree-me'-ro kay sa'-lay]

first in-last out (FILO) [np] el primero entra-el último sale [el pree-me'ro en'-tra — el ool'-tee-mo sa'-lay]

first-generation [adj] primera generación [pree-me'-ra he-ne-ra-syon']

first-order predicate logic [np] lógica predicativa del primer orden [lo'-hee-ka pre-dee-ka-tee'-ba del pree-mer' or'-den]

fixed field [np] campo fijo [kam'-po fee'-ho]

fixed-block length [np] longitud de bloque fijo [lon-hee-tood' day blo'-kay fee'-ho]

fixed-disk file [np] ficheros de discos fijos [fee-che'-ros day dees'-kos fee'-hos]

fixed-point arithmetic [np] aritmética de punto fijo [a-reet-me'-tee-ka day poon'-to fee'-ho]

flag [n] señalador [sen-ya-la-dor']

flagged [adj] apuntador [a-poon-ta-dor']

flat pack [np] plaqueta plana [pla-ke'-ta pla'-na]

flatbed plotter [np] trazador de base plana [tra-sa-dor' day ba'-say pla'-na]

flicker [v] vacilar [ba-see-lar']

floating-point arithmetic [np] aritmética de punto flotante [a-reet-me'-tee-ka day poon'-to flo-tan'-tay]

floppy disk [np] disco flexible [dees'-ko fleck-see'-blay]

floppy-disk drive [np] unidad de disco flexible [oo-nee-dad' day dees'-ko fleck-see'-blay]

flowchart [n] flujograma [floo-ho-gra'-ma]

flowchart template [np] plantilla de flujograma [plan-tee'-ya day floo-ho-gra'-ma]

flowcharting symbol [np] símbolos de flujogramas [seem'-bo-los day floo-ho-gra'-mas]

flowline [n] línea de flujo [lee'-ne-a day floo'-ho]

fluid logic [np] lógica de flúidos [lo'-hee-ka day flwee'-dos]

flush [v] tirar los contenidos [tee-rar' los kon-te-nee'-dos]

folding ratio [np] relación de plegado [re-la-syon' day ple-ga'-do]

font [n] typo de caligrafía [tee'-po day ka-lee-gra-fee'-a]

footer [n] índice de pie [een-dee'-say day pye]

force [v] forzar [for-sar']

foreground processing [np] proceso preferencial [pro-se'-so pre-fe-ren-syal']

foreground program [np] programa preferencial [pro-gra'-ma pre-fe-ren-syal']

forest [n] grupo de árboles [groo'-po day ar'-bo-les]

form feed [np] alimentación por página [a-lee-men-ta-syon' por pa'-hee-na]

form stop [np] parada de papel [pa-ra'-da day pa-pel']

format [n] formato [for-ma'to]

format [n] texto [tecks'-to]

formatter [n] formador de texto [for-ma-dor' day tecks'-to]

forms [n] papel [pa-pel']

forms tractor [n] tractor de arrastre de papel [trak-tor' day ar-ras'-tray day pa-pel']

fourth-generation [adj] cuarta-generación [kwar'-ta he-ne-ra-syon']

four-wire circuit [np] circuito de cuatro alambres [seer-kwee'-to day kwa'-tro a-lam'-bres]

frame [v] encuadrar [en-kwa-drar']

frame [n] encuadre [en-kwa'-dray]

framebuffer [n] cuadro intermedio [kwa'-dro een-ter-me'-dyo]

free field [np] campo libre [kam'-po lee'-bray]

friction-feed [n] alimentación por fricción [a-lee-men-ta-syon' por freek-syon']

friendly interface [np] interfase amiga [een-ter-fa'-say a-mee'-ga]

frob [n] palanca de juego [pa-lan'-ka day hwe'-go]

full-adder [n] adicionador completo [a-dee-syo-na-dor' kom-ple'-to]

full-duplex [n] duplex todo completo [doo'-plex to'-do kom-ple'-to]

full-page display [np] página visual completa [pa'-hee-na bee-swal' kom-ple'-ta]

full-screen [n] pantalla llena [pan-ta'-ya ye'-na]

full-screen editing [np] editor de pantalla llena [e-dee-tor' day pan-ta'-ya ye'-na]

full-text searching [np] búsqueda en el texto [boos'-ke-da en el tex'-to]

function [n] función [foon-syon']

function generator [np] generador de función [he-ne-ra-dor' day foon-syon']

function key [np] tecla de función [tek'-la day foon-syon']

functional design [np] diseño funcional [dee-sen'-yo foon-syo-nal']

funware [n] juego inalterable [hwe'-go ee-nal-te-ra'-blay]

fusible link [np] enlazo fusible [en-la'-so foo-see'-blay]

fuzzy logic [n] lógica de duda [lo'-hee-ka day doo'-da]

G

G flops [np] un billón de puntos por segundo [oon bee-yon' day poon'-tos por se-goon'-do]

gamut [n] gama de colores [ga'-ma day ko-lo'-res]

gap [n] intervalo [een-ter-ba'-lo]

garbage [n] información parásita [een-for-ma-syon' pa-ra'-see-ta]

garbage collection [np] acumulación de información parásitica [a-koo-moo-la-syon' day een-for-ma-syon' pa-ra'-see-tee-ka]

garbage in-garbage out (GIGO) [np] basura entra, basura sale [ba-soo'-ra en'-tra, ba-soo'-ra sa'-lay]

gate [n] puerta [pwer'-ta]

gateway [n] portilla [por-tee'-ya]

gather write [np] escritura agrupada [es-kree-too'-ra a-groo-pa'-da]

gating circuit [np] circuito agitante [seer-kwee'-to a-hee-tan'-tay]

general-purpose computer [np] computador universal [kom-poo-ta-dor' oo-nee-ber-sal']

generate [v] generar [he-ne-rar']

generator [n] generador [he-ne-ra-dor']

generic [adj] genérico [he-ne'-ree-ko]

geocoding [n] geocodificación [he-o-ko-dee-fee-ka-syon']

GERT graphical evaluation and review technique [np] evaluación gráfica y revisión técnica [e-ba-lwa-syon' gra'-fee-ka ee re-bee-syon' tek'-nee-ka]

gibberish [n] galimatías [ga-lee-ma-tee'-as]

GIGO garbage in-garbage out [np] basura entra, basura sale [ba-soo'-ra en'-tra, ba-soo'-ra sa'-lay]

glare [n] deslumbrante [des-loom-bran'-tay]

glitch [n] una interrupción [oo'-na een-ter-roop-syon']

global [adj] global [glo-bal']

global character [np] carácter global [ka-rak'-ter glo-bal']

global operation [np] operación global [o-pe-ra-syon' glo-bal']

global search and replace [np] búsque globalmente y reponga [boos'-kay glo-bal-men'-tay ee re-pon'-ga]

global variable [np] variable global [ba-rya'-blay glo-bal']

gnomon [n] objeto de dirección/dimensión [ob-he'-to day dee-rek-syon' dee-men-syon']

go down [v] tener una avería [te-ner' oo'-na a-be-ree'-a]

grabber [n] asidor [a-see-dor']

graceful degradation [np] degradación con garbo [de-gra-da-syon' kon gar'-bo]

grade [n] calidad [ka-lee-dad']

grandfather file [np] archivo de primera generación [ar-chee-bo day pree-me'-ra he-ne-ra-syon']

graph [n] gráfico [gra'-fee-ko]

graph plotter [np] trazador de curvas [tra-sa-dor' day koor'-bas]

graphic limits [np] límite gráfico [lee'-mee-tay gra'-fee-ko]

graphic panel [np] panel gráfico [pa-nel' gra'-fee-ko]

graphical evaluation and review technique (GERT) [np] evaluación gráfica y revisión técnica [e-ba-lwa-syon' gra'-fee-ka ee re-bee-syon' tek'-nee-ka]

graphics [n] gráfica [gra'-fee-ka]

graphics [n] dibujos [dee-boo'-hos]

graphics digitizer [np] digitilizador de gráfica [dee-hee-tee-lee-sa-dor' day gra'-fee-ka]

graphics display [np] representación gráfica [re-pre-sen-ta-syon' gra'-fee-ka]

graphics printer [np] impresora gráfica [eem-pre-so'-ra gra'-fee-ka]

graphics program [np] programa de gráfica [pro-gra'-ma day gra'-fee-ka]

graphics resolution [np] resolución de gráfica [re-so-loo-syon' day gra'-fee-ka]

graphics screen [np] pantalla gráfica [pan-ta'-ya gra'-fee-ka]

graphics tablet [np] tableta gráfica [ta-ble'-ta gra'-fee-ka]

graphics terminal [np] terminal gráfico [ter-mee-nal' gra'-fee-ko]

graphics-input hardware [np] equipo para entrar dibujos [e-kee'-po pa'-ra en-trar' dee-boo'-hos]

graphics-output hardware [np] equipo para sacar dibujos [e-kee'-po pa'-ra sa-kar' dee-boo'-hos]

graphic-data structure [np] estructurado de datos gráficos [es-trook-too-ra'-do day da'-tos gra'-fee-kos]

graphic-display mode [np] modo de presentación gráfica [mo'-do day pre-sen-ta-syon' gra'-fee-ka]

graphic-display resolution [np] resolución de presentación gráfica [re-so-loo-syon' day pre-sen-ta-syon' gra'-fee-ka]

graphic-display terminal [np] terminal de presentación gráfica [ter-mee-nal' day pre-sen-ta-syon' gra'-fee-ka]

graphic-input device [np] aparato para entrar dibujos [a-pa-ra'-to pa'-ra en-trar' dee-boo'-hos]

graphic-output device [np] aparato para sacar dibujos [a-pa-ra'-to pa'-ra sa-kar' dee-boo'-hos]

gray code [np] escala de gris [es-ka'-la day grees]

greater than [adj] más grande que [mas gran'-day kay]

grid [n] cuadriculado [kwa-dree-koo-la'-do]

grid chart [np] tabla de información [ta'-bla day een-for-ma-syon']

gridding [n] encuadrillado [en-kwa-dree-ya'-do]

gridsheet [n] hoja cuadriculada electrónica [o'-ha kwa-dree-koo-la'-da e-lek-tro'-nee-ka]

group [n] grupo [groo'-po]

group mark [np] marca de grupo [mar'-ka day groo'-po]

guard band [np] banda de guardar [ban'-da day gwar-dar']

guest computer [np] computador anfitríon [kom-poo-ta-dor' an-fee-tree'-on]

gulp [n] un trago de bit [oon tra'-go day beet]

gynoid [n] androide [an-droy'-day]

H

hacker [n] computomaníaco [kom-poo-to-ma-nee'-a-ko]

half subtractor [np] semi-sustractor [se'-mee soos-trak-tor']

halftoning [n] medio tono [me'-dyo to'-no]

half-adder [n] semi-sumador [se'-mee soo-ma-dor']

half-duplex [n] semi-duplex [se'-mee doo'-plex]

half-word [n] media palabra [me'-dya pa-la'-bra]

halt [n] parada [pa-ra'-da]

handler [n] enpuñado [en-poon-ya'-do]

handshaking [n] comunicación amiga [kom-moo-nee-ka-syon' a-mee'-ga]

hands-on [n] experiencia práctica [ex-pe-ryen'-sya prak'-tee-ka]

hang-up [v] colgar [kol-gar']

hard copy [np] copia impresa [ko'-pya eem-pre'-sa]

hard copy [np] salida impresa [sa-lee'-da eem-pre'-sa]

hard disk [np] disco duro [dees'-ko doo'-ro]

hard error [n] error duro [air-ror' doo'-ro]

hard failure [np] fallo duro [fa'-yo doo'-ro]

hard hyphen [np] guión duro [gyon doo'-ro]

hard sector [np] sector duro [sek-tor' doo'-ro]

hardware [n] equipo físico [e-kee'-po fee'-see-ko]

hardware key [np] llave del equipo físico [ya'-be del e-kee'-po fee'-see-ko]

hard-clip area [np] área fuera de límite [a'-re-a fwe'-ra day lee'-mee-tay]

harness [n] grupo de cables [groo'-po day ka'-bles]

hash [n] estática en la pantalla [es-ta'-tee-ka en la pan-ta'-ya]

hash totals [np] total de números [to-tal' day noo'-me-ros]

hashing [n] de tecla a direccional [day tek'-la a dee-rek-syo-nal']

head [n] cabeza [ka-be'-sa]

head crash [np] choque en el disco [cho'-kay en el dees'-ko]

head gap [np] entrehierro [en-tre-yer'-ro]

head slot [np] ventana en el disco flexible [ben-ta'-na en el dees'-ko fleck-see'-blay]

header [n] cabecera [ka-be-se'-ra]

header label [np] etiqueta de cabecera [e-tee-ke'-ta day ka-be-se'-ra]

heap [n] montón de almacenamiento [mon-ton' day al-ma-se-na-myen'-to]

heap sort [np] clasificación del árbol [kla-see-fee-ka-syon' del ar'-bol]

heuristic [adj] heurística [e-oo-rees'-tee-ka]

heuristic learning [np] aprendizaje heurístico [a-pren-dee-sa'-hay e-oo-rees'-tee-ko]

heuristic program [np] programa heurístico [pro-gra'-ma e-oo-rees'-tee-ko]

hexadecimal notation [np] notación hexadecimal [no-ta-syon' eck-sa-de-see-mal']

hidden line [np] línea oculta [lee'-ne-a o-kool'-ta]

hidden-line removal [np] remoción de línea oculta [re-mo-syon' day lee'-ne-a o-kool'-ta]

hierarchical model [np] modelo jerárquico [mo-de'-lo he-rar'-kee-ko]

hierarchical network [np] red jerárquica [red he-rar'-kee-ka]

hierarchical structure [np] estructura jerárquica [es-trook-too'-ra he-rar'-kee-ka]

hierarchy [n] jerarquía [he-rar-kee'-a]

high order [np] orden superior [or'-den soo-pe-ryor']

high resolution [np] resolución de orden superior [re-so-loo-syon' day or'-den soo-pe-ryor']

highlighting [n] destacando [des-ta-kan'-do]

high-level language [np] lenguaje de alto nivel [len-gwa'-hay day al'-to nee-bel']

high-level recovery [np] recuperación de alto nivel [re-koo-pe-ra-syon' day al'-to nee-bel']

hit [n] emparejar [em-pa-re-har']

hi-res graphics [np] gráfica de gran resolución [gra'-fee-ka day gran re-so-loo-syon']

hold [v] mantener [man-te-ner']

Hollerith code [np] código Hollerith [ko'-dee-go Hollerith]

hologram [n] holograma [o-lo-gra'-ma]

holographic memory [np] memoria holográfica [me-mo'-rya o-lo-gra'-fee-ka]

holography [n] holografía [o-lo-gra-fee'-a]

home computing [np] cálculo inicial [kal'-koo-lo ee-nee-syal']

HOME key [n] tecla de inicio [tek'-la day ee-nee'-syo]

homebrew [n] computador hecho en casa [kom-poo-ta-dor' e'-cho en ka'-sa]

homeostasis [n] homeostasis [o-me-o-sta'-sees]

home-grown software [np] soporte lógico hecho en casa [so-por'-tay lo'-hee-ko e'-cho en ka'-sa]

homunculus [n] modelo del cerebro [mo-de'-lo del se-re'-bro]

hopper [n] depósito de alimentación [de-po'-see-to day a-lee-men-ta-syon']

horizontal feed [np] alimentación horizontal [a-lee-men-ta-syon' o-ree-son-tal']

horizontal scrolling [np] enrollamiento horizontal [en-ro-ya-myen'-to o-ree-son-tal']

host computer [np] computador anfitrión [kom-poo-ta-dor' an-feet-ryon']

hot site [np] instalación de emergencia [een-sta-la-syon' day e-mer-hen'-sya]

hot zone [np] zona caliente [so'-na ka-lyen'-tay]

hub [n] centro [sen'-tro]

hub (tape drive) [n] bobina [bo-bee'-na]

hue [n] color [ko-lor']

human-machine interface [np] interfase entre humanos y máquinas [een-ter-fa'-say en'-tray oo-ma'-nos ee ma'-kee-nas]

hybrid computer [np] computador híbrido [kom-poo-ta-dor ee'-bree-do]

I

IC integrated circuit [np] circuito integrado [seer-kwee'-to een-te-gra'-do]

icon [n] icono [ee-ko'-no]

identifier [n] identificador [ee-den-tee-fee-ka-dor']

identity element [np] elemento de identidad [e-le-men'-to day ee-den-tee-dad']

identity unit [np] unidad de identidad [oo-nee-dad' day ee-den-tee-dad']

idle characters [np] carácter sin uso [ka-rak'-ter seen oo'-so]

idle time [np] tiempo pasivo [tyem'-po pa-see'-bo]

IDP integrated data processing [np] proceso integrado de datos [pro-se'-so een-te-gra'-do day da'-tos]

if-then operation [np] operación condicional [o-pe-ra-syon' kon-dee-syo-nal']

ignore character [np] carácter de supresión [ka-rak'-ter day soo-pre-syon']

illegal character [np] carácter inválido [ka-rak'-ter een-ba'-lee-do]

illuminate [v] iluminador [ee-loo-mee-na-dor']

image [n] imagen [ee-ma'-hen]

image enhancement [np] intensificación de imagen [een-ten-see-fee-ka-syon' day ee-ma'-hen]

image processing [np] procesamiento de imagen [pro-se-sa-myen'-to day ee-ma'-hen]

immediate access [np] acceso inmediato [ak-se'-so een-me-dya'-to]

impact printer [np] impresora de martillo [eem-pre-so'-ra day mar-tee'-yo]

impact printer [np] impresora a percusión [eem-pre-so'-ra a per-koo-syon']

implementation [n] realización [re-a-lee-sa-syon']

in queue [adv] estar en espera [es-tar' en es-pe'-ra]

inactive [adj] inactivo [ee-nak-tee'-bo]

inactive window [np] ventana inactiva [ben-ta'-na ee-nak-tee'-ba]

incidence matrix [np] matriz de extensión [ma-trees' day ex-ten-syon']

incidental time [np] tiempo de actividades anexas [tyem'-po day ak-tee-bee-da'-des a-neck'-sas]

inclusive OR operation [np] operación O inclusivo [o-pe-ra-syon' O een-kloo-see'-bo]

incremental plotter [np] trazador incremental [tra-sa-dor' een-kre-men-tal']

incremental representation [np] representación incremental [re-pre-sen-ta-syon' een-kre-men-tal']

incremental spacing [np] espacio incremental [es-pa'-syo een-kre-men-tal']

indent [v] sangrar [san-grar']

indentation [n] sangría [san-gree'-a]

index [v] poner en un índice [po-ner' en oon een-dee'-say]

index [n] índice [een-dee'-say]

index hole [np] hueco de índice [we'-ko day een-dee'-say]

indexed sequential access method (ISAM) [np] método de acceso secuencial indicado [me'-to-do day ak-se'-so se-kwen-syal' een-dee-ka'-do]

indirect address [np] dirección indirecta [dee-rek-syon' een-dee-rek'-ta]

ineffective time [np] tiempo ineficaz [tyem'-po ee-ne-fee-kas']

information [n] información [een-for-ma-syon']

information banks [np] bancos de información automatizada [ban'-kos day een-for-ma-syon' ow-to-ma-tee-sa'-da]

information processing [np] proceso de la información [pro-se'-so day la een-for-ma-syon']

information retrieval [np] recuperación de la información [re-koo-pe-ra-syon' day la een-for-ma-syon']

information system [np] sistema de información [sees-te'-ma day een-for-ma-syon']

information theory [np] teoría de la información [te-o-ree'-a day la een-for-ma-syon']

inherited error [np] error hereditario [air-ror' e-re-dee-ta'-ryo]

inhibit [v] inhibir [een-ee-beer']

inhibit pulse [np] impulso de bloqueo [eem-pool'-so day blo-ke'-o]

inhibiting signal [np] señal inhibidora [sen-yal' een-ee-bee-do'-ra]

initialization [n] inicialización [ee-nee-sya-lee-sa-syon']

initialize [v] inicializar [ee-nee-sya-lee-sar']

ink ribbon [np] cinta entintada [seen'-ta en-teen-ta'-da]

input [v] introducir [een-tro-doo-seer']

input [n] entrada [en-tra'-da]

input buffer [np] memoria intermedia de entrada [me-mo'-rya een-ter-me'-dya day en-tra'-da]

input device [np] dispositivo de entrada [dees-po-see-tee'-bo day en-tra'-da]

input stream [np] grupos de entrada [groo'-pos day en-tra'-da]

inputting [v] entrándolo [en-tran'-do-lo]

input/output buffer [np] memoria intermedia de entrada/salida [me-mo'-rya een-ter-me'-dya day en-tra'-da sa-lee'-da]

input/output device [np] dispositivo de entrada/salida [dees-po-see-tee'-bo day en-tra'-da sa-lee'-da]

input/output port [np] puerta de entrada/salida [pwer'-ta day en-tra'-da sa-lee'-da]

input/output (I/O) [np] entrada/salida [en-tra'-da sa-lee'-da]

inquiry [n] petición [pe-tee-syon']

inquiry terminal [np] terminal de interrogación [ter-mee-nal' day een-ter-ro-ga-syon']

inscribe [v] marcar [mar-kar']

insert [v] insertar [een-ser-tar']

insertion point [np] punto de inserción [poon'-to day een-ser-syon']

install [v] instalar [een-sta-lar']

instruction [n] instrucción [een-strook-syon']

instruction code [np] código de instrucción [ko'-dee-go day een-strook-syon']

instruction format [np] formato de la instrucción [for-ma'-to day la een-strook-syon']

instruction mnemonic [np] instrucción mnemotécnica [een-strook-syon' ne-mo-tek'-nee-ka]

instruction set [np] juego de instrucciones [hwe'-go day een-strook-syo'-nes]

instruction time [np] tiempo de una instrucción [tyem'-po day oo'-na een-strook-syon']

instruction word [np] palabra de la instrucción [pa-la'-bra day la een-strook-syon']

instruction-address register [np] registro de instrucción-dirección [re-hees'-tro day een-strook-syon' dee-rek-syon']

integral memory [np] memoria integral [me-mo'-rya een-te-gral']

integrated circuit (IC) [np] circuito integrado [seer-kwee'-to een-te-gra'-do]

integrated data processing (IDP) [np] proceso integrado de datos [pro-se'-so een-te-gra'-do day da'-tos]

integrated injection logic [np] lógica de injección integrada [lo'-hee-ka day een-hek-syon' een-te-gra'-da]

integrated software [np] soporte lógico integrado [so-por'-tay lo'-hee-ko een-te-gra'-do]

integrator [n] integrador [een-te-gra-dor']

integrity [n] integridad [een-te-gree-dad']

intelligent language [np] lenguaje inteligente [len-gwa'-hay een-te-lee-hen'-tay]

intelligent terminal [np] terminal inteligente [ter-mee-nal' een-te-lee-hen'-tay]

intensity [n] intensidad [een-ten-see-dad']

interactive [adj] interactivo [een-te-rak-tee'-bo]

interactive computing [np] cálculo interactivo [kal'-koo-lo een-te-rak-tee'-bo]

interactive display [np] representación interactiva [re-pre-sen-ta-syon' een-te-rak-tee'-ba]

interactive graphics [np] gráfica interactiva [gra'-fee-ka een-te-rak-tee'-ba]

interactive mode [np] modo interactivo [mo'-do een-te-rak-tee'-bo]

interactive processing [np] procesamiento interactivo [pro-se-sa-myen'-to een-te-rak-tee'-bo]

interactive query [np] interrogación interactiva [een-ter-ro-ga-syon' een-te-rak-tee'-ba]

interactive terminal [np] terminal interactivo [ter-mee-nal' een-te-rak-tee'-bo]

interface [n] acoplamiento mutuo [a-ko-pla-myen'-to moo'-two]

interlace [v] entrelazar [en-tre-la-sar']

interleaving [n] interfolición [een-ter-fo-lee-syon']

interlock [v] interbloquear [een-ter-blo-ke-ar']

interlude [n] descanso [des-kan'-so]

intermediate storage [np] memoria intermedia [me-mo'-rya een-ter-me'-dya]

internal clock [np] reloj interno [re-lo' een-ter'-no]

internal modem [np] módem interno [mo'-dem een-ter'-no]

interpolation [n] interpolación [een-ter-po-la-syon']

interpolator [n] interpolador [een-ter-po-la-dor']

interpret [v] interpretar [een-ter-pre-tar']

interpreter [n] interpretadora [een-ter-pre-ta-do'-ra]

interrecord gap (IRG) [np] intervalo entre archivos [een-ter-ba'-lo en'-tray ar-chee'-bos]

interrupt [v] interrumpir [een-ter-room-peer']

interrupt [n] interrupción [een-ter-roop-syon']

interrupt priority [np] prioridad de interrupción [pryo-ree-dad' day een-ter-roop-syon']

intersystem communications [np] comunicaciones entre sistemas [ko-moo-nee-ka-syo'-nes en'-tray sees-te'-mas]

interval timer [np] reloj automático de intervalos [re-lo' ow-to-ma'-tee-ko day een-ter-ba'-los]

inter-record gap [np] separación entre registros [se-pa-ra-syon' en'-tray re-hees'-tros]

invariant [adj] constante [kon-stan'-tay]

inverse video [np] video inverso [bee-de'-o een-ber'-so]

inversion [n] inversión [een-ber-syon']

invert [v] invertir [een-ber-teer']

inverted file [np] archivo inverso [ar-chee'-bo een-ber'-so]

inverter [n] inversor [een-ber-sor']

invisible refresh [np] regeneración invisible [re-he-ne-ra-syon' een-bee-see'-blay]

in-line [adj] líneal [lee'-ne-al]

in-line coding [np] código líneal [ko'-dee-go lee'-ne-al]

in-line processing [np] procesamiento líneal [pro-se-sa-myen'-to lee'-ne-al]

IRG interrecord gap [np] intervalo entre archivos [een-ter-ba'-lo en'-tray ar-chee'-bos]

ISAM indexed sequential access method [np] método de acceso secuencial indicado [me'-to-do day ak-se'-so se-kwen-syal' een-dee-ka'-do]

isolation [n] aislamiento [aees-la-myen'to]

item design [np] diseño de elementos [dee-sen'-yo day e-le-men'-tos]

iteration [n] iteración [ee-te-ra-syon']

iterative [adj] iterativo [ee-te-ra-tee'-bo]

I/O input/output [np] entrada/salida [en-tra'-da sa-lee'-da]

J

jaggies [n] dentado [den-ta'-do]

jam [n] atascamiento [a-tas-ka-myen'-to]

JCL job control language [np] lenguaje de control de trabajos [len-gwa'-hay day kon-trol' day tra-ba'-hos]

jitter [n] salto pequeño [sal'-to pe-kwen'-yo]

job [n] trabajo [tra-ba'-ho]

job control language (JCL) [np] lenguaje de control de trabajos [len-gwa'-hay day kon-trol' day tra-ba'-hos]

job control system [np] sistema de control de trabajos [sees-te'-ma day kon-trol' day tra-ba'-hos]

job queue [np] turno en espera del trabajo [toor'-no en es-pe'-ra del tra-ba'-ho]

job scheduler [np] planificador de trabajos [pla-nee-fee-ka-dor' day tra-ba'-hos]

join [v] unir [oo-neer']

joy stick [np] palanca de juego [pa-lan'-ka day hwe'-go]

jump [v] saltar [sal-tar']

jump [n] salto [sal'-to]

junk [n] desperdicio [des-per-dee'-syo]

justify [v] justificar [hoos-tee-fee-kar']

K

KCS kilo core seconds [np] kilonúcleo segundos [kee-lo-noo'-kle-o se-goon'-dos]

keep-out areas [np] área que no permite circuitos [a'-re-a kay no per-mee'-tay seer-kwee'-tos]

kernel [n] núcleo primitivo [noo'-kle-o pree-mee-tee'-bo]

kerning [n] sin espacio blanco entre letras [seen es-pa'-syo blan'-ko en'-tray le'-tras]

key [n] tecla [tek'-la]

key bounce [np] picado de tecla [pee-ka'-do day tek'-la]

key punch [np] perforadora de tecla [per-fo-ra-do'-ra day tek'-la]

key stations [np] terminal clave [ter-mee-nal' kla'-bay]

keyboard [v] teclear [tek-le-ar']

keyboard [n] teclado [tek-la'-do]

keyboarding [n] tecleando [tek-le-an'-do]

keyword [n] palabra clave [pa-la'-bra kla'-bay]

key-to-disk [n] teclado de registro sobre disco [tek-la'-do day re-hees'-tro so'-bray dees'-ko]

key-to-tape [n] teclado de registro sobre cinta [tek-la'-do day re-hees'-tro so'-bray seen'-ta]

key-word-in-context (KWIC) [np] contenido pre-selecionado de palabras [kon-te-nee'-do pre se-le-syo-na'-do day pa-la'-bras]

kilo core seconds (KCS) [np] kilonúcleo segundos [kee-lo-noo'-kle-o se-goon'-dos]

kilobit [n] kilobit [kee-lo-beet']

kilobyte [n] kilo-octero [kee'-lo ok-te'-ro]

kludge [n] arreglo improvisado [ar-reg'-lo eem-pro-bee-sa'-do]

knowledge acquisition [np] adquisición de conocimiento [ad-kee-see-syon' day ko-no-see-myen'-to]

knowledge base [np] base de conocimiento [ba'-say day ko-no-see-myen'-to]

knowledge engineering [np] ingeniería de conocimiento [een-he-nye-ree'-a day ko-no-see-myen'-to]

knowledge industries [np] industria de conocimiento [een-doos'-trya day ko-no-see-myen'-to]

knowledge representation [np] representación de conocimiento [re-pre-sen-ta-syon' day ko-no-see-myen'-to]

knowledge work [np] trabajo de conocimiento [tra-ba'-ho day ko-no-see-myen'-to]

KWIC key-word-in-context [np] contenido pre-selecionado de palabras [kon-te-nee'-do pre se-le-syo-na'-do day pa-la'-bras]

L

label [n] etiqueta [e-tee-ke'-ta]

lag [n] retrasado [re-tra-sa'-do]

land [n] área para montar circuitos [a'-re-a pa'-ra mon-tar' seer-kwee'-tos]

language [n] lenguaje [len-gwa'-hay]

language subset [np] subgrupo de lenguaje [soob-groo'-po day len-gwa'-hay]

large scale integration (LSI) [np] integración en gran escala [een-te-gra-syon' en gran es-ca'-la]

laser printer [np] impresora de laser [eem-pre-so'-ra day la-ser']

last in-last out (LILO) [np] el último entra - el último sale [el ool'-tee-mo en'-tra — el ool'-tee-mo sa'-lay]

latency [n] latencia [la-ten'-sya]

layer [n] capas gráficas [ka'-pas gra'-fee-kas]

layering [n] capas asociadas de gráfica [ka'-pas a-so-sya'-das day gra'-fee-ka]

layout [n] plan [plan]

layout sheet [n] papel de planeamiento [pa-pel' day pla-ne-a-myen'-to]

leader [n] delantero [de-lan-te'-ro]

leading [n] distancia de líneas [dees-tan'-sya day lee'-ne-as]

leading edge [np] punta delantera [poon'-ta de-lan-te'-ra]

leaf [n] nodo del árbol [no'-do del ar'-bol]

LED light-emitting diode [np] diodo luminoso [dyo'-do loo-mee-no'-so]

left shift [np] desplazamiento a la izquierda [des-pla-sa-myen'-to a la ees-kyer'-da]

left-justified [adj] justificado a la izquierda [hoos-tee-fee-ka'-do a la ees-kyer'-da]

less than [adj] menos que [me'-nos kay]

letter quality [np] qualidad de letra [ka-lee-dad' day le'-tra]

letter shift [np] traslado de letra [tras-la'-do day le'-tra]

letter-quality printer [np] impresora de qualidad de letra [eem-pre-so'-ra day ka-lee-dad' day le'-tra]

lexicon [n] léxico [leck'-see-ko]

library [n] biblioteca [bee-blyo-te'-ka]

loop structure [np] estructura de bucle [es-trook-too'-ra day boo'-klay]

loophole [n] desviación [des-bya-syon']

looping [n] repetición [re-pe-tee-syon']

loosely coupled [np] debilitadamente aclopado [de-bee-lee-ta-da-men'-tay ak-lo-pa'-do]

loss [n] pérdida [per'-dee-da]

low activity [np] actividad baja [ak-tee-bee-dad' ba'-ha]

low order [np] orden inferior [or'-den een-fe-ryor']

low resolution [np] resolución inferior [re-so-loo-syon' een-fe-ryor']

low-level language [np] lenguaje de bajo nivel [len-gwa'-hay day ba'-ho nee-bel']

low-res graphics [np] gráfica de baja resolución [gra'-fee-ka day ba'-ha re-so-loo-syon']

LP linear programming [np] programación lineal [pro-gra-ma-syon' lee-ne-al']

LPM lines per minute [np] líneas-por-minuto [lee'-ne-as por mee-noo'-to]

LSI large scale integration [np] integración en gran escala [een-te-gra-syon' en gran es-ka'-la]

LU logic unit [np] unidad lógica [oo-nee-dad' lo'-hee-ka]

LU logical unit [np] unidad lógica [oo-nee-dad' lo'-hee-ka]

luminance [n] luminiscente [loo-mee-nees-sen'-tay]

luminance decay [np] decadencia de luminosidad [de-ka-den'-sya day loo-mee-no-see-dad']

luminosity [n] luminosidad [loo-mee-no-see-dad']

M

MAC multi-access computing [np] cálculo de acceso múltiple [kal'-koo-lo day ak-se'-so mool'-tee-play]

machine address [np] dirección de máquina [dee-rek-syon' day ma'-kee-na]

machine code [np] código de máquina [ko'-dee-ho day ma'-kee-na]

machine independent [np] independiente de la máquina [een-de-pen-dyen'-tay day la ma'-kee-na]

machine intelligence [np] inteligencia de la máquina [een-te-lee-hen'-sya day la ma'-kee-na]

machine language [np] lenguaje de la máquina [len-gwa'-hay day la ma'-kee-na]

machine room [np] cuarto de máquinas [kwar'-to day ma'-kee-nas]

machine room [np] sala de máquinas [sa'-la day ma'-kee-nas]

machine word [np] palabra de máquina [pa-la'-bra day ma'-kee-na]

machine-dependent [n] dependiente de la máquina [de-pen-dyen'-tay day la ma'-kee-na]

machine-readable [adj] legible por la máquina [le-hee'-blay por la ma'-kee-na]

machine-run [adj] pasada de máquina [pa-sa'-da day ma'-kee-na]

machine-sensible [adj] legible por la máquina [le-hee'-blay por la ma'-kee-na]

macro- [pre] macro- [ma'-kro]

macro assembler [np] macro ensamblador [ma'-kro en-sam-bla-dor']

macro instruction [np] macro instrucción [ma'-kro een-strook-syon']

macroprogramming [n] macroprogramación [ma-kro-pro-gra-ma-syon']

magnetic bubble memory [np] memoria de burbuja magnética [me-mo'-rya day boor-boo'-ha mag-ne'-tee-ka]

magnetic card [np] tarjeta magnética [tar-he'-ta mag-ne'-tee-ka]

magnetic cell [np] célula magnética [se'-loo-la mag-ne'-tee-ka]

magnetic core [np] núcleo magnético [noo'-kle-o mag-ne'-tee-ko]

magnetic disk [np] disco magnético [dees'-ko mag-ne'-tee-ko]

magnetic drum [np] tambor magnético [tam-bor' mag-ne'-tee-ko]

magnetic ink [np] tinta magnética [teen'-ta mag-ne'-tee-ka]

magnetic ink character recognition [np] reconocimiento de carácteres de tinta magnética [re-ko-no-see-myen'-to day ka-rak'-te-res day teen'-ta mag-ne'-tee-ka]

magnetic media [np] medios magnéticos [me'-dyos mag-ne'-tee-kos]

magnetic memory [np] memoria magnética [me-mo'-rya mag-ne'-tee-ka]

magnetic tape [np] cinta magnética [seen'-ta mag-ne'-tee-ka]

magnetostriction [n] magnetoestricción [mag-ne-to-es-treek-syon']

magstripe [n] cinta magnética [seen'-ta mag-ne'-tee-ka]

mail-merging [n] fusión postal [foo-syon' pos-tal']

main memory [np] memoria principal [me-mo'-rya preen-see-pal']

main storage [np] almacenamiento principal [al-ma-se-na-myen'-to preen-see-pal']

mainframe [n] computador principal [kom-poo-ta-dor' preen-see-pal']

maintenance [n] mantenimiento [man-te-nee-myen'-to]

major sort key [np] llave mayor de clasificar [ya'-bay ma-yor' day kla-see-fee-kar']

majority element [np] elemento mayoritario [e-le-men'-to ma-yo-ree-ta'-ryo]

management graphics [np] gráfica administradora [gra'-fee-ka ad-mee-nee-stra-do'-ra]

manipulated variable [np] variable manipulada [ba-rya'-blay ma-nee-poo-la'-da]

manual control [np] control manual [kon-trol' man-wal']

manual input [np] entrada manual [en-tra'-da man-wal']

man-machine interaction [np] interacción hombre-máquina [een-te-rak-syon' om'-bray ma'-kee-na]

man-machine interface [np] acoplamiento mutuo hombre-máquina [a-ko-pla-myen'-to moo'-two om'-bray ma'-kee-na]

map [n] mapa [ma'-pa]

mapping [n] mapeando [ma-pe-an'-do]

marginal test [np] prueba marginal prwe'-ba mar-hee-nal']

mark [n] marca [mar'-ka]

mark scanning [np] exploración de las marcas [ex-plo-ra-syon' day las mar'-kas]

mark sensing [np] lectura de marcas [lek-too'-ra day mar'-kas]

marker [n] marcador [mar-ka-dor']

mask [v] enmascarar [en-mas-ka-rar']

mask [n] máscara [mas'-ka-ra]

masking [n] enmascaramiento [en-mas-ka-ra-myen'-to]

mass storage [np] memoria de gran capacidad [me-mo'-rya day gran ka-pa-see-dad']

master clock [np] reloj maestro [re-lo' ma-es'-tro]

master file [np] fichero maestro [fee-che'-ro ma-es'-tro]

master record [np] registro maestro [re-hees'-tro ma-es'-tro]

master tape [np] cinta maestra [seen'-ta ma-es'-tra]

master-instruction tape (MIT) [np] cinta de instrucciones maestras [seen'-ta day een-strook-syo'-nes ma-es'-tras]

master-slave system [np] sistema del maestro-esclavo [sees-te'-ma del ma-es'-tro es-kla'-bo]

match [v] enparejar [en-pa-re-har']

matching [adj] correspondiente [kor-res-pon-dyen'-tay]

mathematical programming [np] programación matemática [pro-gra-ma-syon' ma-te-ma'-tee-ka]

matrix [n] matriz [ma-trees']

matrix arithmetic [np] aritmética de matriz [a-ree-me'-tee-ka day ma-trees']

matrix element [np] elemento de matriz [e-le-men'-to day ma-trees']

matrix inversion [np] inversión de matriz [een-ber-syon' day ma-trees']

matrix printer [np] impresora de matriz [eem-pre-so'-ra day ma-trees']

matrix storage [np] memoria de matriz [me-mo'-rya day ma-trees']

mature system [np] sistema maduro [sees-te'-ma ma-doo'-ro]

mean repair time [np] tiempo medio para reparación [tyem'-po me'-dyo pa'-ra re-pa-ra-syon']

mean time between failures [np] tiempo medio entre fallos [tyem'-po me'-dyo en'-tray fa'-yos]

medium [n] medio [me'-dyo]

megabit [n] megabit [me-ga-beet']

megabyte [n] megabyte [me-ga-bee'-tay]

memory [n] memoria [me-mo'-rya]

memory chip [np] plaqueta de almacenamiento de memoria [pla-ke'-ta day al-ma-se-na-myen'-to day me-mo'-rya]

memory dump [np] vuelco de la memoria [bwel'-ko day la me-mo'-rya]

memory map [np] mapa de la memoria [ma'-pa day la me-mo'-rya]

memory protection [np] protección de la memoria [pro-tek-syon' day la me-mo'-rya]

memory sniffing [np] husmeo de la memoria [oos-me'-o day la me-mo'-rya]

menu-display [n] visual menú [bee-swal' me-noo']

menu-driven software [np] soporte lógico que funciona con un menú [so-por'-tay lo'-hee-ko kay foon-syo'-na kon oon me-noo']

merge [v] fusionar [foo-syo-nar']

merge [n] fusión [foo-syon']

message queuing [np] en espera de mensajes [en es-pe'-ra day men-sa'-hes]

message retrieval [np] recuperación de mensajes [re-koo-pe-ra-syon' day men-sa'-hes]

message routing [np] encaminamiento de mensajes [en-ka-mee-na-myen'-to day men-sa'-hes]

message switching [np] conmutación de mensajes [kon-moo-ta-syon' day men-sa'-hes]

metal oxide semiconductor (MOS) [np] semiconductor de óxido metálico [se-mee-kon-dook-tor' day ock'-see-do me-ta'-lee-ko]

micro- [pre] micro- [mee'-kro]

microchip [n] microplaqueta [mee-kro-pla-ke'-ta]

microcode [n] microcódigo [mee-kro-ko'-dee-go]

microcomputer [n] microcomputador [mee-kro-kom-poo-ta-dor']

microcontroller [n] microcontrolador [mee-kro-kon-tro-la-dor']

microelectronics [n] microelectrónica [mee-kro-e-lek-tro'-nee-ka]

microfiche [n] microficha [mee-kro-fee'-cha]

microfilm [n] microfilm [mee-kro-feelm']

microfilm [n] micropelícula [mee-kro-pe-lee'-koo-la]

microform [n] microformas [mee-kro-for'-mas]

micrographics [n] micrográfica [mee-kro-gra'-fee-ka]

microinstruction [n] microinstrucción [mee-kro-een-strook-syon']

microminiature chip [np] plaqueta microminiatura [pla-ke'-ta mee-kro-mee-nya-too'-ra]

microprocessor [n] microprocesador [mee-kro-pro-se-sa-dor'

microprogram [n] microprograma [mee-kro-pro-gra'-ma]

microprogramming [n] microprogramación [mee-kro-pro-gra-ma-syon']

microsecond [n] microsegundo [mee-kro-se-goon'-do]

microsystem [n] microsistema [mee-kro-sees-te'-ma]

microwave hop [n] salto de microondas [sal'-to day mee-kro-on'-das]

milli- [pre] mili- [mee'-lee]

minicomputer [n] minicomputador [mee-nee-kom-poo-ta-dor']

minidiskette [n] minidisco [mee-nee-dees'-ko]

minifloppy disk [np] minidisco flexible [mee-nee-dees'-ko fleck-see'-blay]

minimal tree [np] árbol óptimo [ar'-bol op'-tee-mo]

minimax [adj] minimáximo [mee-nee-mack'-see-mo]

minimum-access code [np] código de acceso mínimo [ko'-dee-go day ak-se'-so mee'-nee-mo]

minus zone [np] zona negativa [so'-na ne-ga-tee'-ba]

mirroring [np] retrovisor [re-tro-bee-sor']

MIT master-instruction tape [np] cinta de instrucciones maestras [seen'-ta day een-strook-syo'-nes ma-es'-tras]

mixed-base notation [np] notación con base múltiple [no-ta-syon' kon ba'-say mool'-tee-play]

mnemonic [n] mnemotécnica [ne-mo-tek'-nee-ka]

mnemonic operation code [np] código de operación mnemotécnico [ko'-dee-go day o-pe-ra-syon ne-mo-tek'-nee-ko]

mode [n] modo [mo'-do]

model [v] diseñar [dee-sen-yar']

model [v] modelar [mo-de-lar']

model [n] modelo [mo-de'-lo]

model building [np] construcción de modelos [kon-strook-syon' day mo-de'-los]

modeling [adj] modelado [mo-de-la'-do]

modem [n] módem [mo'-dem]

modification [n] modificación [mo-dee-fee-ka-syon']

modifier [n] modificador [mo-dee-fee-ka-dor']

modify [v] modificar [mo-dee-fee-kar']

modular coding [np] codigo modular [ko'-dee-go mo-doo-lar']

modular programming [np] programación modular [pro-gra-ma-syon' mo-doo-lar']

modular system [np] sistema modular [sees-te'-ma mo-doo-lar']

modularity [n] en modularción [en mo-doo-lar-syon']

modularization [n] modularisación [mo-doo-la-ree-sa-syon']

modulation [n] modulación [mo-doo-la-syon']

modulator [n] modulador [mo-doo-la-dor']

module [n] módulo [mo'-doo-lo]

modulo-N check [np] verificación de modulo-N [be-ree-fee-ka-syon' day mo'-doo-lo e'-nay]

monitor [v] observar [ob-ser-bar']

monitor [n] monitor [mo-nee-tor']

monolithic [adj] monolítico [mo-no-lee'-tee-ko]

Monte Carlo method [np] método Montecarlo [me'-to-do Montecarlo]

MOS metal oxide semiconductor [np] semiconductor de óxido metálico [se-mee-kon-dook-tor' day ock'-see-do me-ta'-lee-ko]

MOS field-effect transistor (MOSFET) [np] transistor MOS de efecto de campo [tran-sees-tor' MOS day e-fek'-to day kam'-po]

MOSFET MOS field-effect transistor [np] transistor MOS de efecto de campo [tran-sees-tor' MOS day e-fek'-to day kam'-po]

motherboard [n] placa madre [pla'-ka ma'-dray]

mouse [n] ratón [ra-ton']

mouse button [np] botón de ratón [bo-ton' day ra-ton']

MPX multiplexer [n] multiplexar [mool-tee-pleck-sar']

multiaccess [n] acceso múltiple [ak-se'-so mool'-tee-play]

multilayered software [np] soporte lógico en multicapas [so-por'-tay lo'-hee-ko en mool-tee-ka'-pas]

multipart forms [np] papel continuo de muchas partes [pa-pel' kon-tee'-nwo day moo'-chas par'-tes]

multiplex [n] múltiplex [mool'-tee-plex]

multiplexer channel [np] canal del multiplexer [ka-nal' del mool-tee-pleck-ser']

multiplexer (MPX) [n] multiplexar [mool-tee-pleck-sar']

multiplexing [n] múltiplexado [mool'-tee-pleck-sa-do]

multiplexor [n] multiplexar [mool-tee-pleck-sar']

multiple-address instruction [np] instrucción de direcciones múltiples [een-strook-syon' day dee-rek-syo'-nes mool'-tee-ples]

multiple-length arithmetic [np] aritmética de longitud múltiple [a-reet-me'-tee-ka day lon-hee-tood' mool'-tee-play]

multiple-length number [np] número de longitud múltiple [noo'-me-ro day lon-hee-tood' mool'-tee-play]

multiplier [n] multiplicador [mool-tee-plee-ka-dor']

multipoint network [np] red de puntos múltiples [red day poon'-tos mool'-tee-ples]

multiprocessor [n] procesador múltiple [pro-se-sa-dor' mool'-tee-play]

multiprogramming [n] multiprogramación [mool-tee-pro-gra-ma-syon']

multiuser system [np] sistema para usuarios múltiples [sees-te'-ma pa'-ra oo-swa'-ryos mool'-tee-ples]

multi-access computing (MAC) [np] cálculo de acceso múltiple [kal'-koo-lo day ak-se'-so mool'-tee-play]

music synthesizer [np] sintetizador de música [seen-te-tee-sa-dor' day moo'-see-ka]

musical language [np] lenguaje musical [len-gwa'-hay moo-see-kal']

musicomp [n] sintetizador musical [seen-te-tee-sa-dor' moo-see-kal']

N

naive user [np] usuario candido [oo-swa'-ryo kan-dee'-do]

NAND-gate [n] puerta NY [pwer'-ta NY]

NAND-operation [n] operación NY [o-pe-ra-syon' NY]

native compiler [np] compiladora natal [kom-pee-la-do'-ra na-tal']

native language [np] lenguaje natal [len-gwa'-hay na-tal']

NDRO non-destructive read operation [np] operación de lectura no destructiva [o-pe-ra-syon' day lek-too'-ra no des-trook-tee'-ba]

negation [n] negación [ne-ga-syon']

negative acknowledgement [np] confirmación negativa [kon-feer-ma-syon' ne-ga-tee'-ba]

negator [n] negador [ne-ga-dor']

neither-nor operation [np] operación ni-no [o-pe-ra-syon' ni-no]

nerd [n] borde [bor'-day]

nest [v] jerarquizar [he-rar-kee-sar']

nest [n] nido [nee'-do]

nested block [np] bloque ennidado [blo'-kay en-nee-da'-do]

nested loop [np] lazo enninado [la'-so en-nee-da'-do]

nesting [n] ennidar [en-nee-dar']

network [n] red [red]

network analysis [np] análisis de redes [a-na'-lee-sees day re'-des]

network system [np] sistema de redes [sees-te'-ma day re'-des]

neural net [np] malla neural [ma'-ya ne-oo-ral']

neural network [np] red neural [red ne-oo-ral']

nibble [n] nibble [neeb'-blay]

nil pointer [np] apuntador nulo [a-poon-ta-dor' noo'-lo]

niladic [adj] operación sin operando [o-pe-ra-syon' seen o-pe-ran'-do]

nine's complement [np] complemento a nueves [kom-ple-men'-to a nwe'-bes]

node [n] nodo [no'-do]

noise [n] ruido [rwee'-do]

noisy mode [np] modo ruidoso [mo'-do rwe-do'-so]

nonconductor [n] nonconductivo [non-kon-dook-tee'-bo]

nondestructive read [np] lectura no destructiva [lek-too'-ra no des-trook-tee'-ba]

nonerasable storage [np] memoria imborrable [me-mo'-rya eem-bor-ra'-blay]

nongraphic character [np] carácter nongráfico [ka-rak'-ter non-gra'-fee-ko]

nonimpact printer [np] impresora sin percusión [eem-pre-so'-ra seen per-coo-syon']

nonlinear programming [np] programación no lineal [pro-gra-ma-syon' no lee-ne-al']

nonoverlap processing [np] procesamiento sin extenderse sobre [pro-se-sa-myen'-to seen ex-ten-der'-say so'-bray]

nonreflective ink [np] tinta nonreflectora [teen'-ta non-re-flek-to'-ra]

nonvolatile memory [np] memoria nonvolátil [me-mo'-rya non-vo-la'-teel]

non-destructive read operation (NDRO) [np] operación de lectura no destructiva [o-pe-ra-syon' day lek-too'-ra no des-trook-tee'-ba]

normalize [v] normalizar [nor-ma-lee-sar']

NOR-gate [n] puerta NI [pwer'-ta NI]

NOR-operation [n] operación NI [o-pe-ra-syon' NI]

NOT-AND operation [np] operación NO-Y [o-pe-ra-syon' NO-Y]

NOT-gate [n] puerta NO [pwer'-ta NO]

NOT-operation [n] operación NO [o-pe-ra-syon' NO]

no-address instruction [np] instrucción sin dirección [een-strook-syon' seen dee-rek-syon']

no-op [n] sin operación [seen o-pe-ra-syon']

nucleus [n] núcleos [noo'-kle-os]

null [n] nulo [noo'-lo]

null cycle [np] ciclo nulo [see'-klo noo'-lo]

null string [np] serie nula [se'-ryay noo'-la]

number crunching [np] crujido de números [kroo-hee'-do day noo'-me-ros]

number system [np] sistema de numeración [sees-te'-ma day noo-me-ra-syon']

numeric [adj] numérico [noo-me'-ree-ko]

numerical analysis [np] análisis numérico [a-na'-lee-sees noo-me'-ree-ko]

numerical control [np] control numérico [kon-trol' noo-me'-ree-ko]

O

oasis [n] oasis [o-a'-sees]

object code [np] código objeto [ko'-dee-go ob-he'-to]

object language [np] lenguaje objeto [len-gwa'-hay ob-he'-to]

object program [np] programa objeto [pro-gra'-ma ob-he'-to]

obscure [adj] oscuro [os-koo'-ro]

OCR optical character recognition [np] reconocimiento óptico de carácteres [re-ko-no-see-myen'-to op'-tee-ko day ka-rak'-te-res]

octal [n] octal [ok-tal']

octal notation [np] notación octal [no-ta-syon' ok-tal']

odd parity [np] imparidad [eem-pa-ree-dad']

odd-even check [np] control de paridad par-impar [kon-trol' day pa-ree-dad' par — eem-par']

off load [v] descargar [des-kar-gar']

off-line [adj] fuera de linea [fwe'-ra day lee'-ne-a]

off-the-shelf [adj] en-el-estante [en el es-tan'-tay]

one level storage [np] memoria de un solo nivel [me-mo'-rya day oon so'-lo nee-bel']

one state [np] estado de uno [es-ta'-do day oo'-no]

one's complement [np] complemento a uno [kom-ple-men'-to a oo'-no]

one-dimensional array [np] arreglo de una dimensión [ar-reg'-lo day oo'-na dee-men-syon']

one-for-one [adj] uno por uno [oo'-no por oo'-no]

one-plus-one address [np] dirección de uno más uno [dee-rek-syon' day oo'-no mas oo'-no]

on-line [adj] en línea [en lee'-ne-a]

on-line data base [np] base de datos en línea [ba'-say day da'-tos en lee'-ne-a]

on-line data reduction [np] reducción de datos en línea [re-dook-syon' day da'-tos en lee'-ne-a]

on-line fault tolerant system [np] sistema tolerante de averías en línea [sees-te'-ma to-le-ran'-tay day a-be-ree'-as en lee'-ne-a]

on-line problem solving [np] solución del problema en línea [so-loo-syon' del pro-ble'-ma en lee'-ne-a]

opacity [n] opacidad [o-pa-see-dad']

open loop [np] circuito abierto [seer-kwee'-to a-byer'-to]

open routine [np] rutina de apertura [roo-tee'-na day a-per-too'-ra]

operating ratio [np] relación de utilización [re-la-syon' day oo-tee-lee-sa-syon']

operating station [np] estación operativa [es-ta-syon' o-pe-ra-tee'-ba]

operating system (OS) [np] sistema operativo [sees-te'-ma o-pe-ra-tee'-bo]

operation [n] operación [o-pe-ra-syon']

operational research [np] investigación operativa [een-bes-tee-ga-syon' o-per-ra-tee'-ba]

operator [n] operador [o-pe-ra-dor']

optical character [np] carácter óptico [ka-rak'-ter op'-tee-ko]

optical character reader [np] leedora óptica de carácteres [le-e-do'-ra op'-tee-ka day ka-rak'-te-res]

optical character recognition (OCR) [np] reconocimiento óptico de carácteres [re-ko-no-see-myen'-to op'-tee-ko day ka-rak'-te-res]

optical communications [np] comunicaciones ópticas [ko-moo-nee-ka-syo'-nes op'-tee-kas]

optical fiber technology [np] tecnología de las fibras ópticas [tek-no-lo-hee'-a day las fee'-bras op'-tee-kas]

optical fibre technology [np] tecnología de las fibras ópticas [tek-no-lo-hee'-a day las fee'-bras op'-tee-kas]

optical mark recognition [np] reconocimiento óptico de las marcas [re-ko-no-see-myen'-to op'-tee-ko day las mar'-kas]

optical page reader [np] leedor óptico de páginas [le-e-dor' op'-tee-ko day pa'-hee-nas]

optical scanner [np] explorador óptico [ex-plo-ra-dor' op'-tee-ko]

optimal merge tree [np] fusión óptima del árbol [foo-syon' op'-tee-ma del ar'-bol]

optimization [n] optimización [op-tee-me-sa-syon']

optimize [v] optimizar [op-tee-mee-sar']

optimum programming [np] programación óptima [pro-gra-ma-syon' op'-tee-ma]

option key [np] tecla de opción [tek'-la day op-syon']

opto-electronics [n] óptica-electrónico [op'-tee-ka e-lek-tro'-nee-ko]

op-code [n] código de operación [ko'-dee-go day o-pe-ra-syon']

order [v] ordenar [or-de-nar']

order [n] orden [or'-den]

order code [np] código de orden [ke'-dee-go day or'-den]

organization and methods (O&M) [np] organización y métodos [or-ga-nee-sa-syon' ee me'-to-dos]

origin [n] origen [o-ree'-hen]

orphan [n] quedó huérfano [ke-do' wer'-fa-no]

OR-gate [n] puerta O [pwer'-ta O]

OR-operation [n] operación O [o-pe-ra-syon' O]

OS operating system [np] sistema operativo [sees-te'-ma o-pe-ra-tee'-bo]

oscillating sort [np] clasificación oscilante [kla-see-fee-ka-syon' os-see-lan'-tay]

oscillography [n] oscilográfica [os-see-lo-gra'-fee-ka]

outdegree [n] de canto del árbol [day kan'-to del ar'-bol]

output [v] salir [sa-leer']

output [n] salida [sa-lee'-da]

output area [np] área de salida [a'-re-a day sa-lee'-da]

output buffer [np] memoria intermedia de salida [me-mo'-rya een-ter-me'-dya day sa-lee'-da]

output device [np] dispositivo de salida [dees-po-see-tee'-bo day sa-lee'-da]

output media [np] medios de salida [me'-dyos day sa-lee'-da]

output stream [np] grupos de salida [groo'-pos day sa-lee'-da]

outputting [n] salida de buena información [sa-lee'-da day bwe'-na een-for-ma-syon']

overflow [v] derramarse [der-ra-mar'-say]

overflow [n] desbordamiento [des-bor-da-myen'-to]

overlap [v] extenderse sobre [ex-ten-der'-say so'-bray]

overlap processing [np] procesamiento de superposición [pro-se-sa-myen'-to day soo-per-po-see-syon']

overlapping [n] superposicionamiento [soo-per-po-see-syo-na-myen'-to]

overlay [v] obscurecer [ob-skoo-re-ser']

override [v] anular [a-noo-lar']

overrun [n] exedió [eck-se-dyo']

overscan [v] sobreexplorar [so-bre-ex-plo-rar']

overstriking [n] sobreimprimir [so-bre-eem-pree-meer']

overwrite [v] sobreescribir [so-bre-es-kree-beer']

O&M organization and methods [np] organización y métodos [or-ga-nee-sa-syon' ee me'-to-dos]

P

pack [v] empaquetar [em-pa-ke-tar']

pack of cards (paper) [np] baraja de tarjetas [ba-ra'-ha day tar-he'-tas]

pack up [n] empaque [em-pa'-kay]

packet switching [np] conmutación de paquetes [kon-moo-ta-syon' day pa-ke'-tes]

packet-switched network [np] red de commutación de paquetes [red day kon-moo-ta-syon' day pa-ke'-tes]

packing [v] empacar [em-pa-kar']

packing density [np] densidad de empaquetamiento [den-see-dad' day em-pa-ke-ta-myen'-to]

padding [n] relleno [re-ye'-no]

paddle [n] paleta [pa-le'-ta]

page [n] página [pa'-hee-na]

page printer [np] impresora de páginas [eem-pre-so'-ra day pa'-hee-nas]

page turning [np] volteador de páginas [bol-te-a-dor' day pa'-hee-nas]

paged memory [np] memoria organizada en páginas [me-mo'-rya or-ga-nee-sa'-da en pa'-hee-nas]

pagination [n] paginación [pa-hee-na-syon']

paging [n] organización de páginas [or-ga-nee-sa-syon' day pa'-hee-nas]

paintbrush [n] brocha de pintar [bro'-cha day peen-tar']

painting [n] pintura [peen-too'-ra]

palette [n] paleta [pa-le'-ta]

pane [n] hoja de vidrio [o'-ha day bee'-dryo]

panning [n] desplazamiento [des-pla-sa-myen'-to]

paper tape [np] cinta de papel [seen'-ta day pa-pel']

paper throw [np] salto de papel [sal'-to day pa-pel']

paper-tape punch [np] perforadora de cinta de papel [per-fo-ra-do'-ra day seen'-ta day pa-pel']

paper-tape reader [np] leedora de cinta de papel [le-e-do'-ra day seen'-ta day pa-pel']

paradigm [n] paradigma [pa-ra-deeg'-ma]

parallel access [np] acceso paralelo [ak-se'-so pa-ra-le'-lo]

parallel conversion [np] conversión paralela [kon-ber-syon' pa-ra-le'-la]

parallel interface [np] interfase en paralelo [een-ter-fa'-say en pa-ra-le'-lo]

parallel processing [np] proceso en paralelo [pro-se'-so en pa-ra-le'-lo]

parallel running [np] funcionamiento en paralelo [foon-syo-na-myen'-to en pa-ra-le'-lo]

parallel transfer [np] transferencia en paralelo [trans-fe-ren'-sya en pa-ra-le'-lo]

parameter [n] parámetro [pa-ra'-me-tro]

parametric [adj] parámetrica [pa-ra'-me-tree-ka]

parent [n] fichero padre [fee-che'-ro pa'-dray]

parity bit [np] bit de paridad [beet day pa-ree-dad']

parity check [np] control de paridad [kon-trol' day pa-ree-dad']

parity error [np] error de paridad [air-ror' day pa-ree-dad']

parser [n] analizador de carácteres [a-na-lee-sa-dor' day ka-rak'-te-res]

parsing [n] analización [a-na-lee-sa-syon']

part operation [np] operación parcial [o-pe-ra-syon' par-syal']

partial carry [np] arrastre parcial [ar-ras'-tray par-syal']

passing parameters [np] parámetro superficial [pa-ra'-me-tro soo-per-fee-syal']

password [n] contraseña [kon-tra-sen'-ya]

paste [v] pegar [pe-gar']

patch [v] remendar [re-men-dar']

patch [v] componer [kom-po-ner']

patch [n] parche [par'-chay]

patchboard [n] tablero de conectadores [ta-ble'-ro day ko-nek-ta-do'-res]

patchcord [n] cable de conexión [ka'-blay day ko-nek-syon']

path [v] cursar [koor-sar']

path [n] curso [koor'-so]

path [n] paso [pa'-so]

pattern recognition [np] reconocimiento de configuración [re-ko-no-see-myen'-to day kon-fee-goo-ra-syon']

PQCM plug compatible manufacturer [np] fabricante de tapónes compatibles [fa-bree-kan'-tay day ta-po'-nes kom-pa-tee'-bles]

pedestal [n] pedestal [pe-des-tal']

peek [n] mirada rápida [mee-ra'-da ra'-pee-da]

perforated tape [np] cinta con perforación [seen'-ta kon per-fo-ra-syon']

perforation rate [np] régimen de perforación [re'-hee-men day per-fo-ra-syon']

perforator [n] perforador [per-fo-ra-dor']

performance monitor [np] monitor de ejecución [mo-nee-tor' day e-he-koo-syon']

perfs [n] agujeros [a-goo-he'-ros]

peripheral controller [np] controlador periférico [kon-tro-la-dor' pe-ree-fe'-ree-ko]

peripheral processor [np] procesador periférico [pro-se-sa-dor' pe-ree-fe'-ree-ko]

peripheral transfer [np] transferencia periférica [trans-fe-ren'-sya pe-ree-fe'-ree-ka]

peripheral unit [np] unidad periférica [oo-nee-dad' pe-ree-fe'-ree-ka]

peripheral-limited [adj] limitado por los periféricos [lee-mee-ta'-do por los pe-ree-fe'-ree-kos]

permanent memory [np] memoria permanente [me-mo'-rya per-ma-nen'-tay]

personal computer [np] computador personal [kom-poo-ta-dor' per-so-nal']

petri nets [np] petri nets [pe'-tree nets]

photoelectric devices [np] aparato fotoeléctrico [a-pa-ra'-to fo-to-e-lek'-tree-ko]

photoresist [n] fotoresistivo [fo-to-re-sees-tee'-bo]

photo-optic memory [np] memoria fotográfica óptica [me-mo'-rya fo-to-gra'-fee-ka op'-tee-ka]

physical file [np] fichero físico [fee-che'-ro fee'-see-ko]

pica [n] pica [pee'-ka]

picture graph [np] gráfico en barras [gra'-fee-ko en bar'-ras]

piggyback board [np] tablero electrónico con trasera [ta-ble'-ro e-lek-tro'-nee-ko kon tra-se'-ra]

piggyback file [np] archivo con trasera [ar-chee'-bo kon tra-se'-ra]

pinboard [n] tablero de estacas [ta-ble'-ro day es-ta'-kas]

pitch [n] grado de inclinación [gra'-do day een-klee-na-syon']

pixel [n] pixel [peek-sel']

plaintext [n] texto plano [tex'-to pla'-no]

platen [n] rollo [ro'-yo]

platter [n] platillo [pla-tee'-yo]

playback head [np] cabeza reproductora [ka-be'-sa re-pro-dook-to'-ra]

plotter [n] trazadora [tra-sa-do'-ra]

plug [v] tapar [ta-par']

plug [n] tapón [ta-pon']

plug compatible manufacturer (PCM) [np] fabricante de tapónes compatibles [fa-bree-kan'-tay day ta-po'-nes kom-pa-tee'-bles]

plug in [v] enchufar [en-choo-far']

plug in [n] cicuito de enchufe [seer-kwee'-to day en-choo'-fay]

plugboard [n] tablero de enchufe [ta-ble'-ro day en-choo'-fay]

plus zone [np] zona positiva [so'-na po-see-tee'-ba]

PM preventive maintenance [np] mantenimiento preventivo [man-te-nee-myen'-to pre-ben-tee'-bo]

PN Polish notation [np] notación polaca [no-ta-syon' po-la'-ka]

pneumatic computer [np] computador neumático [kom-poo-ta-dor' ne-oo-ma'-tee-ko]

poaching [adj] furtivo [foor-tee'-bo]

pointer [n] indicador [een-dee-ka-dor']

point-mode display [np] representación de modo puntual [re-pre-sen-ta-syon' day mo'-do poon-twal']

poke [v] poner rápido [po-ner' ra'-pee-do]

Polish notation (PN) [np] notación polaca [no-ta-syon' po-la'-ka]

polling [n] elección [e-lek-syon']

polygon clipping [np] recorte polígonal [re-kor'-tay po-lee'-go-nal]

pooler [n] convertidor de teclado [kon-ber-tee-dor' day tek-la'-do]

pop [v] dar un tirón [dar oon tee-ron']

port [n] portilla [por-tee'-ya]

portability [n] cualidad portátil [kwa-lee-dad' por-ta'-teel]

portable computer [np] computador portátil [kom-poo-ta-dor' por-ta'-teel]

positional notation [np] notación posicional [no-ta-syon' po-see-syo-nal']

post edit [v] post-editar [post e-dee-tar']

post mortem dump [np] vaciado póstumo [ba-sya'-do pos'-too-mo]

post mortem routine [np] rutina póstuma [roo-tee'-na pos'-too-ma]

power down [v] apagar [a-pa-gar']

power on [v] prender [pren-der']

pragmatics [n] pragmática [prag-ma'-tee-ka]

precanned routines [n] rutinas enlatadas [roo-tee'-nas en-la-ta'-das]

precision [n] precisión [pre-see-syon']

prefix notation [np] notación por prefijos [no-ta-syon por pre-fee'-hos]

preprocessor [n] preprocesador [pre-pro-se-sa-dor']

preset parameter [np] parámetro definido previamente [pa-ra'-me-tro de-fee-nee'-do pre-bya-men'-tay]

press [n] golpe seco [gol'-pay se'-ko]

preventive maintenance (PM) [np] mantenimiento preventivo [man-te-nee-myen'-to pre-ben-tee'-bo]

pre-edit [v] pre-editar [pre e-dee-tar']

pre-read head [np] cabeza de lectura previa [ka-be'-sa day lek-too'-ra pre'-bya]

pre-sort [v] pre-separar [pre se-pa-rar']

pre-sort [n] pre-separado [pre se-pa-ra'-do]

pre-store [v] pre-almacenar [pre al-ma-se-nar']

PRF pulse repetition frequency [np] frequencia de repetición de impulsos [fre-kwen'-sya day re-pe-tee-syon' day eem-pool'-sos]

primary cluster [np] agrupación primordial [a-groo-pa-syon' pree-mor-dyal']

primary colors [np] colores primordiales [ko-lo'-res pree-mor-dya'-les]

primary storage [np] memoria principal [me-mo'-rya preen-see-pal']

primitive [adj] primitivo [pree-mee-tee'-bo]

primitive data type [np] typo de datos primitivos [tee'-po day da'-tos pree-mee-tee'-bos]

primitive element [np] elemento primitivo [e-le-men'-to pree-mee-tee'-bo]

print barrel [np] cilindro impresor [see-leen'-dro eem-pre-sor']

print format [np] formato de impresión [for-ma'-to day eem-pre-syon']

print wheel [np] rueda de impresión [rwe'-da day eem-pre-syon']

printer [n] impresora [eem-pre-so'-ra]

printer stand [np] pedestal de impresora [pe-des-tal' day eem-pre-so'-ra]

printing punch [np] perforadora de impresión [per-fo-ra-do'-ra day eem-pre-syon']

printout [v] imprimir [eem-pree-meer']

printout [n] impresión [eem-pre-syon']

priority indicator [np] indicador de prioridad [een-dee-ka-dor' day pryo-ree-dad']

priority processing [np] proceso por prioridad [pro-se'-so por pryo-ree-dad']

privacy [n] privado [pree-ba'-do]

private code [np] código reservado [ko'-dee-go re-ser-ba'-do]

probability [n] probabilidad [pro-ba-bee-lee-dad']

problem definition [np] definición del problema [de-fee-nee-syon' del pro-ble'-ma]

problem solving [np] solución del problema [so-loo-syon' del pro-ble'-ma]

problem-oriented language [np] lenguaje orientado a los problemas [len-gwa'-hay o-ryen-ta'-do a los pro-ble'-mas]

procedure [n] procedimiento [pro-se-dee-myen'-to]

procedure-oriented language [np] lenguaje orientado a los procedimientos [len-gwa'-hay o-ryen-ta'-do a los pro-se-dee-myen'-tos]

process [v] procesar [pro-se-sar']

process [n] proceso [pro-se'-so]

process control [np] control de procesos [kon-trol' day pro-se'-sos]

process conversion [np] conversión de procesos [kon-ber-syon' day pro-se'-sos]

processing [n] procesamiento [pro-se-sa-myen'-to]

processor [n] procesador [pro-se-sa-dor']

processor-bound [adj] procesador vinculado [pro-se-sa-dor' been-koo-la'-do]

processor-limited [adj] procesador limitado [pro-se-sa-dor' lee-mee-ta'-do]

production run [np] pasada de producción [pa-sa'-da day pro-dook-syon']

productive time [np] tiempo de producción [tyem'-po day pro-dook-syon']

program [v] programar [pro-gra-mar']

program [n] programa [pro-gra'-ma]

program chaining [np] encadenación del programa [en-ka-de-na-syon' del pro-gra'-ma]

program compatibility [np] compatibilidad de programas [kom-pa-tee-bee-lee-dad' day pro-gra'-mas]

program flowchart [np] flujograma de programa [floo-ho-gra'-ma day pro-gra'-ma]

program generator [np] generador de programas [he-ne-ra-dor' day pro-gra'-mas]

program library [np] biblioteca de programas [bee-blyo-te'-ka day pro-gra'-mas]

program modification [np] modificación del programa [mo-dee-fee-ka-syon' del pro-gra'-ma]

program package [np] colección de programas [ko-lek-syon' day pro-gra'-mas]

program parameter [np] parámetro del programa [pa-ra'-me-tro del pro-gra'-ma]

program specification [np] especificación del programa [es-pe-see-fee-ka-syon' del pro-gra'-ma]

program stack [np] pila del programa [pee'-la del pro-gra'-ma]

program testing [np] ensayo del programa [en-sa'-yo del pro-gra'-ma]

programmable [adj] programable [pro-gra-ma'-blay]

programmable function key [np] tecla funcional programable [tek'-la foon-syo-nal' pro-gra-ma'-blay]

programmable read-only memory (PROM) [np] memoria fija programable [me-mo'-rya fee'-ha pro-gra-ma'-blay]

programmed [n] programado [pro-gra-ma'-do]

programmer [n] programador [pro-gra-ma-dor']

programming [n] programación [pro-gra-ma-syon']

programming aids [np] ayuda de programación [a-yoo'-da day pro-gra-ma-syon']

programming language [np] lenguaje de programación [len-gwa'-hay day pro-gra-ma-syon']

projecting [adj] proyectando [pro-yek-tan'-do]

PROM programmable read-only memory [np] memoria fija programable [me-mo'-rya fee'-ha pro-gra-ma'-blay]

prompt [n] guía [gee'-a]

proof [n] prueba [prwe'-ba]

proof total [np] comprobación total [kom-pro-ba-syon' to-tal']

propagated error [np] error propagado [air-ror' pro-pa-ga'-do]

propagation delay [np] retardo de propagación [re-tar'-do day pro-pa-ga-syon']

proportional control [np] control proporcional [kon-trol' pro-por-syo-nal']

protect [v] proteger [pro-te-her']

protected location [np] posición protegida [po-see-syon' pro-te-hee'-da]

protected record [np] registro protegido [re-hees'-tro pro-te-hee'-do]

protection [n] protección [pro-tek-syon']

protocol [n] protocolo [pro-to-ko'-lo]

proving [n] sistema probado [sees-te'-ma pro-ba'-do]

proving time [np] tiempo de ensayo [tyem'-po day en-sa'-yo]

pseudocode [n] pseudocódigo [se-oo-do-ko'-dee-go]

pseudoinstruction [n] pseudo-instrucción [se-oo'-do een-strook-syon']

pseudooperation [n] pseudo-operación [se-oo'-do o-pe-ra-syon']

pseudorandom [n] pseudo-casual [se-oo'-do ka-swal']

public domain software [np] soporte lógico en dominio público [so-por'-tay lo'-hee-ko en do-mee'-nyo poob'-lee-ko]

puck [n] ventanita [ben-ta-nee'-ta]

pull-down menu [np] menú de tirar [me-noo' day tee-rar']

pulse [n] impulso [eem-pool'-so]

pulse modulation [np] modulación de pulsación [mo-doo-la-syon' day pool-sa-syon']

pulse repetition frequency (PRF) [np] frequencia de repetición de impulsos [fre-kwen'-sya day re-pe-tee-syon' day eem-pool'-sos]

pulse train [np] tren de impulsos [tren day eem-pool'-sos]

punch [v] perforar [per-fo-rar']

punch [n] perforadora [per-fo-ra-do'-ra]

punch card [np] tarjeta de perforación [tar-he'-ta day per-fo-ra-syon']

punch verifier [np] verificador de perforación [be-ree-fee-ka-dor' day per-fo-ra-syon']

punched card [np] tarjeta perforada [tar-he'-ta per-fo-ra'-da]

punched tape [np] cinta perforada [seen'-ta per-fo-ra'-da]

punching position [np] posición de perforación [po-see-syon' day per-fo-ra-syon']

punching rate [np] velocidad de perforación [be-lo-see-dad' day per-fo-ra-syon']

purge [n] purga [poor'-ga]

push-down list [np] lista de abajo hacia arriba [lees'-ta day a-ba'-ho a'-sya ar-ree'-ba]

push-pop stack [np] pila de empuje y vaciado [pee'-la day em-poo'-hay ee ba-sya'-do]

push-up list [np] lista de empuje al final [lees'-ta day em-poo'-hay al fee-nal']

put [v] colocar [ko-lo-kar']

Q

quantization [n] cuantificación [kwan-tee-fee-ka-syon']

quantize [v] cuantificar [kwan-tee-fee-kar']

quantizer [n] cuantificador [kwan-tee-fee-ka-dor']

quasi-instruction [n] cuasi-instrucción [kwa'-see een-strook-syon']

query [n] interrogación [een-ter-ro-ga-syon']

query by example [np] ejemplo por interrogación [e-hem'-plo por een-ter-ro-ga-syon']

query language [np] lenguaje de interrogación [len-gwa'-hay day een-ter-ro-ga-syon']

queuing [n] esperando [es-pe-ran'-do]

queuing theory [np] teoría de esperar [te-o-ree'-a day es-pe-rar']

R

radix [n] base [ba'-say]

radix [n] raíz [ra-ees']

radix complement [np] complemento de la base [kom-ple-men'-to day la ba'-say]

radix point [np] punto de la base [poon'-to day la ba'-say]

ragged left [np] lado izquierdo roto [la'-do ees-kyer'-do ro'-to]

ragged right [np] lado derecho roto [la'-do de-re'-cho ro'-to]

RAM random-access memory [np] memoria de acceso casual [me-mo'-rya day ak-se'-so ka-swal']

ramdomly [adv] casualmente [ka-swal-men'-tay]

random [adj] casual [ka-swal']

random access [np] acceso casual [ak-se'-so ka-swal']

random files [np] ficheros casuales [fee-che'-ros ka-swa'-les]

random number generator [np] generador de números casuales [he-ne-ra-dor' day noo'-me-ros ka-swa'-les]

random-access memory (RAM) [np] memoria de acceso casual [me-mo'-rya day ak-se'-so ka-swal']

range [n] margen [mar'-hen]

range check [np] examinación de la variación [ek-sa-mee-na-syon' day la ba-rya-syon']

range independent [np] independiente del margen [een-de-pen-dyen'-tay del mar'-hen]

rank [n] rango [ran'-go]

rapid-access loop [np] bucle de acceso rápido [boo'-klay day ak-se'-do ra'-pee-do]

raster [n] presentación de líneas [pre-sen-ta-syon' day lee'-ne-as]

raster display [np] presentación visual de líneas [pre-sen-ta-syon' bee-swal' day lee'-ne-as]

raster fill [np] llenado entre líneas [ye-na'-do en'-tray lee'-ne-as]

raster graphics [np] dibujo con líneas [dee-boo'-ho kon lee'-ne-as]

raster scan [np] escudriñado de líneas [es-koo-dreen-ya'-do day lee'-ne-as]

raw data [np] datos sin procesar [da'-tos seen pro-se-sar']

read [v] leer [le-er']

read [n] lectura [lek-too'-ra]

read head [np] cabeza de lectura [ka-be'-sa day lek-too'-ra]

read out [np] lectura de salida [lek-too'-ra day sa-lee'-da]

read out [np] información de salida [een-for-ma-syon' day sa-lee'-da]

read rate [np] velocidad de lectura [be-lo-see-dad' day lek-too'-ra]

read time [np] tiempo de lectura [tyem'-po day lek-too'-ra]

reader [n] leedor [le-e-dor']

read-only memory (ROM) [np] memoria de lectura fija [me-mo'-rya day lek-too'-ra fee'-ha]

read-write channel [np] canal de lectura-escritura [ka-nal' day lek-too'-ra es-kree-too'-ra]

read-write head [np] cabeza de lectura-escritura [ka-be'-sa day lek-too'-ra es-kree-too'-ra]

real storage [np] memoria real [me-mo'-rya re-al']

real time [np] tiempo real [tyem'-po re-al']

real-time clock [np] reloj binario [re-lo' bee-na'-ryo]

real-time clock [np] reloj de tiempo real [re-lo' day tyem'-po re-al']

real-time processing [np] proceso en tiempo real [pro-se'-so en tyem'-po re-al']

reasonableness check [np] verificación de tolerancia [be-ree-fee-ka-syon' day to-le-ran'-sya]

reboot [n] reanudación [re-a-noo-da-syon']

recompile [v] recompilar [re-kom-pee-lar']

reconfiguration [n] reconfiguración [re-kon-fee-goo-ra-syon']

reconstitution [n] reconstitución [re-kon-stee-too-syon']

record [v] registrar [re-hees-trar']

record [n] registro [re-hees'-tro]

record blocking [np] bloqueo de registro [blo-ke'-o day re-hees'-tro]

record head [np] cabeza de registro [ka-be'-sa day re-hees'-tro]

record layout [np] arreglo del registro [ar-reg'-lo del re-hees'-tro]

record length [np] longitud de registro [lon-hee-tood' day re-hees'-tro]

recording density [np] densidad de registro [den-see-dad' day re-hees'-tro]

recover [v] restablecer [re-stab-le-ser']

recovery [n] recuperación [re-koo-pe-ra-syon']

recursion [n] recursión [re-koor-syon']

recursive [adj] recursivo [re-koor-see'-bo]

reduce format [np] formato reducido [for-ma'-to re-doo-see'-do]

redundancy [n] redundancia [re-doon-dan'-sya]

redundancy check [np] verificación por redundancia [be-ree-fee-ka-syon' por re-doon-dan'-sya]

redundant code [np] código redundante [ko'-dee-go re-doon-dan'-tay]

red-green-blue monitor (RGB) [np] monitor rojo-verde-azul [mo-nee-tor' ro'-ho ber'-day a-sool']

reel [n] carrete [kar-re'-tay]

reel number [np] número de carrete [noo'-me-ro day kar-re'-tay]

reentrant [n] reentrada [re-en-tra'-da]

reentrant code [np] código de reentrada [ko'-dee-go day re-en-tra'-da]

reentrant subroutine [np] subrutina de reentrada [soob-roo-tee'-na day re-en-tra'-da]

reference address [np] dirección de referencia [dee-rek-syon' day re-fe-ren'-sya]

reference listing [np] lista de referencias [lees'-ta day re-fe-ren'-syas]

reflectance [n] reflectora [re-flek-to'-ra]

reflectance ink [np] tinta reflectora [teen'-ta re-flek-to'-ra]

refresh [v] regenerar [re-he-ne-rar']

refresh circuitry [np] circuito regenerado [seer-kwee'-to re-he-ne-ra'-do]

refresh display [np] representación regenerada [re-pre-sen-ta-syon' re-he-ne-ra'-da]

refresh rate [np] velocidad de regeneración [be-lo-see-dad' day re-he-ne-ra-syon']

refreshed display [np] visual regenerado [bee-swal' re-he-ne-ra'-do]

regenerate [v] regenerarse [re-he-ne-rar'-say]

regeneration [n] regeneración [re-he-ne-ra-syon']

regenerative read [np] lectura regenerativa [lek-too'-ra re-he-ne-ra-tee'-ba]

regenerative storage [np] memoria regenerativa [me-mo'-rya re-he-ne-ra-tee'-ba]

register [n] registro [re-hees'-tro]

regression testing [np] prueba de regresión [prwe'-ba day re-gre-syon']

relational expression [np] expresión de relación [ex-pre-syon' day re-la-syon']

relational model [np] modelo de relación [mo-de'-lo day re-la-syon']

relational operator [np] operador de relación [o-pe-ra-dor' day re-la-syon']

relative address [np] dirección relativa [dee-rek-syon' re-la-tee'-ba]

relative addressing [np] direccionado relativo [dee-rek-syo-na'-do re-la-tee'-bo]

relative code [np] código relativo [ko'-dee-go re-la-tee'-bo]

relay [n] reemisor [re-e-mee-sor']

relay [n] relé [re-lay']

relay center [np] centro de retransmisión [sen'-tro day re-trans-mee-syon']

release [v] soltar [sol-tar']

release [v] libertar [lee-ber-tar']

release [n] soltura [sol-too'-ra]

reliability [n] confiabilidad [kon-fya-bee-lee-dad']

reliable [adj] confiable [kon-fya'-blay]

reload [v] recargar [re-kar-gar']

relocatable address [np] dirección reubicable [dee-rek-syon' re-oo-bee-ka'-blay]

relocatable code [np] código reubicable [ko'-dee-go re-oo-bee-ka'-blay]

relocate [v] reubicar [re-oo-bee-kar']

relocate [n] resituado [re-see-twa'-do]

remark [n] notar [no-tar']

remote batch processing [np] procesamiento remoto de lotes [pro-se-sa-myen'-to re-mo'-to day lo'-tes]

remote computing system [np] sistema de cálculo a distancia [sees-te'-ma day kal'-koo-lo a dees-tan'-sya]

remote console [np] consola remota [kon-so'-la re-mo'-ta]

remote job entry [np] entrada de trabajos a distancia [en-tra'-da day tra-ba'-hos a dees-tan'-sya]

remote processing [np] proceso a distancia [pro-se'-so a dees-tan'-sya]

remote site [np] localidad distante [lo-ka-lee-dad' dees-tan'-tay]

remote terminal [np] terminar teledirigido [ter-mee-nar' te-le-dee-ree-hee'-do]

remote testing [np] ensayo a distancia [en-sa'-yo a dees-tan'-sya]

reorganize [v] reorganizar [re-or-ga-nee-sar']

repagination [n] repaginación [re-pa-hee-na-syon']

repaint [v] repintar [re-peen-tar']

repair time [np] tiempo de reparación [tyem'-po day re-pa-ra-syon']

repeat key [np] tecla de repetición [tek'-la day re-pe-tee-syon']

repertoire [n] repertorio [re-per-to'-ryo]

repetition instruction [np] instrucción de repetición [een-strook-syon' day re-pe-tee-syon']

repetitive addressing [np] direccionado repetitivo [dee-rek-syo-na'-do re-pe-tee-tee'-bo]

replication [n] réplica [rep'-lee-ka]

report file [np] archivo de reporte [ar-chee'-bo day re-por'-tay]

report generator [np] generador de informes [he-ne-ra-dor' day een-for'-mes]

report program [np] programa de informes [pro-gra'-ma day een-for'-mes]

reproducer [n] reproductor [re-pro-dook-tor']

reroute [v] reencaminar [re-en-ka-mee-nar']

reroute information [np] desviación de información [des-bya-syon' day een-for-ma-syon']

rerun [v] repetir la pasada [re-pe-teer' la pa-sa'-da]

rerun [n] repetición de pasada [re-pe-tee-syon' day pa-sa'-da]

rerun point [np] punto de reanudación de pasada [poon'-to day re-a-noo-da-syon' day pa-sa'-da]

rescue dump [np] vaciado de rescate [ba-sya'-do day res-ka'-tay]

reserve [v] reservar [re-ser-bar']

reset [v] reajustar [re-a-hoos-tar']

reset pulse [np] impulso de reposición [eem-pool'-so day re-po-see-syon']

reside [v] residir [re-see-deer']

resident routine [np] rutina residente [roo-tee'-na re-see-den'-tay]

residual error [np] error residual [air-ror' re-see-dwal']

residual value [np] valor residual [ba-lor' re-see-dwal']

residue check [np] verificación por residuo [be-ree-fee-ka-syon' por re-see'-dwo]

resilience [n] resiliencia [re-see-lyen'-sya]

resistor-transistor logic (RTL) [np] lógica de resistencia-transistor [lo'-hee-ka day re-sees-ten'-sya tran-sees-tor']

resizing [n] redimensionar [re-dee-men-syo-nar']

resource [n] recurso [re-koor'-so]

resource allocation [np] asignación de recursos [a-seeg-na-syon' day re-koor'-sos]

resource file [np] archivo de recurso [ar-chee'-bo day re-koor'-so]

resource leveling [np] nivelación de recursos [nee-be-la-syon' day re-koor'-sos]

response time [np] tiempo de respuesta [tyem'-po day res-pwes'-ta]

restart [v] reanudar [re-a-noo-dar']

restart [n] reanudación [re-a-noo-da-syon']

restart point [np] punto de reanudación [poon'-to day re-a-noo-da-syon']

restore [v] restaurar [res-tow-rar']

retention period [np] período de retención [pe-ree'-o-do day re-ten-syon']

reticle [n] retículo [re-tee'-koo-lo]

retrieval [n] recuperación [re-koo-pe-ra-syon']

retrofit [n] retroapto [re-tro-ap'-to]

return [v] retornar [re-tor-nar']

return [n] retorno [re-tor'-no]

return instruction [np] instrucción de retorno [een-strook-syon' day re-tor'-no]

RETURN key [n] tecla de REGRESO [tek'-la day REGRESO]

reverse Polish notation [np] notación polaca inversa [no-ta-syon' po-la'-ka een-ber'-sa]

reverse video [np] video invertido [bee-de'-o een-ber-tee'-do]

reversible counter [np] contador reversible [kon-ta-dor' re-ber-see'-blay]

review [n] revisión [re-bee-syon']

rewind [v] rebobinar [re-bo-bee-nar']

rewrite [v] reescribir [re-es-kree-beer']

re-entrant procedure [np] procedimiento reentrante [pro-se-dee-myen'-to re-en-tran'-tay]

RGB red-green-blue monitor [np] monitor rojo-verde-azul [mo-nee-tor' ro'-ho ber'-day a-sool']

right shift [np] desplazamiento a la derecha [des-pla-sa-myen'-to a la de-re'-cha]

right-justified [adj] justificado a la derecha [hoos-tee-fee-ka'-do a la de-re'-cha]

ring counter [np] contador en círculo [kon-ta-dor' en seer'-koo-lo]

ring network [np] redes en círculo [re'-des en seer'-koo-lo]

ring shift [np] desplazamiento en círculo [des-pla-sa-myen'-to en seer'-koo-lo]

ripple sort [np] clasificación en onda [kla-see-fee-ka-syon' en on'-da]

roam [v] recorrer [re-kor-rer']

robot [n] autómata [ow-to'-ma-ta]

robotics [n] robótica [ro-bo'-tee-ka]

roll out [np] rodando [ro-dan'-do]

rollback [n] enrollar [en-ro-yar']

rollover [n] rodando [ro-dan'-do]

ROM read-only memory [np] memoria de lectura fija [me-mo'-rya day lek-too'-ra fee'-ha]

root [n] raíz del árbol [ra-ees' del ar'-bol]

rotational delay [np] retraso rotacional [re-tra'-so ro-ta-syo-nal']

round off [v] redondear [re-don-de-ar']

round robin [np] en rotación [en ro-ta-syon']

rounding error [np] error de redondeo [air-ror' day re-don-de'-o]

route [v] encaminar [en-ka-mee-nar']

route [n] ruta [roo'-ta]

routine [n] rutina [roo-tee'-na]

routine maintenance [np] mantenimiento de rutina [man-te-nee-myen'-to day roo-tee'-na]

row [n] fila [fee'-la]

row pitch [np] paso entre filas [pa'-so en'-tray fee'-las]

RTL resistor-transistor logic [np] lógica de resistencia-transistor [lo'-hee-ka day re-sees-ten'-sya tran-sees-tor']

rubber banding [np] banda de jebe [ban'-da day he'-bay]

run [v] pasar [pa-sar']

run [n] pasada [pa-sa'-da]

run time [np] tiempo de pasada [tyem'-po day pa-sa'-da]

S

sample data [np] datos de muestra [da'-tos day mwes'-tra]

sampling [n] muestreo [mwes-tre'-o]

sampling rate [np] frequencia del muestreo [fre-kwen'-sya del mwes-tre'-o]

sans serif [n] sin serif [seen se-reef']

satellite computer [np] computador satélite [kom-poo-ta-dor' sa-te'-lee-tay]

saturated [adj] saturado [sa-too-ra'-do]

scale [n] escala [es-ka'-la]

scale factor [np] factor de la escala [fak-tor' day la es-ka'-la]

scaling [adj] escalada [es-ka-la'-da]

scan [v] explorar [ex-plo-rar']

scan [n] exploración [ex-plo-ra-syon']

scanner [n] explorador [ex-plo-ra-dor']

scanning [adj] escudriñando [es-koo-dreen-yan'-do]

scatter plot [np] trazo de dispersión [tra'-so day dees-per-syon']

scatter read-gather write [np] lea disperso-escriba junto [le'-a dees-per'-so es-kree'-ba hoon'-to]

scheduled maintenance [np] mantenimiento planeado [man-te-nee-myen'-to pla-ne-a'-do]

scheduled maintenance [np] mantenimiento programado [man-te-nee-myen'-to pro-gra-ma'-do]

scheduling [n] planificación [pla-nee-fee-ka-syon']

schema [n] esquema [es-ke'-ma]

schematic [n] esquemático [es-ke-ma'-tee-ko]

schematic symbols [n] símbolos de esquemáticos [seem'-bo-los day es-ke-ma'-tee-kos]

scissoring [adj] recortando [re-kor-tan'-do]

scrapbook [n] álbum de recortes [al'-boom day re-kor'-tes]

scratch [v] borrar [bor-rar']

scratch file [np] fichero de trabajo [fee-che'-ro day tra-ba'-ho]

scratch pad [np] bloc de notas [blok day no'-tas]

screen [n] pantalla [pan-ta'-ya]

screen dump [np] vuelco de pantalla [bwel'-ko day pan-ta'-ya]

screen position [np] posición en la pantalla [po-see-syon' en la pan-ta'-ya]

screen size [np] tamaño de la pantalla [ta-man'-yo day la pan-ta'-ya]

scrolling [n] enrollamiento [en-ro-ya-myen'-to]

search [v] buscar [boos-kar']

search [n] búsqueda [boos'-ke-da]

search and replace [np] búsque y reponga [boos'-kay ee re-pon'-ga]

search string [np] series de búsqueda [se'-ryes day boos'-ke-da]

search time [np] tiempo de búsqueda [tyem'-po day boos'-ke-da]

secondary key [np] llave secundaria [ya'-bay se-koon-da'-rya]

secondary storage [np] almacenamiento de memoria secundaria [al-ma-se-na-myen'-to day me-mo'-rya se-koon-da'-rya]

second-generation [adj] segunda-generación [se-goon'-da he-ne-ra-syon']

second-level address [np] dirección de segundo nivel [dee-rek-syon' day se-goon'-do nee-bel']

secure kernel [np] núcleo primitivo asegurado [nook'-le-o pree-mee-tee'-bo a-se-goo-ra'-do]

segment [v] segmentar [seg-men-tar']

segment [n] segmento [seg-men'-to]

segment mark [np] marca de segmento [mar'-ka day seg-men'-to]

segmented program [np] programa segmentado [pro-gra'-ma seg-men-ta'-do]

select [v] seleccionar [se-lek-syo-nar']

selector [n] selector [se-lek-tor']

selector channel [np] canal selector [ka-nal' se-lek-tor']

self-adapting [adj] autoadaptado [ow-to-a-dap-ta'-do]

self-checking number [np] número autoverificador [noo'-me-ro ow-to-be-ree-fee-ka-dor']

self-organizing [adj] autoestructurado [ow-to-es-trook-too-ra'-do]

semantic [adj] semántico [se-man'-tee-ko]

semaphores [n] semáforado [se-ma'-fo-ra-do]

semiautomatic [adj] semiautomático [se-mee-ow-to-ma'-tee-ko]

semiconductor [n] semiconductor [se-mee-kon-dook-tor']

semiconductor array [np] hilera de semiconductores [ee-le'-ra day se-mee-kon-dook-to'-res]

semiconductor memory [np] memoria de semiconductores [me-mo'-rya day se-mee-kon-dook-to'-res]

semirandom access [np] acceso semicasual [ak-se'-so se-mee-ka-swal']

send only (SO) [np] envio solo [en'-byo so'-lo]

sense [v] detectar [de-tek-tar']

sense probe [np] sonda de sentir [son'-da day sen-teer']

sensors [n] sensor [sen-sor']

separator [n] separador [se-pa-ra-dor']

sequence [v] secuenciar [se-kwen-syar']

sequence [n] secuencia [se-kwen'-sya]

sequence check [np] verificación de secuencia [be-ree-fee-ka-syon' day se-kwen'-sya]

sequential access [np] acceso secuencial [ak-se'-so se-kwen-syal']

sequential data set [np] conjunto de datos secuenciales [kon-hoon'-to day da'-tos se-kwen-sya'-les]

sequential device [np] aparato de secuencia [a-pa-ra'-to day se-kwen'-sya]

sequential file [np] fichero secuencial [fee-che'-ro se-kwen-syal']

sequential logic [np] lógica de secuencia [lo'-hee-ka day se-kwen'-sya]

sequential processing [np] proceso secuencial [pro-se'-so se-kwen-syal']

sequential search [np] búsqueda en secuencia [boos'-ke-da en se-kwen'-sya]

serial access [np] acceso en serie [ak-se'-so en se'-ryay]

serial interface [np] interfase en series [een-ter-fa'-say en se'-ryes]

serial port [np] portilla de series [por-tee'-ya day se'-ryes]

serial printer [np] impresora en serie [eem-pre-so'-ra en se'-ryay]

serial processing [np] proceso en serie [pro-se'-so en se'-ryay]

serial transfer [np] transferencia en series [trans-fe-ren'-sya en se'-ryes]

serial transmission [np] transmisión en series [trans-mee-syon' en se'-ryes]

serial-parallel converter [np] convertidor serie-paralelo [kon-ber-tee-dor' ser'-ryay pa-ra-le'-lo]

service bit [np] bit de servicio [beet day ser-bee'-syo]

service programs [np] programa de servicio [pro-gra'-ma day ser-bee'-syo]

service routine [np] rutina de servicio [roo-tee'-na day ser-bee'-syo]

serviceability [n] aptitude de servicio [ap-tee-too'-day day ser-bee'-syo]

set [v] ajustar [a-hoos-tar']

set [n] conjunto [kon-hoon'-to]

setup [n] preparación [pre-pa-ra-syon']

setup time [np] tiempo de preparación [tyem'-po day pre-pa-ra-syon']

shade [np] sombra [som'-bra]

shading symbols [np] símbolo de sombreado [seem'-bo-lo day som-bre-a'-do]

shadow printing [np] impresión de obscuridad [eem-pre-syon' day ob-skoo-ree-dad']

shared files [np] ficheros compartidos [fee-che'-ros kom-par-tee'-dos]

shareware [np] soporte lógico en dominio público [so-por'-tay lo'-hee-ko en do-mee'-nyo poob'-lee-ko]

sharpness [n] agudo [a-goo'-do]

shielding [adj] resguardador [res-gwar-da-dor']

shift [v] desplazar [des-pla-sar']

shift [n] desplazamiento [des-pla-sa-myen'-to]

SHIFT key [n] tecla de desplazamiento [tek'-la day des-pla-sa-myen'-to]

shift register [np] registro de desplazamiento [re-hees'-tro day des-pla-sa-myen'-to]

shift-click [n] golpe seco con mayúscula [gol'-pay se'-ko kon ma-yoos'-koo-la]

shutdown [n] cierre [syer'-ray]

sibling [n] hijos nodales [ee'-hos no-da'-les]

sift [v] cerner [ser-ner']

sifting [adj] cerniendo [ser-nyen'-do]

sign [n] signo [seeg'-no]

sign bit [n] bit de signo [beet day seeg'-no]

sign check indicator [np] indicador del signo de verificación [een-dee-ka-dor' del seeg'-no day be-ree-fee-ka-syon']

sign digit [np] dígito de signo [dee'-hee-to day seeg'-no]

sign flag [np] señalador del signo [sen-ya-la-dor' del seeg'-no]

signal [n] señal [sen-yal']

signal distance [np] distancia de señal [dees-tan'-sya day sen-yal']

signaling rate [np] velocidad de transmisión de señal [be-lo-see-dad' day trans-mee-syon' day sen-yal']

signal-to-noise ratio [np] relación de señal-ruido [re-la-syon' day sen-yal' rwee'-do]

significant digits [np] dígitos significativos [dee'-hee-tos seeg-nee-fee-ka-tee'-bos]

signing-on [adj] inscribirse [een-skree-beer'-say]

silicon [n] silicio [see-lee'-syo]

silicon chip [np] plaqueta de silicio [pla-ke'-ta day see-lee'-syo]

silicon wafer [np] oblea de silicio [ob-le'-a day see-lee'-syo]

simplex [n] simplex [seem-plex']

simulation [n] simulación [see-moo-la-syon']

simulator [n] simulador [see-moo-la-dor']

simultaneous access [np] acceso simultáneo [ak-se'-so see-mool-ta'-ne-o]

simultaneous processing [np] procesamiento simultáneo [pro-se-sa-myen'-to see-mool-ta'-ne-o]

single address instruction [np] instrucción de una sola dirección [een-strook-syon' day oo'-na so'-la dee-rek-syon']

single-sided disk [np] disco de un lado [dees'-ko day oon la'-do]

single-step operation [np] operación de un paso [o-pe-ra-syon' day oon pa'-so]

skeletal code [np] código esquemático [ko'-dee-go es-ke-ma'-tee-ko]

sketch pad [np] bloc de dibujo [blok day dee-boo'-ho]

sketching [adj] dibujando [dee-boo-han'-do]

skew [n] sesgado [ses-ga'-do]

skip [v] omitir [o-mee-teer']

slab [n] parte de la palabra [par'-tay day la pa-la'-bra]

slack time [np] tiempo flotante [tyem'-po flo-tan'-tay]

slave storage [np] memoria sin parte residente [me-mo'-rya seen par'-tay re-see-den'-tay]

slew [v] jalarlo [ha-lar'-lo]

slide [n] diapositivos [dya-po-see-tee'-bos]

slide show package [np] paquete de gráficos diapositivos [pa-ke'-tay day gra'-fee-kos dya-po-see-tee'-bos]

smart [adj] inteligente [een-te-lee-hen'-tay]

smart machines [np] máquina inteligente [ma'-kee-na een-te-lee-hen'-tay]

smart terminal [np] terminal sávido [ter-mee-nal' sa'-bee-do]

smash [n] encontronazo [en-kon-tro-na'-so]

smooth scrolling [np] enrollamiento suave [en-ro-ya-myen'-to swa'-bay]

SNA systems network architecture [np] estructura de redes de sistemas [es-trook-too'-ra day re'-des day sees-te'-mas]

snapshot dump [np] vaceo instantáneo [ba-se'-o een-stan-ta'-ne-o]

SO send only [np] envio solo [en'-byo so'-lo]

soft clip area [np] área blanda de imagen [a'-re-a blan'-da day ee-ma'-hen]

soft copy [np] copia blanda [ko'-pya blan'-da]

soft hyphen [np] guión blando [gyon blan'-do]

soft keys [np] teclas blandas [tek'-las blan'-das]

soft return [np] regreso blando [re-gre'-so blan'-do]

software [n] soporte lógico [so-por'-tay lo'-hee-ko]

software engineering [np] ingeniería de soporte lógicos [een-he-nye-ree'-a day so-por'-tay lo'-hee-kos]

software generator [np] generador de soportes lógicos [he-ne-ra-dor' day so-por'-tes lo'-hee-kos]

software house [np] casa especializada en programación [ka'-sa es-pe-sya-lee-sa'-da en pro-gra-ma-syon']

software package [np] paquete de soporte lógico [pa-ke'-tay day so-por'-tay lo'-hee-ko]

solid-state memory [np] memoria de estado sólido [me-mo'-rya day es-ta'-do so'-lee-do] son file [np] fichero hijo [fee-che'-ro ee'-ho]

sort [v] clasificar [kla-see-fee-kar']

sort [n] clasificación [kla-see-fee-ka-syon']

sorter [n] clasificadora [kla-see-fee-ka-do'-ra]

sorting [adj] clasificando [kla-see-fee-kan'-do]

sorting routine [np] rutina de clasificación [roo-tee'-na day kla-see-fee-ka-syon']

sort-merge [adj] clasificación-fusión [kla-see-fee-ka-syon' foo-syon']

source [n] fuente [fwen'-tay]

source code [np] código fuente [ko'-dee-go fwen'-tay]

source data automation [np] automatización de la fuente de datos [ow-to-ma-tee-sa-syon' day la fwen'-tay day da'-tos]

source data capture [np] captura de datos fuente [kap-too'-ra day da'-tos fwen'-tay]

source document [np] documento fuente [do-koo-men'-to fwen'-tay]

source language [np] lenguaje fuente [len-gwa'-hay fwen'-tay]

source program [np] programa de fuente [pro-gra'-ma day fwen'-tay]

space character [np] carácter blanco [ka-rak'-ter blan'-ko]

spacebar [n] tecla de espaciar [tek'-la day es-pa-syar']

spanning tree [np] árbol con brotes [ar'-bol kon bro'-tes]

sparse array [np] arreglo escaso [ar-re'-glo es-ka'-so]

special character [np] carácter especial [ka-rak'-ter es-pe-syal']

special-purpose computer [np] computador especializado [kom-poo-ta-dor es-pe-sya-lee-sa'-do]

specification [n] especificación [es-pe-see-fee-ka-syon']

speech recognition [np] reconocimiento del hablar [re-ko-no-see-myen'-to del a-blar']

speech synthesizer [np] sintetizador del hablar [seen-te-tee-sa-dor' del a-blar']

spider configuration [np] configuración en telaraña [kon-fee-goo-ra-syon' en te-la-ran'-ya]

spike [n] sobretensión transitoria [so-bre-ten-syon' tran-see-to'-rya]

splicer [n] empalmadora [em-pal-ma-do'-ra]

spline [n] suavizador [swa-bee-sa-dor']

split screen [np] pantalla dividida [pan-ta'-ya dee-bee-dee'-da]

split window [np] ventana dividida [ben-ta'-na dee-bee-dee'-da]

splitting a window [np] ventana en separación [ben-ta'-na en se-pa-ra-syon']

spool [v] bobinar [bo-bee-nar']

spool [n] bobina [bo-bee'-na]

spooler [n] bobinadora [bo-bee-na-do'-ra]

spooling [adj] bobinado [bo-bee-na'-do]

spreadsheet [n] hoja electrónica [o'-ha e-lek-tro'-nee-ka]

sprites [n] duendecillo [dwen-de-see'-yo]

sprocket holes [np] perforaciones marginales [per-fo-ra-syo'-nes mar-hee-na'-les]

sprocket pulse [np] impulso de sincronización [eem-pool'-so day seen-kro-nee-sa-syon']

stack [n] pila [pee'-la]

stack pointer [np] puntero de pila [poon-te'-ro day pee'-la]

stacker [n] casillero receptor [ka-see-ye'-ro re-sep-tor']

stair-stepping [adj] escalónado [es-ka-lo'-na-do]

standard form [np] formato normalizado [for-ma'-to nor-ma-lee-sa'-do]

standard interface [np] interfase normalizada [een-ter-fa'-say nor-ma-lee-sa'-da]

standard subroutine [np] subrutina normal [soob-roo-tee'-na nor-mal']

standardization [n] normalización [nor-ma-lee-sa-syon']

standardize [v] normalizar [nor-ma-lee-sar']

stand-alone [n] computador sólo [kom-poo-ta-dor' so'-lo]

stand-alone graphics system [np] sistema gráfico sólo [sees-te'-ma gra'-fee-ko so'-lo]

star bit [n] bit de comienzo [beet day ko-myen'-so]

star network [np] redes en estrella [re'-des en es-tre'-ya]

start time [np] tiempo de arranque [tyem'-po day ar-ran'-kay]

startup [n] inicializador [ee-nee-sya-lee-sa-dor']

start-stop time [np] tiempo de arranque-espera [tyem'-po day ar-ran'-kay es-pe'-ra]

statement [n] declaración [de-kla-ra-syon']

statement label [n] etiqueta de declaración [e-tee-ke'-ta day de-kla-ra-syon']

state-of-the-art [adj] estado de arte [es-ta'-do day ar'-tay]

static [adj] estática [es-ta'-tee-ka]

static dump [np] vuelco estático de la memoria [bwel'-ko es-ta'-tee-ko day la me-mo'-rya]

static refresh [np] regenerador estático [re-he-ne-ra-dor' es-ta'-tee-ko]

static storage [np] memoria estática [me-mo'-rya es-ta'-tee-ka]

static subroutine [np] subrutina estática [soob-roo-tee'-na es-ta'-tee-ka]

statitizing [n] listo para ejecución [lees'-to pa'-ra e-he-koo-syon']

status [n] categoría [ka-te-go-ree'-a]

status report [np] reporte de categoría [re-por'-tay day ka-te-go-ree'-a]

status word [np] palabra de estado [pa-la'-bra day es-ta'-do]

step [n] paso [pa'-so]

step change [np] cambio de paso [kam'-byo day pa'-so]

stochastic procedures [np] procedimiento estochastico [pro-se-dee-myen'-to es-to-chas-tee'-ko]

storage [n] almacenamiento de memoria [al-ma-se-na-myen'-to day me-mo'-rya]

storage allocation [np] asignación de almacenamiento de memoria [a-seeg-na-syon' day al-ma-se-na-myen'-to day me-mo'-rya]

storage block [np] bloque de almacenamiento de memoria [blo'-kay day al-ma-se-na-myen'-to day me-mo'-rya]

storage capacity [np] capacidad de almacenamiento de memoria [ka-pa-see-dad' day al-ma-se-na-myen'-to day me-mo'-rya]

storage density [np] densidad de almacenamiento de memoria [den-see-dad' day al-ma-se-na-myen'-to day me-mo'-rya]

storage device [np] dispositivo del almacenamiento de memoria [dees-po-see-tee'-bo del al-ma-se-na-myen'-to day me-mo'-rya]

storage display [np] presentacion de almacenamiento de memoria [pre-sen-ta-syon' day al-ma-se-na-myen'-to day me-mo'-rya]

storage dump [np] volcado del almacenamiento de memoria [bol-ka'-do del al-ma-se-na-myen'-to day me-mo'-rya]

storage key [np] llave de bloque [ya'-bay day blo'-kay]

storage memory [np] memoria de núcleos [me-mo'-rya day nook'-le-os]

storage pool [np] fuente de almacenamiento [fwen'-tay day al-ma-se-na-myen'-to]

storage tube [np] tubo de almacenamiento de memoria [too'-bo day al-ma-se-na-myen'-to day me-mo'-rya]

store [v] almacenar [al-ma-se-nar']

stored program [np] programa almacenado [pro-gra'-ma al-ma-se-na'-do]

store-and-forward [adj] guarde y envie [gwar'-day ee en'-bye]

streamer [n] cinta de serpentina [seen'-ta day ser-pen-tee'-na]

stress testing [np] prueba de tensión [prwe'-ba day ten-syon']

string [n] serie [se'-rye]

string handling [np] manejo de series [ma-ne'-ho day se'-ryes]

string length [np] largo de las series [lar'-go day las se'-ryes]

string manipulation [np] manipulación en series [ma-nee-poo-la-syon' en se'-ryes]

strobe [n] estroboscópico [es-tro-bos-ko'-pee-ko]

stroke [n] trazo [tra'-so]

stroke writer [np] escritor de trazos [es-kree-tor day tra'-sos]

structure [n] estructura [es-trook-too'-ra]

structure chart [np] flujo de estructura [floo'-ho day es-trook-too'-ra]

structured flowchart [np] flujorama estructurado [floo-ho-ra'-ma es-trook-too-ra'-do]

structured program [np] programa estructurado [pro-gra'-ma es-trook-too-ra'-do]

stylus [n] estilo [es-tee'-lo]

subdirectory [n] subdirectorio [soob-dee-rek-to'-ryo]

subprogram [n] subprograma [soob-pro-gra'-ma]

subroutine [n] subrutina [soob-roo-tee'-na]

subschema [n] subesquema [soo-bes-ke'-ma]

subscriber station [np] estación de una red [es-ta-syon' day oo'-na red]

subset [n] subgrupo [soob-groo'-po]

substrate [n] subestrato [soo-bes-tra'-to]

substring [n] subserie [soob-se'-rye]

subsystem [n] subsistema [soob-sees-te'-ma]

subtracter [n] sustractor [soos-trak-tor']

subtree [n] subárbol [soob-ar'-bol]

suite [n] suite [swee'-tay]

summation check [np] comprobación de suma [kom-pro-ba-syon' day soo'-ma]

superscript [n] sobreescritura [so-bre-es-kree-too'-ra]

supervisor [n] supervisor [soo-per-bee-sor']

supervisory control [np] control de supervisión [kon-trol' day soo-per-bee-syon']

supervisory program [np] programa de supervisión [pro-gra'-ma day soo-per-bee-syon']

supplementary maintenance [np] mantenimiento suplementario [man-te-nee-myen'-to soo-ple-men-ta'-ryo]

suppress [v] suprimir [soo-pree-meer']

suppression [n] supresión [soo-pre-syon']

surge [n] sobretensión [so-bre-ten-syon']

surging [n] sobretensión oleada [so-bre-ten-syon' o-le-a'-da]

suspend [v] suspender [soos-pen-der']

swapping [adj] intercambiando [een-ter-kam-byan'-do]

swim [adj] nadando en la pantalla [na-dan'-do en la pan-ta'-ya]

switch [v] conmutar [kon-moo-tar']

switch [adj] conmutable [kon-moo-ta'-blay]

switch [n] conmutador [kon-moo-ta-dor']

switched line [np] línea conmutada [lee'-ne-a kon-moo-ta'-da]

switched-message network [np] red de conmutación de mensajes [red day kon-moo-ta-syon' day men-sa'-hes]

switching center [np] centro de conmutación [sen'-tro day kon-moo-ta-syon']

symbol [n] símbolo [seem'-bo-lo]

symbolic address [np] dirección simbólica [dee-rek-syon' seem-bo'-lee-ka]

symbolic coding [np] código simbólico [ko'-dee-go seem-bo'-lee-ko]

symbolic editor [np] programa de edición simbólica [pro-gra'-ma day e-dee-syon' seem-bo'-lee-ka]

symbolic language [np] lenguaje simbólico [len-gwa'-hay seem-bo'-lee-ko]

symbolic logic [np] lógica simbólica [lo'-hee-ka seem-bo'-lee-ka]

symbolic programming [np] programación simbólica [pro-gra-ma-syon' seem-bo'-lee-ka]

symbolic table [np] tabla simbólica [ta'-bla seem-bo'-lee-ka]

sync character [np] carácter de sincronización [ka-rak'-ter day seen-kro-nee-sa-syon']

synchronization [n] sincronización [seen-kro-nee-sa-syon']

synchronizer [n] síncronizador [seen-kro-nee-sa-dor']

synchronous communications [np] comunicación síncronizada [ko-moo-nee-ka-syon' seen-kro-nee-sa'-da]

synchronous computer [np] computador síncrono [kom-poo-ta-dor' seen-kro'-no]

synchronous operation [np] operación síncrona [o-pe-ra-syon' seen-kro'-na]

syntax [n] sintaxis [seen-tak'-sees]

synthesizer [n] sintetizador [seen-te-tee-sa-dor']

synthetic language [np] lenguaje sintético [len-gwa'-hay seen-te'-tee-ko]

SYSGEN systems generation [np] generación de sistemas [he-ne-ra-syon' day sees-te'-mas]

SYSOP system operator [np] operador del sistema [o-pe-ra-dor' del sees-te'-ma]

system [np] sistema [sees-te'-ma]

system analysis [np] análisis de sistemas [a-na'-lee-sees day sees-te'-mas]

system analyzer [np] análizador de sistema [a-na'-lee-sa-dor day sees-te'-ma]

system diagnostics [np] diagnóstico de sistema [dyag-nos'-tee-ko day sees-te'-ma]

system generation [np] generación del sistema [he-ne-ra-syon' del sees-te'-ma]

system installation [np] instalación de sistema [een-sta-la-syon' day sees-te'-ma]

system loader [np] cargador de sistema [kar-ga-dor day sees-te'-ma]

system operator (SYSOP) [np] operador del sistema [o-pe-ra-dor' del sees-te'-ma]

system programmer [np] programador de sistema [pro-gra-ma-dor' day sees-te'-ma]

system reset [np] reajuste del sistema [re-a-hoos'-tay del sees-te'-ma]

system testing [np] prueba del sistema [prwe'-ba del sees-te'-ma]

systematic search [np] búsqueda sistemática [boos'-ke-da sees-te-ma'-tee-ka]

systems analyst [np] analista de sistemas [a-na-lees'-ta day sees-te'-mas]

systems generation (SYSGEN) [np] generación de sistemas [he-ne-ra-syon' day sees-te'-mas]

systems network architecture (SNA) [np] estructura de redes de sistemas [es-trook-too'-ra day re'-des day sees-te'-mas]

systems programming [np] programación de sistemas [pro-gra-ma-syon' day sees-te'-mas]

T

table [n] tabla [ta'-bla]

table look-up (TLU) [np] consulta de tablas [kon-sool'-ta day ta'-blas]

tablet [n] tableta [ta-ble'-ta]

tabular display [np] representación tabular [re-pre-sen-ta-syon' ta-boo-lar']

tabular language [np] lenguaje tabular [len-gwa'-hay ta-boo-lar']

tabulate [v] tabular [ta-boo-lar']

tabulation [n] tabulación [ta-boo-la-syon']

tabulator [n] tabuladora [ta-boo-la-do'-ra]

tag [n] etiqueta [e-tee-ke'-ta]

tail [n] cabo [ka'-bo]

tailor-made [adj] creado especialmente [kre-a'-do es-pe-syal-men'-tay]

tandem computers [np] computadores en tándem [kom-poo-ta-do'-res en tan'-dem]

tandem system [np] sistema en tándem [sees-te'-ma en tan'-dem]

tape [n] cinta [seen'-ta]

tape drive [np] impulsor de cinta [eem-pool-sor' day seen'-ta]

tape feed [np] alimentador de cinta [a-lee-men-ta-dor' day seen'-ta]

tape library [np] biblioteca de cintas [bee-blyo-te'-ka day seen'-tas]

tape mark [np] marca de cinta [mar'-ka day seen'-ta]

tape operating system (TOS) [np] sistema de cintas operacional [sees-te'-ma day seen'-tas o-pe-ra-syo-nal']

tape punch [np] preforadora de cinta [pre-fo-ra-do'-ra day seen'-ta]

tape reader [np] leedora de cinta [le-e-do'-ra day seen'-ta]

tape transport [np] transportador de cinta [trans-por-ta-dor' day seen'-ta]

tape unit [np] unidad de cinta [oo-nee-dad' day seen'-ta]

tape verifier [np] verificadora de cinta [be-ree-fee-ka-do'-ra day seen'-ta]

target disk [np] disco de blanco [dees'-ko day blan'-ko]

target language [np] lenguaje asestado [len-gwa'-hay a-ses-ta'-do]

task [n] tarea [ta-re'-a]

telecommunication [n] telecomunicación [te-le-ko-moo-nee-ka-syon']

telecommuting [n] teleconmutar [te-le-kon-moo-tar']

Telematics [n] teleautomático [te-le-ow-to-ma'-tee-ko]

telemedicine [n] telemedicina [te-le-me-dee-see'-na]

telemetry [n] telemetría [te-le-met-ree'-a]

Telenet [n] teleseries [te-le-se'-ryes]

telephone data set [np] equipo de datos telefónicos [e-kee'-po day da'-tos te-le-fo'-nee-kos]

telephone switching [np] conmutación telefónica [kon-moo-ta-syon' te-le-fo'-nee-ka]

telephonic communication [np] comunicación telefónica [ko-moo-nee-ka-syon' te-le-fo'-nee-ka]

teleprinter [n] teleimpresor [te-le-eem-pre-sor']

teleprocessing [n] teleproceso [te-le-pro-se'-so]

teletext [n] teletexto [te-le-tex'-to]

temporary storage [np] almacenamiento de memoria temporal [al-ma-se-na-myen'-to day me-mo'-rya tem-po-ral']

ten's complement [np] complemento a diez [kom-ple-men'-to a dyes]

ten-key pad [np] teclado de a diez [tek-la'-do day a dyes]

terminal [n] terminal [ter-mee-nal']

terminal emulation [np] emulación del terminal [e-moo-la-syon' del ter-mee-nal']

terminal error [np] error final [air-ror' fee-nal']

termination [n] terminación [ter-mee-na-syon']

test [v] probar [pro-bar']

test [n] prueba [prwe'-ba]

test data [np] datos del ensayo [da'-tos del en-sa'-yo]

test driver [np] conductor de prueba [kon-dook-tor' day prwe'-ba]

test plan [np] plan de prueba [plan day prwe'-ba]

test program [np] programa de ensayo [pro-gra'-ma day en-sa'-yo]

test run [np] pasada de ensayo [pa-sa'-da day en-sa'-yo]

testbed [n] banca de prueba [ban'-ka day prwe'-ba]

text [n] texto [tex'-to]

text editing [np] editación de texto [e-dee-ta-syon' day tex'-to]

text editor [np] editor de texto [e-dee-tor' day tex'-to]

text file [np] archivo de texto [ar-chee'-bo day tex'-to]

text processing [np] procesamiento de texto [pro-se-sa-myen'-to day tex'-to]

text window [np] ventana de texto [ben-ta'-na day tex'-to]

texture [n] textura [tex-too'-ra]

thimble [n] dedal [de-dal']

thimble printer [np] impresora de dedal [eem-pre-so'-ra day de-dal']

thin-film memory [np] memoria de película delgada [me-mo'-rya day pe-lee'-koo-la del-ga'-da]

third-generation [adj] tercera-generación [ter-se'-ra he-ne-ra-syon']

third-party lease [np] alquiler a una tercera persona [al-kee-ler' a oo'-na ter-se'-ra per-so'-na]

thrashing [adj] revolverse [re-bol-ber'-say]

threaded [adj] enhebrar [en-e-brar']

threaded tree [np] árbol enhebrado [ar'-bol en-e-bra'-do]

three-address intruction [np] instrucción de tres-direcciones [een-strook-syon' day tres dee-rek-syo'-nes]

three-dimensional (3-D) [np] tridimensional [tree-dee-men-syo-nal']

three-input element [np] elemento con tres-entradas [e-le-men'-to kon tres en-tra'-das]

threshold element [np] elemento de umbral [e-le-men'-to day oom-bral']

throughput [n] capacidad de tratamiento utíl [ka-pa-see-dad' day tra-ta-myen'-to oo-teel']

thumbwheel [n] giratablas [hee-ra-ta'-blas]

tick mark [np] marca apuntadora [mar'-ka a-poon-ta-do'-ra]

tightly coupled [adj] fuertamente acoplado [fwer-ta-men'-tay a-ko-pla'-do]

tilting screen [np] pantalla ladeadora [pan-ta'-ya la-de-a-do'-ra]

time quantum [np] cuántico tiempo [kwan'-tee-ko tyem'-po]

time scale [np] escala de tiempo [es-ka'-la day tyem'-po]

time slice [np] unidad de tiempo [oo-nee-dad' day tyem'-po]

timer [n] marcador [mar-ka-dor']

time-clock [n] reloj marcador [re-lo' mar-ka-dor']

time-division multiplexing [np] múltiplexado tiempo dividido [mool'-tee-plek-sa-do tyem'-po dee-bee-dee'-do]

time-sharing [n] tiempo compartido [tyem'-po kom-par-tee'-do]

TLU table look-up [np] consulta de tablas [kon-sool'-ta day ta'-blas]

toggle [n] conmutador [kon-moo-ta-dor']

token [n] señal [sen-yal']

tone [n] matiz [ma-tees']

top-down programming [np] programación de arriba-abajo [pro-gra-ma-syon' day ar-ree'-ba a-ba'-ho]

TOS tape operating system [np] sistema de cintas operacional [sees-te'-ma day seen'-tas o-pe-ra-syo-nal']

touch-sensitive panel [np] panel de tocada sensitiva [pa-nel' day to-ka'-da sen-see-tee'-ba]

touch-sensitive tablet [np] tableta de tocada sensitiva [ta-ble'-ta day to-ka'-da sen-see-tee'-ba]

TPI tracks per inch [np] pista por pulgadas [pees'-ta por pool-ga'-das]

trace [n] traza [tra'-sa]

track [n] pista [pees'-ta]

track ball [np] boleador [bo-le-a-dor']

track label [np] etiqueta de pista [e-tee-ke'-ta day pees'-ta]

tracking [adj] rastreando [ras-tre-an'-do]

tracking symbol [np] símbolo de rastreo [seem'-bo-lo day ras-tre'-o]

tracks per inch (TPI) [np] pista por pulgadas [pees'-ta por pool-ga'-das]

tradeoff [n] cambio de factores [kam'-byo day fak-to'-res]

trailer label [np] etiqueta de cola [e-tee-ke'-ta day ko'-la]

trailer record [np] registro de cola [re-hees'-tro day ko'-la]

train printer [np] impresor de cadena [eem-pre-sor' day ka-de'-na]

tranceiver [n] transceptor [trans-sep-tor']

transaction [n] transacción [tran-sak-syon']

transaction data [np] datos de transacción [da'-tos day tran-sak-syon']

transaction processing [np] proceso de transacciones [pro-se'-so day tran-sak-syo'-nes]

transborder [n] transfrontera [trans-fron-te'-ra]

transcribe [v] transcribir [trans-kree-beer']

transcriber [n] copiador [ko-pya-dor']

transducer [n] transductor [trans-dook-tor']

transfer [v] transferir [trans-fe-reer']

transfer [n] transferencia [trans-fe-ren'-sya]

transfer check [np] verificación de transferencia [be-ree-fee-ka-syon' day trans-fe-ren'-sya]

transfer control [np] transferencia de control [trans-fe-ren'-sya day kon-trol']

transfer function [np] función de transferencia [foon-syon' day trans-fe-ren'-sya]

transfer instruction [np] instrucción de transferencia [een-strook-syon' day trans-fe-ren'-sya]

transfer rate [np] índice de transferencia [een'-dee-say day trans-fe-ren'-sya]

transform [v] transformar [trans-for-mar']

transient [adj] transitorio [tran-see-to'-ryo]

transient program [np] programa transitorio [pro-gra'-ma tran-see-to'-ryo]

transient suppressors [np] suprimidor transitorio [soop-ree-mee-dor' tran-see-to'-ryo]

transistor [n] transistor [tran-sees-tor']

transistor-transistor logic (TTL) [np] lógica de transistor-transistor [lo'-hee-ka day tran-sees-tor']

transition [n] transición [tran-see-syon']

translate [v] traducir [tra-doo-seer']

translator [n] traductor [tra-dook-tor']

transliterate [v] transliterar [trans-lee-te-rar']

transmission [n] transmisión [trans-mee-syon']

transmission interface [np] interfase de transmisión [een-ter-fa'-say day trans-mee-syon']

transmission speed [np] velocidad de transmisión [be-lo-see-dad' day trans-mee-syon']

transmit [v] transmitir [trans-mee-teer']

transparency [n] transparencia [trans-pa-ren'-sya]

transparent [adj] transparente [trans-pa-ren'-tay]

transponder [n] transponder [trans-pon-der']

trap [v] atrapar [a-tra-par']

trap [n] trampa [tram'-pa]

trapdoor [n] escotilla [es-ko-tee'-ya]

trapping [n] interruptor [een-ter-roop-tor']

tree [n] árbol [ar'-bol]

tree diagram [np] esquema del árbol [es-ke'-ma del ar'-bol]

tree sort [np] clasificación del árbol [kla-see-fee-ka-syon' del ar'-bol]

tree structure [np] estructura del árbol [es-trook-too'-ra del ar'-bol]

tree traversal [np] travesaño del árbol [tra-be-san'-yo del ar'-bol]

trichromatic [adj] tricolor [tree-ko-lor']

trigger [v] disparar [dees-pa-rar']

trigger [n] disparador [dees-pa-ra-dor']

trigger circuit [np] circuito de disparo [seer-kwee'-to day dees-pa'-ro]

triple precision [np] presición triple [pre-see-syon' tree'-play]

tristimulus values [np] valores de trimatiz [ba-lo'-res day tree-ma-tees']

troubleshooting [n] localización de errores [lo-ka-lee-sa-syon' day air-ro'-res]

truncate [v] truncar [troon-kar']

truncation error [np] error de truncamiento [air-ror' day troon-ka-myen'-to]

trunk [n] línea telefónica [lee'-ne-a te-le-fo'-nee-ka]

trunk circuit [np] circuito común [seer-kwee'-to ko-moon']

trunk link [np] enlace común [en-la'-say ko-moon']

truth table [np] tabla de decisión lógica [ta'-bla day de-see-syon' lo'-hee-ka]

TTL transistor-transistor logic [np] lógica de transistor-transistor [lo'-hee-ka day tran-sees-tor']

tube [n] tubo [too'-bo]

tuning [n] sintonización [seen-to-nee-sa-syon']

turn off [v] desconectar [des-ko-nek-tar']

turn on [v] conectar [ko-nek-tar']

turnaround [n] giro total [hee'-ro to-tal']

turnkey operation [np] operación con llave en mano [o-pe-ra-syon' kon ya'-bay en ma'-no]

turtle [np] tortuga automatizada [tor-too'-ga ow-to-ma-tee-sa'-da]

turtle graphics [np] gráfica de tortuga [gra'-fee-ka day tor-too'-ga]

tweak [n] ajuste fino [a-hoos'-tay fee'-no]

twin control [np] doble control [do'-blay kon-trol']

twinkle box [np] caja de centello [ka'-ha day sen-te'-yo]

two pass [np] dos pasos [dos pa'-sos]

two's complement [np] complemento a dos [kom-ple-men'-to a dos]

two-address instruction [np] instrucción con dos direcciones [een-strook-syon' kon dos dee-rek-syo'-nes]

two-dimensional storage np] memoria bidimensional [me-mo'-rya bee-dee-men-syo-nal']

type [v] escribir con el teclado [es-kree-beer kon el tek-la'-do]

type [n] tipo [tee'-po]

type ahead [np] escribiendo con adelanto [es-kree-byen'-do kon a-de-lan'-to]

type bar [np] barra de tipos [bar'-ra day tee'-pos]

type drum [np] tambor de tipos [tam-bor' day tee'-pos]

type font [np] clases de tipógrafos [kla'-ses day tee-po'-gra-fos]

typeball [n] bola de tipógraficos [bo'-la day tee-po'-gra-fos]

typeface [n] tipógrafos [tee-po'-gra-fos]

typematic [adj] tecla repetitiva [tek'-la re-pe-tee-tee'-ba]

typeover [n] dobletipo [do-ble-tee'-po]

typesize [n] tamaño del tipo [ta-man'-yo del tee'-po]

typewriter [n] máquina de escribir [ma'-kee-na day es-kree-beer']

typewriter terminal [np] terminal con teclado [ter-mee-nal' kon tek-la'-do]

U

ultrafiche [n] ultraficha [ool-tra-fee'-cha]

unary operation [np] operación unaria [o-pe-ra-syon' oo-na'-rya]

unattended operation [np] operación sin personal [o-pe-ra-syon' seen per-so-nal']

unattended time [np] tiempo sin personal [tyem'-po seen per-so-nal']

unconditional branch instruction [np] instrucción de bifurcación incondicional [een-strook-syon' day bee-foor-ka-syon' een-kon-dee-syo-nal']

unconditional transfer [np] transferencia incondicional [trans-fe-ren'-sya een-kon-dee-syo-nal']

uncontrolled loop [np] bucle sin control [boo'-klay seen kon-trol']

underflow [n] subdesbordamiento [soob-des-bor-da-myen'-to]

undisturbed output signal [np] señal de salida no cambiada [sen-yal' day sa-lee'-da no kam-bya'-da]

undo [v] deshacer [des-a-ser']

unibus [n] un conductor común [oon kon-dook-tor' ko-moon']

unipolar [adj] unipolar [oo-nee-po-lar']

unit [n] unidad [oo-nee-dad']

unit record [np] registro unitario [re-hees'-tro oo-nee-ta'-ryo]

universal identifier [np] identificador universal [ee-den-tee-fee-ka-dor' oo-nee-ber-sal']

universal product code [np] código del producto universal [ko'-dee-go del pro-dook'-to oo-nee-ber-sal']

universal Turing machine [np] máquina de Turing universal [ma'-kee-na day Turing oo-nee-ber-sal']

unordered tree [np] árbol desordenado [ar'-bol de-sor-de-na'-do]

unpack [v] desempaquetar [de-sem-pa-ke-tar']

unpaged segment [np] segmento no paginado [seg-men'-to no pa-hee-na'-do]

unused time [np] tiempo no empleado [tyem'-po no em-ple-a'-do]

unwind [v] desenredar [de-sen-re-dar']

update [v] actualizar [ak-twa-lee-sar']

upload [n] ascenso de archivos [as-sen'-so day ar-chee'-bos]

upper case [np] mayúscula [ma-yoos'-koo-la]

uptime [n] tiempo productivo [tyem'-po pro-dook-tee'-bo]

upward compatible [np] sistema compatible [sees-te'-ma kom-pa-tee'-blay]

up-and-running [adj] restablecido y corre [res-ta-ble-see'-do ee kor'-ray]

user [n] usuario [oo-swa'-ryo]

user group [np] grupo de usuarios [groo'-po day oo-swa'-ryos]

user-defined function [np] función definida por el usuario [foon-syon' de-fee-nee'-da por el oo-swa'-ryo]

user-defined key [np] tecla definida por el usuario [tek'-la de-fee-nee'-da por el oo-swa'-ryo]

user-friendly [adj] fácil para el usuario [fa'-seel pa'-ra el oo-swa'-ryo]

utility program [np] programa de utilidad [pro-gra'-ma day oo-tee-lee-dad']

utilization ratio [np] relación de utilización [re-la-syon' day oo-tee-lee-sa-syon']

V

VAB voice answer back [np] respondedor de voz [res-pon-de-dor' day bos]

validity check [np] verificación de validez [be-ree-fee-ka-syon' day ba-lee-des']

value [n] valor [ba-lor']

value parameter [np] parámetro de valor [pa-ra'-me-tro day ba-lor']

value-added network [np] serie con valor añadido [se'-ryay kon ba-lor' an-ya-dee'-do]

variable [n] variable [ba-rya'-blay]

variable field [np] campo variable [kam'-po ba-rya'-blay]

variable name [np] nombre de variable [nom'-bray day ba-rya'-blay]

variable word length [np] largo de la palabra variable [lar'-go day la pa-la'-bra ba-rya'-blay]

variable-length record [np] registro de tamaño variable [re-hees'-tro day ta-man'-yo ba-rya'-blay]

VDT video display terminal [np] terminal de representación de video [ter-mee-nal' day re-pre-sen-ta-syon' day bee-de'-o]

VDU visual display unit [np] unidad de visualización [oo-nee-dad' day bee-swa-lee-sa-syon']

vector arithmetic [np] aritmética vectorial [a-reet-me'-tee-ka bek-to-ryal']

vector display [np] presentación vectorial [pre-sen-ta-syon' bek-to-ryal']

vector processing [np] proceso vectorial [pro-se'-so bek-to-ryal']

vector-mode display [np] representación en modo vectorial [re-pre-sen-ta-syon' en mo'-do bek-to-ryal']

verification [n] verificación [be-ree-fee-ka-syon']

verify [v] verificar [be-ree-fee-kar']

vertical recording [np] registro vertical [re-hees'-tro ber-tee-kal']

vertical scrolling [np] enrollamiento vertical [en-ro-ya-myen'-to ber-tee-kal']

video [n] video [bee-de'-o]

video digitizer [np] digitizador de video [dee-hee-tee-sa-dor' day bee-de'-o]

video display terminal (VDT) [np] terminal de representación de video [ter-mee-nal day re-pre-sen-ta-syon' day bee-de'-o]

video game [np] juego de video [hwe'-go day bee-de'-o]

video game machine [np] aparato de juego de video [a-pa-ra'-to day hwe'-go day bee-de'-o]

video generator [np] generador de video [ge-ne-ra-dor' day bee-de'-o]

video monitor [np] monitor de video [mo-nee-tor' day bee-de'-o]

video terminal [np] terminal de video [ter-mee-nal' day bee-de'-o]

videodisk [np] videodisco [bee-de-o-dees'-ko]

vidicon [n] vidicon [bee-dee-kon']

viewport [n] vistaportador [bees-ta-por-ta-dor']

virgin tape [np] cinta virgen [seen'-ta beer'-hen]

virtual [adj] virtual [beer-twal']

virtual address [np] dirección virtual [dee-rek-syon' beer-twal']

virtual machine [np] máquina virtual [ma'-kee-na beer-twal']

virtual storage operating system (VSOS) [np] systema virtual en operación [sees-te'-ma beer-twal' en o-pe-ra-syon']

virtual storage (VS) [np] almacenamiento de memoria virtual [al-ma-se-na-myen'-to day me-mo'-rya beer-twal']

vision recognition [np] reconocimiento de vista [re-ko-no-see-myen'-to day bees'-ta]

visual display unit (VDU) [np] unidad de visualización [oo-nee-dad' day bee-swa-lee-sa-syon']

visual page [np] página de visualización [pa'-hee-na day bee-swa-lee-sa-syon']

vocabulary [n] vocabulario [bo-ka-boo-la'-ryo]

voder [n] sintetizador de voz [seen-te-tee-sa-dor' day bos]

voice answer back (VAB) [np] respondedor de voz [res-pon-de-dor' day bos]

voice communications [np] comunicación de voz [ko-moo-nee-ka-syon' day bos]

voice grade channel [np] canal de rango vocal [ka-nal' day ran'-go bo-kal']

voice input [np] entrada de voz [en-tra'-da day bos]

voice mail [np] correo por voz [kor-re'-o por bos]

voice output [np] salida de voz [sa-lee'-da day bos]

voice recognition [np] reconocimiento de voz [re-ko-no-see-myen'-to day bos]

voice response [np] respuesta vocal [res-pwes'-ta bo-kal']

voice synthesis [np] sintetiza la voz [seen-te-tee'-sa la bos]

volatile memory np] memoria volátil [me-mo'-rya bo-la'-teel]

volume [n] volumen [bo-loo'-men]

VS virtual storage [np] almacenamiento de memoria virtual [al-ma-se-na-myen'-to day me-mo'-rya beer-twal']

VSOS virtual storage operating system [np] systema virtual en operación [sees-te'-ma beer-twal' en o-pe-ra-syon']

W

wafer [n] oblea [o-ble'-a]

wait state [np] estado de espera [es-ta'-do day es-pe'-ra]

wait time [np] tiempo de espera [tyem'-po day es-pe'-ra]

wand [n] varilla [ba-ree'-ya]

warm boot [np] arranque secundario [ar-ran'-kay se-goon-da'-ryo]

warm-up time [np] tiempo de calentura [tyem'-po day ka-len-too'-ra]

weed [v] eliminar [e-lee-mee-nar']

wetzel [n] wetzel [wet-sel']

wheel printer [np] impresora de ruedas [eem-pre-so'-ra day rwe'-das]

white noise [np] sonido de continuidad [so-nee'-do day kon-tee-nwee-dad']

widow [n] quedó viudo [ke-do' byoo'-do]

wild card [np] relación de nombres [re-la-syon' day nom'-bres]

window [n] ventana [ben-ta'-na]

windowing [adj] ventaneando [ben-ta-ne-an'-do]

word [n] palabra [pa-la'-bra]

word length [np] longitud de palabra [lon-hee-tood' day pa-la'-bra]

word processing center [np] centro de procesador de texto [sen'-tro day pro-se-sa-dor' day tex'-to]

word processing operator [np] operador de proceso del texto [o-pe-ra-dor' day pro-se'-so del tex'-to]

word processing program [np] programa de proceso de texto [pro-gra'-ma day pro-se'-so day tex'-to]

word processing (WP) [np] proceso de texto [pro-se'-so day tex'-to]

word processor [np] procesador de la palabra [pro-se-sa-dor' day la pa-la'-bra]

word wrap [np] retorno automático de la palabra [re-tor'-no ow-to-ma'-tee-ko day la pa-la'-bra]

words-per-minute (WPM) [n] palabras-por-minuto [pa-la'-bras por mee-noo'-to]

word-oriented [adj] orientado a la palabra [o-ryen-ta'-do a la pa-la'-bra]

work area [np] zona de trabajo [so'-na day tra-ba'-ho]

work tape [np] cinta de maniobra [seen'-ta day ma-nyo'-bra]

worksheet [n] hoja electrónica [o'-ha e-lek-tro'-nee-ka]

workstation [n] puesto de trabajo [pwes'-to day tra-ba'-ho]

WP word processing [np] proceso de texto [pro-se'-so day tex'-to]

WPM words-per-minute [n] palabras-por-minuto [pa-la'-bras por mee-noo'-to]

wraparound [n] retorno automático [re-tor'-no ow-to-ma'-tee-ko]

write [v] escribir [es-kree-beer']

write head [np] cabeza de escritura [ka-be'-sa day es-kree-too'-ra]

write protect [np] protección de escritura [pro-tek-syon' day es-kree-too'-ra]

write time [np] tiempo de escritura [tyem'-po day es-kree-too'-ra]

write-enable ring [np] anillo que permite escribir [a-nee'-yo kay per-mee'-tay es-kree-beer']

write-inhibit ring [np] anillo que no permite escribir [a-nee'-yo kay no per-mee'-tay es-kree-beer']

write-protect notch [np] ventanilla que proteje escritura [ben-ta-nee'-ya kay pro-te'-hay es-kree-too'-ra]

write-protect ring [np] anillo que proteje escritura [a-nee'-yo kay pro-te'-hay es-kree-too'-ra]

X

Xenographic printer [np] impresora xerográfica [eem-pre-so'-ra se-ro-gra'-fee-ka]

XOR exclusive OR operation [np] operación O exclusivo [o-pe-ra-syon' O ex-kloo-see'-bo]

X-Y plotter [np] trazador X-Y [tra-sa-dor' X Y]

Z

Zap [v] suprimir [soo-pree-meer']

zero state [np] estado cero [es-ta'-do se'-ro]

zero suppression [np] supresión de ceros [soo-pre-syon' day se'-ros]

zeroize [adj] llenando de ceros [ye-nan'-do day se'-ros]

zero-address instruction [np] instrucción de dirección cero [een-strook-syon' day dee-rek-syon' se'-ro]

zero-output signal [np] señal de salida cero [sen-yal' day sa-lee'-da se'-ro]

zone [n] zona [so'-na]

zone bit [np] bit de zona [beet day so'-na]

zone digit [np] dígito de zona [dee'-hee-to day so'-na]

zooming [adj] aumentando [ow-men-tan'-do]

HIPPOCRENE FOREIGN LANGUAGE DICTIONARIES

Modern • Up-to-Date • Easy-to-Use • Practical

Afrikaans-English/English-Africaans Dictionary
0134 ISBN 0-7818-0052-8 $11.95 pb

Albanian-English Dictionary
0744 ISBN 0-7818-0021-8 $14.95 pb

English-Albanian Dictionary
0518 ISBN 0-7818-0021-8 $14.95 pb

Arabic-English Dictionary
0487 ISBN 0-7818-0153-2 $14.95 pb

English-Arabic Dictionary
0519 ISBN 0-7818-0152-4 $14.95 pb

Arabic-English Learner's Dictionary
0033 ISBN 0-7818-0155-9 $24.95 hc

English-Arabic Learner's Dictionary
0690 ISBN 0-87052-914-5 $14.95 pb

Armenian-English/English-Armenian Concise Dictionary
0490 ISBN 0-7818-0150-8 $11.95 pb

Western Armenian-English/English-Western Armenian
0059 ISBN 0-7818-0207-5 $9.95 pb

Bulgarian-English/English-Bulgarian Practical Dictionary
0331 ISBN 0-87052-145-4 $8.95 pb

Byelorussian-English/English-Byelorussian Concise Dictionary
1050 ISBN 0-87052-114-4 $9.95 pb

Cambodian-English/English-Cambodian Standard Dictionary
0143 ISBN 0-87052-818-1 $14.95 pb

Catalan-English/English-Catalan Dictionary
0451 ISBN 0-7818-0099-4 $8.95 pb

Classified and Illustrated Chinese-English Dictionary (Mandarin)
0027 ISBN 0-87052-714-2 $19.95 hc

An Everyday Chinese-English Dictionary (Mandarin)
0721 ISBN 0-87052-862-9 $12.95 hc

Czech-English/English-Czech Concise Dictionary
0276 ISBN 0-87052-981-1 $9.95 pb

Danish-English English-Danish Practical Dictionary
0198 ISBN 0-87052-823-8 $12.95 pb

Dutch-English/English-Dutch Concise Dictionary
0606 ISBN 0-87052-910-2 $8.95 pb

Estonian-English/English-Estonian Concise Dictionary
1010 ISBN 0-87052-081-4 $11.95 pb

Finnish-English/English-Finnish Concise Dictionary
0142 ISBN 0-87052-813-0 $8.95 pb

French-English/English-French Practical Dictionary
0199 ISBN 0-7818-0178-8 $8.95 pb

Georgian-English English-Georgian Concise Dictionary
1059 ISBN 0-87052-121-7 $8.95 pb

German-English/English-German Practical Dictionary
0200 ISBN 0-88254-813-1 $6.95 pb

English-Hebrew/Hebrew English Conversational Dictionary
0257 ISBN 0-87052-625-1 $7.95 pb

Hindi-English/English-Hindi Practical Dictionary
0442 ISBN 0-7818-0084-6 $16.95 pb

English-Hindi Practical Dictionary
0923 ISBN 0-87052-978-1 $11.95 pb

Hindi-English Practical Dictionary
0186 ISBN 0-87052-824-6 $11.95 pb

English-Hungarian/Hungarian-English Dictionary
2039 ISBN 0-88254-986-3 $9.95 hc

Hungarian-English/English-Hungarian Concise Dictionary
0254 ISBN 0-87052-891-2 $7.95 pb

Icelandic-English/English-Icelandic Concise Dictionary
0147 ISBN 0-87052-801-7 $8.95 pb

Indonesian-English/English-Indonesian Practical Dictionary
0127 ISBN 0-87052-810-6 $8.95 pb

Irish-English/English-Irish Dictionary and Phrasebook
1037 ISBN 0-87052-110-1 $7.95 pb

Italian-English/English-Italian Practical Dictionary
0201 ISBN 0-88254-816-6 $6.95 pb

Japanese-English/English-Japanese Concise Dictionary
0474 ISBN 0-7818-0162-1 $9.95 pb

Korean-English/English-Korean Dictionary
1016 ISBN 0-87052-092-X $9.95 pb

Latvian-English/English-Latvian Dictionary
0194 ISBN 0-7818-0059-5 $14.95 pb

Lithuanian-English/English-Lithuanian Concise Dictionary
0489 ISBN 0-7818-0151-6 $11.95 pb

Malay-English/English-Malay Dictionary
0428 ISBN 0-7818-0103-6 $16.95 pb

Nepali-English/English Nepali Concise Dictionary
1104 ISBN 0-87052-106-3 $8.95 pb

Norwegian-English English-Norwegian Dictionary (Revised Edition)
0202 ISBN 0-7818-0199-0 $11.95 pb

Persian-English Dictionary
0350 ISBN 0-7818-0055-2 $16.95 pb

English-Persian Dictionary
0365 ISBN 0-7818-0056-0 $16.95 pb

Polish-English/English Polish Practical Dictionary
0450 ISBN 0-7818-0085-4 $11.95 pb

Polish-English/English-Polish Concise Dictionary (Completely Revised)
0268 ISBN 0-7818-0133-8 $8.95 pb

Polish-English/English-Polish Standard Dictionary
0665 ISBN 0-87052-882-3 $22.50 hc

Polish-English/English-Polish Standard Dictionary
0207 ISBN 0-87052-882-3 $16.95 pb

Portugese-English/English-Portugese Dictionary
0477 ISBN 0-87052-980-3 $14.95 pb

English-Punjabi Dictionary
0144 ISBN 0-7818-0060-9 $14.95 hc

Romanian-English/English-Romanian Dictionary
0488 ISBN 0-87052-986-2 $19.95 pb

Russian-English/English-Russian Standard Dictionary
0440 ISBN 0-7818-0083-8 $16.95 pb

English-Russian Standard Dictionary
1025 ISBN 0-87052-100-4 $11.95 pb

Russian-English Standard Dictionary
0578 ISBN 0-87052-964-1 $11.95 pb

Russian-English/English-Russian Concise Dictionary
0262 ISBN 0-7818-0132-X $11.95 pb

Concise Sanskrit-English Dictiontary
0164 ISBN 0-7818-0203-2 $14.95 pb

English-Sinhalese/Sinhalese-English Dictionary
0319 ISBN 0-7818-0219-9 $24.95 hc

Slovak-English/English-Slovak Concise Dictionary
1052 ISBN 0-87052-115-2 $8.95 pb

Spanish-English/English-Spanish Practical Dictionary
0211 ISBN 0-7818-0179-6 $8.95 pb

Swedish-English/English-Swedish Dictioanry
0761 ISBN 0-87052-871-8 $19.95 hc

English-Tigrigna Dictionary
0330 ISBN 0-7818-0220-2 $34.95 hc

English-Turkish/Turkish-English Concise Dictionary
0338 ISBN 0-7818-0161-3 $8.95 pb

English-Turkish/Turkish-English Pocket Dictionary
0148 ISBN 0-87052-812-2 $14.95 pb

Ukrainian-English/English Ukrainian Practical Dictionary
1055 ISBN 0-87052-116-0 $8.95 pb

Ukrainian-English/English-Ukrainian Standard Dictionary
0006 ISBN 0-7818-0189-3 $16.95 pb

Urdu-English Gem Pocket Dictionary
0289 ISBN 0-87052-911-0 $6.95 pb

English-Urdu Gem Pocket Dictionary
0880 ISBN 0-87052-912-9 $6.95 hc

English-Urdu Dictionary
0368 ISBN 0-7818-0222-9 $24.95 hc

Urdu-English Dictionary
0368 ISBN 0-7818-0222-9 $24.95 hc

Uzbek-English/English-Uzbek
0004 ISBN 0-7818-0165-6 $11.95 pb

Vietnamese-English/English-Vietnamese Standard Dictionary
0529 ISBN 0-87052-924-2 $19.95 pb

Welsh-English/English-Welsh Dictionary
0116 ISBN 0-7818-0136-2 $19.95 pb

English-Yiddish/Yiddish-English Conversational Dictionary (Romanized)
1019 ISBN 0-87052-969-2 $7.95 pb

(Prices subject to change)

TO PURCHASE HIPPOCRENE BOOKS contact your local bookstore, or write to: HIPPOCRENE BOOKS, 171 Madison Avenue, New York, NY 10016. Please enclose check or money order, adding $4.00 shipping (UPS) for the first book and .50 for each additional book.